CONFLICT RESOLUTION

THEORY, RESEARCH, AND PRACTICE

JAMES A. SCHELLENBERG

STATE UNIVERSITY OF NEW YORK PRESS

Chapter 10 contains material that is reprinted from *Keeping Faith: Memoirs of a President* by Jimmy Carter with permission of Jimmy Carter © 1982

Chapter 12 contains material that is reprinted from "Conflict Resolution in County Seat Wars" by James A. Schellenberg in *Journal of the West,* vol. 13 no. 4 (October 1974) with permission of Journal of the West, Inc. © 1974.

Published by
State University of New York Press, Albany

© 1996 State University of New York

For information, address State University of New York Press,
State University Plaza, Albany, NY 12246

Production by M. R. Mulholland
Marketing by Fran Keneston

Library of Congress Cataloging-in-Publication Data

Schellenberg, James A., 1932–
      Conflict resolution : theory, research, and practice / James A. Schellenberg.
          p.   cm.
      Includes bibliographical references and index.
      ISBN 0-7914-3101-0 (HC : alk. paper). — ISBN 0-7914-3102-9 (PB : alk. paper)
      1. Conflict management.   I. Title.
      HM136.S282   1996
      303.6'9 — dc20
                                                                              95-52851
                                                                                  CIP

10 9 8 7 6 5 4 3 2

To all students with a serious interest in conflict resolution
—theory, research, or practice—
this book is respectfully dedicated.

CONTENTS

PREFACE

Scholarly work in the study of conflict has expanded greatly in recent decades, as has the work of professionals who apply their efforts to the area of conflict resolution. However, there is relatively little contact between the academics and the conflict resolution professionals. The primary purpose of the present book is to fill this need for bridging the gap between scholarly theory and research, on the one hand, and, on the other, practical work in conflict resolution.

My sense of the need for such a book was confirmed when I helped to establish a graduate program in conflict resolution at Indiana State University. There was no book that I felt could serve well as a basic text for the foundation course in this program. I decided to supply one.

As I thought about student needs (as well as those of intelligent people generally—even if not taking a class in the subject), I became convinced that the field needs books that are fairly easy to read. Dealing with subjects in a sophisticated way does not require that we bore our readers to death. I therefore have put into this book a series of case studies that should help make the subject matter more concrete and interesting than would otherwise be the case. I have also tried to use a writing style that is direct and informative, and which avoids drawing out any subject at too great a length. I hope that I have succeeded at these tasks better than in my previous books on social conflict.

A number of persons—including at one critical time in my initial planning, the late James Laue—have encouraged me to undertake the present book. I am grateful to them, as I am to SUNY Press for their willingness to take on this project for their publication list. Among others who should be acknowledged are my students in our Conflict Resolution Program at Indiana State, who over a period of three years have patiently borne with me as I developed the materials into their present form. It is to such students that I dedicate this book.

I

INTRODUCTION

PROLOGUE: OUT OF THE GARDEN

How conflict became a central part of our world is the subject of several great myths. Three of these myths are especially prominent in traditions of the West. These myths also suggest basic ways that we should try to deal with conflicts.

Human society, according to one story, started out with everything working perfectly under the direct supervision of the Almighty. Then humans began to make judgments of their own about what they should or should not do. According to the most famous version of the story, this occurred in the Garden of Eden after Adam and Eve ate fruit from the tree of the knowledge of good and evil. In any event, according to this scenario, a world of constant conflict was the result. True, humans sought the guidance of their God for dealing with this new world of conflict, but they were mostly on their own. They had to develop their own ways of organizing society and keeping rule breakers in line. They could never go back—at least, not in their earthly lives—to the idyllic conditions with which their world began.[1]

A second story is quite different. Here human society is seen as originally one of constant conflict and turmoil. There were no standards of right and wrong, and physical might always prevailed. However, not even the strongest man could provide for his own security, for others could always temporarily band together and kill him. Thus, this original "state of nature" was one described as a war of all against all. One of the great storytellers of this view characterized such early human life as "solitary, poor, nasty, brutish, and short." But humans did have the sense to see that this constant state of conflict could be overcome if they would but yield to some higher authority. This higher authority could then set standards of right and wrong and enforce obedience. So it is, this story concludes, that the state and formal government came into existence, based on the need for an authoritative system that could provide security for its people. The state thus provides the basis for the future progress of human society.[2]

A third story is in some ways similar to both of the first two, but it also has its own distinctive view. This story holds that humans were originally in a state that was neither perfect bliss nor unlimited warfare. Rather, it was a condition of partly organized society—where basic patterns of organization emerged out of fundamental features of human nature. Already at the early dawn of humanity there was a sense of right and wrong, with certain human rights rooted in the basic conditions of life together. However, what was lacking was an instrument to settle disputes over these rights. This brought people together to agree upon a governmental system, with those in authority (to quote a famous American statement inspired largely by this third myth) "deriving their just powers from the consent of the governed." According to this view, the way we organize to resolve our conflicts may continually change, and with such changes so do we change our governments; but unchanged is the basic human nature that derives from the fundamental conditions of human society.[3]

It should be clear that myths such as these point to different views as to the fundamental nature of human conflict resolution. According to the first myth, resolving our conflicts is always something of a hit-or-miss affair. The only ultimate standard is the will of God, and this is not easily deciphered for most mundane matters. The second myth gives us more of an earthly answer: follow the guidance of whoever is in authority. Although such authority is ultimately arbitrary, it is our only clear guide to proper conduct in our lives with one another. The third myth suggests that we together must work out our conflicts with due respect for one another's basic human needs and interests. There is no ultimate formula for conflict resolution, only those temporary standards we develop; these, in turn, are based upon our fundamental human natures, which provide a bedrock of general moral guidelines.

Factual evidence does not much affect myths such as those we have been considering. We can neither prove nor disprove their fundamental validity. Rather, they reflect basic philosophies on the nature of our social world, and they rise or fall as these philosophies wax or wane. However, we should recognize that there have been important changes in dominant views over approximately the last six centuries of Western history. Six hundred years ago, the first of these myths reflected the dominant spirit of the times. Over the next three centuries or so, the main movement was from the first to the second—from a world of ultimate divine authority to one of arbitrary human authority. For about the past three hundred years, the main movement has been from the second to the third basic viewpoint. Our problems are more and more seen as human in origin, and they are to be solved by ordinary people through whatever means of democratic participation they may devise.

We should not neglect to point out that there are some common elements in all the myths we have examined. All of them see the world in profoundly moral terms. They may differ in what they see as the source of morality, but all three of our myths emphasize the importance of moral standards for intelligent conflict resolution. All of them also see the present human condition as fundamentally changed from its original pattern. For better or worse, we are now out of the garden—or the "state of nature" or society without civil government, as would, respectively, be the preferred terminologies of our second and third myths—and there's no going back. Finally, all three of our myths imply that there is a central role for human intelligence as we seek to work out solutions for our conflicts. It is significant that it was a tree of knowledge from which Adam and Eve ate in the original Garden of Eden story. In the second myth, the role of human reason was central in leading us to create systems of human authority. And clear thinking is also suggested as a key to successful conflict resolution in our third myth—as people, through mutual persuasion, seek to work out their differences.

Let us summarize the main points we have tried to make so far. First, we tend to approach the subject of conflict not just in a factual manner, but also with strong philosophical assumptions. These assumptions may be expressed in the form of myths, and we have reviewed three of the most prominent of these myths. Second, although we can neither prove nor disprove such philosophies and their associated myths, we can recognize that there have been changes in their popularity. Currently, the view that social conflicts can usually be resolved through democratic participation and persuasion is on the ascendancy. Third, despite their differences, all of these basic views share a profoundly moral emphasis, a basic acceptance of social change, and a respect for human intelligence in properly relating to our changing conditions.

This last point leads us to make another distinction about the way we use our intelligence to resolve our human conflicts. There are two main Western traditions about the use of intelligence for human problem solving. These may be characterized as the "rationalistic" and the "pragmatic" approaches. The former sees human intelligence as useful primarily to seek out general principles to apply to concrete problems. The second sees human intelligence as useful primarily in wisely assessing the detailed realities and managing them as effectively as possible. Of course, we need not make a simple choice between these two styles; most of us seek some combination of both. However, we should recognize that some persons (including scientists and philosophers) place a stronger emphasis in the one direction, while others lean more the other way. Only a few prominent thinkers represent these approaches in nearly pure form (*The Republic* of Plato and Machiavelli's *The Prince* are probably the most classic examples of works that do); however, we can find numerous examples of the influence of one or the other of these approaches as we pursue the literature on conflict resolution.[4]

So what may we conclude? That there are many viewpoints out there that profoundly color the way we may look at the subject of conflict resolution? Yes, indeed. That we must choose one or the other of these positions as a base for our own thinking? No, not necessarily. The present author's view is that there is profound truth to be seen in them all—in all three of the myths we summarized, as well as in both rationalistic and pragmatic approaches to the use of human intelligence—and that the most effective response is to seek some combination of them. However, the reader may have another view. Also, persons

reflecting traditions other than those of the West are especially apt to be critical of the way we have formulated the basic issues. So be it. We are not here
attempting to resolve our intellectual conflicts—just to recognize them and the
role they may play. With this recognition, we are more likely to approach our
subject with a broader framework than otherwise would be the case. And this
search for a broader framework is sometimes the most important first step toward conflict resolution.

1

The Field of Conflict Studies

Past and Present

Background

Over the centuries, many great minds have been drawn to the study of conflict. Some have studied particular conflicts in great depth and detail. For example, we may note the analysis of the Peloponnesian War by that famous historian of ancient Greece, Thucydides. Others have generalized more fully on one type of conflict. Examples include Aristotle's comparative analysis of revolutions and the reflections on the art of war by Sun Tzu, a Chinese warrior and philosopher who also lived more than twenty centuries ago.[1]

Without minimizing the importance of these contributions from past centuries, we need also to recognize that it is only in the twentieth century that the systematic study of conflict has become a field in its own right. In fact, the overwhelming majority of work in this field is a product of the last half of the twentieth century.

A New Discipline?

The jury is still out on whether or not conflict studies is to become a discipline in its own right. Some scholars have argued that this field has now developed its own literature and academic programs and therefore should be treated as an emerging discipline. Others point out that most of the work still comes from persons who identify themselves primarily with one of the more established disciplines, such as history, political science, or sociology. Indeed, the list of disciplines that the systematic study of conflict may draw upon is very long—including the full range of the social sciences and the humanities, as well as mathematics and biology.

But the issue of disciplinary status does not need to be resolved at this point. Whether it is a field where many disciplines come together or a discipline of its own, in either case it has its own central questions and a body of literature increasingly identified as that of conflict studies. Subjects pursued include not only the study of particular conflicts, but also such basic questions as the following: Under what conditions are human societies most likely to engage in warfare, or to become disrupted by revolution or by ethnic conflict? What are the main mechanisms by which conflict—between individuals, between groups, and between nations—is normally controlled without violence? What patterns of individual behavior are most conducive to avoiding conflict, or to pursuing it successfully, or to resolving it once bitter passions have been aroused? What patterns of group structure are most likely to lead to intergroup hostilities, or to successful conflict management? Such are among the organizing questions of the field of conflict studies.

Examples of Work

There are now several academic journals that focus on the study of conflict. Selecting rather randomly an issue of one of these, the *Journal of Conflict Resolution,* we may note something of the range of topics that may be included:

- Decision-making processes leading to the Allied attack on Iraq during the 1992 Persian Gulf War
- Attitudes of Jews and Arabs in Israel toward a Palestinian state
- General social factors influencing decision making during negotiations
- Effects of using a particular form of arbitration
- Factors related to the effectiveness of international mediation
- The dynamics of intransigence in negotiations
- A game theory analysis of the development of cooperation in dyads
- Evidence on the relationship between the polarization of the international system and the likelihood of war

This shows that the field of conflict studies can cover a very broad range of topics.[2]

Basic Concepts

Social Conflict

The field of conflict studies is generally understood as excluding certain kinds of conflict. It does not focus on conflict within individual minds, nor on purely individual reactions to conflict. Rather, its focus is on social conflict: conflict between or among individuals, or between or among groups.

As an initial statement, we may define social conflict as the opposition between individuals and groups on the basis of competing interests, different identities, and/or differing attitudes. Such a definition may narrow slightly the coverage of conflict studies, but it also leaves open a very wide range of subject matter. Note especially that social conflict, in this conception, is not limited to the more violent or confrontational forms of opposition. Violence may or may not be involved, though violence is certainly one of the subjects of special interest. Furthermore, we can include impersonal and unconscious forms of opposition (such as may be seen in market competition), and not only cases of high emotional involvement.[3]

Conflict Resolution

Conflict resolution is of course a central subject in the field of conflict studies. It may therefore be helpful to give an initial definition of what may be meant by this concept. Actually, we will give two definitions: one a broad conception, and the other more focused on what is most commonly studied. Broadly, we may conceive of conflict resolution as any marked reduction in social conflict. More specifically, we may conceive of conflict resolution as a marked reduction in social conflict as a result of a conscious settlement of issues in dispute. Note that with our broad definition, conflict resolution may occur through self-conscious efforts to come to an agreement, or it may come by other means (environmental change, the influence of third parties, victory for one party, and so on). As more narrowly conceived, conflict resolution is seen as a process of conscious settlement of the issues between parties.

In this book we will tend to take the broad view of conflict resolution as any marked reduction in social conflict, just as we will use a broad conceptualization of social conflict itself. The reader should be informed, however, that in some other works, conflict resolution may be viewed more specifically as dispute resolution (our second definition). Also, the terms *conflict management* and *conflict regulation* are sometimes preferred for the broader ways in which we try to reduce conflict or keep it at low levels.

A Question of Attitude

When we begin to consider the phenomena of social conflict, most of us start with a negative attitude. That is, we associate conflict with what is undesirable. Conflict is bad, and the resolution of conflict is good; that, at least, is the association most of us make when we first consider these terms. But we should be careful here. Conflict is so fully a part of all forms of society that we should appreciate its importance—for stimulating new thoughts, for promoting social change, for defining our group relationships, for helping us form our own senses of personal identity, and for many other things we take for granted in our everyday lives. Indeed, nearly all of us have loyalties to a national state that was forged through bitter conflict. The things we love, as well as those we despise, are inexorably shaped by social conflict.[4]

Likewise, we generally associate conflict resolution with what is good and desirable. But let us note that not all attempts to resolve conflict lead to justice or mutual satisfaction. In our international conflicts we are often warned of the dangers of a peace-at-any-price philosophy, and a similar warning needs to be voiced in relation to our everyday conflicts. Attempts to resolve conflict do not always work; and when they do, they can sometimes lead to undesirable consequences.

Most of us feel bad when we think about our conflicts. They worry us. Likewise, we feel good when we sense that a conflict is resolved. That is all very natural. But we should not let such associations with our personal feelings cloud our vision about the broader landscape of social conflict. We are more likely to be rewarded in our study of conflict if we can approach the subject with a neutral attitude—assuming conflict is neither something inherently good or bad, but rather that some conflict is essential for all human social life. With such an attitude, we are more likely to understand what we see occurring in cases of conflict than if we start with a simpleminded moralizing attitude.

Distinctions within Conflict Studies

Macro and Micro

There are a number of ways we can divide the field of conflict studies. None of these will provide categories that are applicable to all studies, but they suggest some of the main ways the work of those in this field may be described.

One important distinction is between focusing on big conflicts (such as wars and revolutions) or focusing on smaller conflicts (such as conflicts within small groups or disputes between neighbors). Sometimes the terms *macro* (for the bigger conflicts) and *micro* (for the smaller ones) are applied to this distinction. Most people doing research in social conflict work either at the macro or the micro level, though they sometimes try to generalize back and forth between them. Likewise, most persons specializing in conflict resolution in their professional responsibilities work either with large groups and organizations or with small groups and at the level of interpersonal relationships.

The term *peace studies* (or *peace and conflict studies* or *peace science)* is frequently applied to the work of scholars who operate at the broader levels of conflict studies. Relations between national states are often a special focus of their interests. Those who work at the micro level often identify their field by the terms *conflict resolution* or *dispute management.* Their focus is more upon the management of conflicts at the interpersonal level or within small groups.

There is, of course, a very wide range of phenomena included in conflict studies—from families to nations, and with many other kinds of social organization in between. There are many different levels at which the phenomena of conflict may be studied, and some scholars are especially interested in the study of conflict processes that may cut across the various levels, macro and micro, as well as shadings in between.

Academics and Practitioners

Another major distinction may be made between those who approach conflict studies as an academic field and those who see it as an area of professional practice. Most political scientists, historians, and sociologists who engage in the study of social conflict are primarily academicians; they are scholars who seek to understand basic forms of conflict, and how they may relate to specific cases. On the other hand, the practicing professionals relate primarily to particular cases, and seek to understand basic forms of conflict only in order to help them with such specific cases. These practitioners may include social workers, clinical psychologists, attorneys, ministers, military strategists, diplomats, and labor-management specialists.

Naturally, there are important differences between the academicians and the practitioners, but they do need each other. The practitioners need to draw upon the academic knowledge base, and the academic scholars need to bear in mind that only if their work proves helpful to the practitioners are they likely to find it well supported. Fortunately, there are also some people who work primarily in the middle: academicians who are especially interested in applications of their theories and research findings, and professional leaders who are especially interested in broader questions about their practice field. For these, the growing literature of the field of conflict studies is especially important.

Generalists and Specialists

A third distinction that is helpful in understanding the range of conflict studies is that between the generalist and the specialist. The generalist is that person who deals with a wide range of ideas and their implications; the specialist focuses more narrowly upon a particular question or issue. Among academics, the generalist is more likely to present ideas that might "save the world"—or, at least, make a wide range of conflicts more manageable. On the other hand, the academic specialist is more likely to focus on a particular problem of research—and on getting the results published. Among practitioners, generalists are more likely to discuss the broader issues of their work, while specialists focus more on technical questions of effective practice.

Although such distinctions as we have made (between macro and micro levels, between academicians and practitioners, and between generalists and specialists) are helpful in seeing the range of conflict studies, we should avoid using them as simple categories for the classification of people or their work. Few people (certainly among those working in conflict studies) fit neatly into a simple subclassification of these variables. Nor is most of their work easily classified in such terms. Indeed, one of the key features of the field of conflict studies is that it brings together persons of very different disciplines—political scientists and social workers, attorneys and anthropologists, social psychologists and ministers, military men and sociologists, and more—who seek to focus on questions they have in common. Conflict studies represents an extremely broad field. But it focuses on its own central themes: how social conflicts occur, and how they may be resolved.

Conflict Theory (and Theories)

Varieties of Conflict Theory

When sociologists and political scientists talk about "conflict theory," they are often thinking about a broad point of view which emphasizes the struggles between groups as giving social and political institutions their present shape. Some of them see themselves as part of this struggle, while others are not personally involved in this way. In either case, such scholars are likely to cite Karl Marx, as well as others who view social conflict as the primary instrument of social change.

To a social worker or minister, the term *conflict theory* may have a very different meaning; it may apply more to the psyches of individuals as they become enmeshed in their interpersonal conflicts. Social workers may cite the work of a great psychologist (such as Sigmund Freud) for leads toward understanding such conflict, while ministers are apt to cite the works of an ancient prophet or contemporary theologian.

Other students of social conflict avoid such terms as "conflict theory." This doesn't mean that they are any less concerned with a theory of conflict, only that their preferred language is different. For example, economists see a very central place for human conflicts of interest in their discipline; however, they tend to talk about them in terms of competition and market mechanisms rather than in terms of conflict theory or conflict resolution. Some mathematicians may specialize in the analysis of conflict, but they are unlikely to call it "conflict theory." Their analysis of conflicts of interest is more likely to be pursued under the name of "game theory," for some rather obscure reasons in the history of mathematics.

The point is that there are many possible versions of conflict theory and many different theories about conflict. However, despite important differences in terminology and focus, there is a common concern in all theories of conflict; this is a concern for conceptualizing how human social conflicts may be expressed and resolved.

Main Perspectives

To provide some help in examining the great variety of theories about social conflict, we can group them into several main types. Each type has a fundamental perspective, though a variety of different theories develop from this perspective. We may identify these main types (or families) of theories as the following:

1. *Individual characteristics theories* look at social conflict in terms of the natures of the individuals who are involved.
2. *Social process theories* look at conflict as a process of social interaction between individuals or groups, and seek to make generalizations about the nature of this process.
3. *Social structural theories* look at conflict as a product of the way society is formed and organized.
4. *Formal theories* seek to understand human social conflicts in logical and mathematical terms.

Practice

Main Approaches

Practitioners who deal with human conflicts are, as we have pointed out, a highly varied lot. They include persons in many different professions, and the forms of conflict are equally diverse. The forms of conflict resolution are as diverse as the forms of social conflict. At first glance, therefore, it may appear hopeless to generalize about the practice of conflict resolution. Nevertheless, we can identify a limited set of approaches usually applied to the resolution of conflicts. These may be summarized as follows:

1. Coercion, or forcing parties in conflict to a particular conclusion.
2. Negotiation and bargaining, or involving the parties in a process of discussion which seeks to bring them into voluntary agreement.
3. Adjudication, or using the power of the state and its legal system to provide an authoritative conclusion.
4. Mediation, or using a third party to help the conflicting parties come to a mutually satisfactory agreement.
5. Arbitration, or using a third party to decide, through prior mutual consent, the issues in dispute.

Although the possibilities of further variation in approaches to conflict resolution (including combinations of the above forms) is endless, most practitioners emphasize one or another of these five approaches.

The Plan of This Book

Research

Empirical research is applicable to questions of both theory and practice. Most of the chapters of this book will make reference to relevant research. However, since research deserves some attention in its own right, we will devote one chapter, Chapter 2, to focus specifically on conflict resolution research.

Theory

Chapters 3 through 6 are primarily theoretical in content. Each is devoted to a general theoretical approach. These chapters focus on, respectively, individual characteristics theories, social process theories, social structural theories, and formal theories. This is not to claim that all the important theoretical work can be neatly classified under one or another of these categories; rather, we mean to show that a wide range of theories should be included in our background understandings, and that the categories we use should be helpful in showing something of this range.

Theories of conflict resolution are closely intertwined with broader assumptions about social conflict. Each of the theory chapters therefore focuses both on conflict and on conflict resolution. One should recognize that each of the main theoretical approaches to understanding social conflict also implies an approach to conflict resolution. If one emphasizes individual characteristics as a foundation for social conflict, then the primary approach to conflict resolution is to change individuals, so that they are less prone to aggressive behavior. If one emphasizes a social process approach, resolution comes by changing the process—by developing new ways to handle conflicts and by avoiding unproductive confrontations. With a social structural approach, resolution is achieved primarily through social reform (or revolution); the society needs to be changed so that primary points of tension are eliminated. With a formal approach to studying conflict, we engage in such activities as solving equations and identifying points of equilibrium; these activities help us give a formal description of the conditions where we would find a reduction of conflict.

Although our approach in Chapters 3 through 6 is primarily theoretical, we also note some research bearing on these theories. We do not dwell at length on these studies, but they should be seen as a critical part of the formulation and revision of theories about conflict resolution.

Finally, each of these theory chapters begins with a biographical or historical account involving a leading theorist of social conflict. This is aimed at making clear the general approach of thought represented by the particular family of theories being considered. This is followed by a brief introduction to some of the other theories and theorists that may be seen as representing the same general approach.

Practice

After the four theory chapters will come six focusing on practice, Chapters 7 through 12. In each of these chapters (excepting the last) we examine one of the common approaches to the practice of conflict resolution: coercion, negotiation and bargaining, adjudication, mediation, and arbitration. As we examine these approaches, we cite the research that seems most appropriate for understanding how each method may work (or sometimes not work) in the practice of conflict resolution.

Each chapter focusing on the practice of conflict resolution will begin with a case study, selected to illustrate in some detail how the approach may apply to a particular case. Discussion then follows on some of the assets and liabilities of particular applications of the same general approach featured in that chapter.

Summary and Conclusions

Summary

The field of conflict studies has a long history, but also a very rapid recent development. The question of whether it now constitutes a discipline in its own right is still a subject of debate. In any event, the field includes a great variety of subjects and approaches.

For organizing our investigations, we will use broad definitions for our central concepts. Social conflict may be understood as "the opposition between individuals and groups on the basis of competing interests, different identities, or differing attitudes." Conflict resolution may be understood as "any marked reduction in social conflict." Students of the field of conflict studies differ in many ways; broad divisions include those focusing on the macro or the micro level, those who are academic scholars or those who are practitioners, and generalists as compared with specialists.

Theories of conflict include those that can be seen in the following broad categories: (1) individual characteristics theories, which look at social conflict in terms of the natures or the individuals involved; (2) social process theories, which look at conflict as a process of social interaction between individuals or groups, seeking to make generalizations about the nature of this process; (3) social structural theories, which look at conflict as a product of the way society is formed and organized; and (4) formal theories, which seek to understand social conflicts in logical and mathematical terms. Main approaches in the practice of conflict resolution include: (a) coercion, or forcing parties in conflict to a particular conclusion; (b) negotiation and bargaining, or involving the parties in a process of discussion that seeks to bring them into voluntary agreement; (c) adjudication, or using the power of the state and its legal system to provide an authoritative conclusion; (d) mediation, or using a third party to help those in conflict come to a mutually satisfactory agreement; and (e) arbitration, or using a third party to decide, through prior mutual consent, the issues in dispute. Separate chapters in this book focus on each of these main types of theory and forms of practice.

Conclusions

There are two main conclusions the reader may draw from this initial chapter:

a.   The field of conflict studies is an extremely rich area for study.

b.   We should look forward to an exciting intellectual adventure as we pursue our study of conflict resolution in the chapters that follow.

2

Conflict Resolution Research

Main Methodologies

Dominance and Altruism at Camp Wancaooah

Human dominance hierarchies pose a persistent background for the study of social conflict. They may be observed in all forms of social conflict, from those in the family to those of the world of national states. We make many generalizations about them—we speak of their natural inevitability or their denial of true democracy—but how well do we really understand how dominance hierarchies work? Not very well, in the view of one social scientist named Ritch Savin-Williams, who set out to try to reduce this area of ignorance.[1]

Savin-Williams chose summer camps for young adolescents as his arena for research. He obtained permission from the sponsors of a well-established camp program for himself and several graduate students to be present, mostly in the roles of camp counselors, to make detailed observations of campers' behavior. A total of ten camp groups (six of boys and four of girls) were studied during the five summers that the research was carried out. Ages of all campers ranged from 11 to 17, though each group was homogeneous in age as well as sex.

Observation focused especially upon five settings in the daily routines of groups: getting up in the morning or going to bed, mealtimes, group discussions, cabin cleanup times, and special group activities. Within these settings, all behaviors were sampled, and detailed recordings were made of those related to dominance or submission. The following are the main categories used for coding interpersonal dominance behaviors: verbal directives (such as asking someone to do something), verbal ridicule (such as name calling or making negative remarks about another camper), physical assertiveness with contact (including both overt aggression and play fighting), recognition (asking for information from, or showing respect for, another in the group), physical displacement (moving away from another), verbal or physical threat (behavior involving the direct challenge of another person), counter dominance (neglecting interaction with another who asserts dominance behaviors), and verbal control (such as interrupting another's speech or arguing with him or her). This yielded a fairly precise count of all such behaviors between all possible members in a camp group.

Results of these observations were analyzed in great detail and related to other information about the young people involved. Probably the most important general finding was that, in all groups, a fairly definite dominance hierarchy had become apparent after only a few days in camp. Structures varied from group to group, but nearly all groups developed hierarchies that remained relatively stable for the rest of the camp experience. In these structures, some individuals were in positions of relative dominance, and others clearly were not. Conflicts tended to be expressed in terms of these structures, and conflict management also followed the lines of a group's hierarchical framework.

Some—but not very dramatic—age differences appeared in Savin-Williams' analyses. Much more notable were the gender differences. Male groups more quickly and more clearly developed dominance structures than did female groups. Conflicts involved in the emergence of these structures tended to be expressed differently by boys and girls. Boys dealt with conflicts more directly and more physically, while girls were more indirect and more verbal in their methods of combat. Also, boys were more likely to have the main interpersonal conflicts within the group resolved by the end of the camp period, leaving with a stronger group identity, as compared with the girls' groups.

Savin-Williams used what he calls an "ethological perspective" for this work, both in the way the data were collected and how interpretations were made. Ethology is the systematic study of animal behavior. It was developed to study the detailed behaviors of various species of animals. Although species vary greatly in particular behaviors, we find strong dominance hierarchies in most of the more social species, including monkeys and apes. What Savin-Williams observed in American adolescents was quite similar to the general way dominance hierarchies have been found to develop in other primate species.[2]

Although dominance hierarchies were the main focus of Savin-Williams' research, he also included altruistic behaviors among the detailed recordings for two groups. Behaviors oriented to the welfare of the group or for special assistance to another member were carefully coded and counted. He did find important individual differences in altruism that continued throughout the camp experience. Interestingly, correlations between helping behavior and dominance scores were quite low, suggesting that there is little systematic relationship between a person's dominance status and altruistic tendency. Gender differences were far less marked for altruism than for dominance behaviors. However, Savin-Williams does suggest that there are at least some small differences. For example, in observing the same type of group activity in groups of the opposite sex, he comments:

When a potential beneficiary was in need of comforting, females were more likely to offer help than were males. In comparison, males were more responsive when the situation offered the opportunity for physical assistance.[3]

Violence in the Family

While behaviors of adolescents in summer camps offer important leads for understanding social conflict, some investigators prefer to focus their studies, literally, closer to home. One such investigator is Richard Gelles.

Gelles was interested in domestic violence long before it became a subject of popular discussion. In fact, when he discussed this as a possible topic for his doctoral dissertation with Murray Straus, his advisor, there was practically no systematic research on the subject. Gelles was not sure it would be possible for social scientists to get reliable information on so private a phenomenon; but Strauss was strongly encouraging for this direction of work. As a result, as Gelles later summarizes his research, "In the winter of 1972 I trudged through the slush and cold of gray New Hampshire days to knock on doors and talk to people about violence and abuse in the home."[4]

A sociologist, Gelles began his study with the goal of obtaining a systematic sample that would include clear cases of domestic violence. However, he also wanted to have a good sample of "normal" families. In order to achieve both of these objectives, he selected a total of eighty cases in the cities of Manchester and Portsmouth, New Hampshire. Twenty of these cases were of homes described by social workers as problem homes. Another twenty ordinary households were selected to match with the first group. They were neighbors of the families in the first group, chosen by a systematic procedure to assure that they were similar except that they had not been identified in advance as having family problems. A third group of twenty homes was identified on the basis of police reports of family violence. For these, in turn, a final group of twenty "normal" neighbors was matched.

Gelles was careful about controlling some obvious possible sources of research bias. He personally conducted the interviews in half the cases of each of the four samples, with a female interviewer handling the other forty cases. Within each sample, furthermore, there was an attempt to obtain equal numbers of husbands and wives as respondents. Gender was controlled in this fashion.

An open-ended interview format was used. That is, there were some basic questions asked all respondents, but there were also attempts to get free responses and to follow up with further questions about any reported instances of family violence. The average length of interviews was slightly over one hour, and most interviews were taped (when no objections were made by the respondent) for further analysis later.

Most notable among the results of this study were indications of the simple frequency of domestic violence. As might be expected, regular violence was present in almost half of the families in samples identified by social workers or the police. What was less expected was the frequency of spousal violence in the other homes, with more than ten percent of the neighbors also reporting fairly regular episodes of spousal violence. Another finding, less widely cited, was that slightly over half of the "normal" families had no reported instances of physical violence in the history of the marriage, with the remaining 30 to 40 percent of these families reporting only rare cases of violence. Of all interspousal violence, both in "problem" families and in "normal" families, the husband was the perpetrator more often than the wife. However, the gender violence ratio was over 2:1 in the problem families and about 5:3 in the "normal" families.

The most common forms of family violence found in Gelles' study were pushing, shoving, punching, kicking, slapping, grabbing, and throwing objects at the other. All of these were more used by husbands than by wives—though wives were also responsible for a fair amount of slapping, grabbing, and throwing objects. Though more rare, hitting with a hard object was used slightly more by wives than by husbands. Guns were never reported to be used, and only once was a knife used (by a wife). However, there were four reported cases of a husband threatening a wife with a knife or gun.

Although the incidence of violence was the subject attracting the most attention among those noting his research, Gelles was even more interested in identifying the conditions under which violence was likely to be practiced in homes. For example, the kitchen was easily the most likely place for violence to occur (followed by the bedroom or the living room). Evenings provided the most frequent time of the day. In general, violence is most apt to occur when the husband and wife are locked in a bitter conflict and find no physical escape from each other.

As for social backgrounds, there is a small (negative) correlation between education and family violence. Also, income and violence are negatively correlated. Occupational status provides a more interesting pattern. Among husbands, middle levels of the occupational structure are associated with more violence than either higher or lower levels; while just the opposite is true for wives, with the least violence for them associated with middle occupational levels. Violence appears more likely when the wife has a higher educational or occupational level than the husband than when the reverse is the case. In commenting on such features of social structure and family violence, Gelles says:

> Certain families, largely by their position in the social structure, suffer greater stress and frustration than do other families as a result of lack of resources and skills and because of certain structural arrangements within the family that tend to be associated with violence.[5]

Gelles' pioneering work on family violence has been followed by many other studies in this area. Many of these later studies have had more sophisticated samples and research techniques. However, their findings have proven to be not greatly different from what Gelles found for eighty New Hampshire homes in the early 1970s.

Experiments in Adjudication

Research we have examined so far in this chapter focuses especially on behavior. Also important is understanding how people think and feel about situations involving disputes and their resolution. To illustrate the kind of work that may be done in this direction, we draw on a study by four social psychologists.

Laurens Walker and three associates designed an experiment that sought to show how people react differently to varied forms of adjudication. Adjudication in this study does not refer to actual court settings, but rather to simulations of different ways that courts may be conducted.[6]

Primary subjects for this study were ninety-nine undergraduate men at a major university who volunteered to take part in a simulation of a business case. The case involved an advertising task, for which subjects played the role of a president of an advertising firm. It was arranged so that an accomplice of the experimenters would be "selected" by the president as his creative director. The president and creative director would then lead their (imaginary) team in competition with another (imaginary) advertising firm to furnish the most creative set of product names for a client company. When the names were submitted, however, company presidents found themselves accused of plagiarizing names thought up by the rival advertising firm. The creative director was naturally the person who would need to answer to any suspicions about such plagiarism. This called for a brief trial procedure, as had been mentioned as a possibility in the instructions at the start of the simulation. The company president and creative director then went into the next room for their "trial."

Another set of sixty-four subjects had been selected to be trial observers. They expected that they would later be involved in other business case simulations, for which their observation of the present case should provide helpful preparation.

The trial was conducted by accomplices of the experimenters. At the end of the trial, a written verdict was presented that found the accused pair either guilty or innocent.

All of this was an elaborate plan to allow the experimenters to vary certain key features of the adjudication process. A central purpose was to compare what the experimenters called "adversarial" and "inquisitional" trial procedures. In an adversarial situation, each accused party was represented by a student attorney, an accomplice who advocated their cause before a student judge. The other side was also represented by an accomplice acting in the role of attorney. In the inquisitional situation, there was only one attorney, who presented the arguments for both sides. The attorneys presented the same arguments in either adversarial or inquisitional conditions.

It should be recognized that adversarial procedures are generally a standard part of trials in the American judicial system. Sometimes special courts (some juvenile courts, for example) as well as some noncourt investigations will use a nonadversarial format, in which an agent of the court will investigate the facts and make recommendations. The present study sought to create forms of these two contrasting styles of adjudication in their simulations.

A second key variable was created by the verdict arranged to be given: either guilty or innocent. There were some further manipulations, but the study can probably best be understood as having the following four kinds of cases:

1. Adversarial trials resulting in a guilty verdict
2. Adversarial trials resulting in an innocent verdict
3. Inquisitional trials resulting in a guilty verdict
4. Inquisitional trials resulting in an innocent verdict

Each of these conditions was experienced by two kinds of subjects (in addition to the accomplices involved): those who were playing the role of a company president accused of plagiarism, and those who were just observing the trial.

At the end of the trial, all subjects filled out questionnaires to express their satisfaction with the trial, the fairness with which it was conducted, and its outcome. Generally similar questionnaires were filled out by both kinds of subjects: participants (the accused company president) and observers (witnesses to the trial).

What would we expect to be the results of such a study as we have described? Would we expect people to generally prefer (as participants or as observers) the less adversarial form of adjudication? If so, we would be wrong. Quite the reverse was indicated by the results of this study. Both participants and observers generally gave higher marks to the adversarial than the inquisitional procedures. Participant subjects gave especially high ratings for the fairness of the adversarial procedures, and they were most satisfied with the judgments coming from it. Not surprisingly, participants preferred an innocent to a guilty verdict (that is, they were less satisfied with procedures when found guilty than when found innocent). However, it was also found that the observers preferred the trials with innocent verdicts.

The investigators appeared somewhat surprised at their results. They considered whether certain features of the design might have made the adversarial procedures seem more proper to the subjects, and thus incline them in that direction. Nevertheless, in their final comments, they caution against moving too rapidly to consider alternatives to the adversarial system of American justice; they end with the opinion that

> The findings of this study suggest that parties to litigation and the observing public would view such [nonadversarial] procedures as unfair and would be greatly concerned about the lack of opportunity afforded the parties for the presentation of their positions.[7]

An Historical "Experiment"

The research just described was done under artificially controlled conditions. Often, however, it is difficult to pose our questions in terms of such restrictive environments. We frequently need methods that allow a more comprehensive range of data to be considered. Especially is this true when we are seeking to understand basic historical changes in the way conflict is handled in society.

A brief essay by Jeffrey Haydu provides us with an example of how we may do research on questions of broad historical changes. The problem Haydu explores is that of the different directions that labor-management relations took early in the twentieth century in two countries: Great Britain and the United States.

We may start with the observation that labor-management relations were especially strained in the United States in the first third of the twentieth century. Although there were unions, they had little influence on how business and industry operated. This lack of an organized voice for labor led to an almost constant conflict between labor and management. Labor's desire to organize and seek greater influence on wages and working conditions was directly (and usually successfully) opposed by management, which sought to minimize all forms of labor organization. When this conflict took the form of a strike, it was apt to be extremely bitter.

Organized labor had a much stronger role in Great Britain during the same period. Management there was much more likely than in America to accept labor unions and use them in helping to plan how work was to be organized. This applied both to individual companies and to industrywide planning.

In trying to understand these different roles of organized labor in the United States and Great Britain, Haydu could not himself directly observe the past, nor could he engage in meaningful surveys or experiments on the way things were several generations ago. What Haydu instead used for his research were the investigations that others had made of particular industrial patterns of the past. He examined what previous scholars had found, and sought to combine these findings into a more general interpretation. By using Great Britain as a framework of comparison for looking at American patterns, Haydu was using an element of experimental design (looking at an 'experimental group' in relation to a 'control group'); but of course he was not actually doing an experiment. He was just trying to put the historical facts together in such a way that he could made sense out of otherwise puzzling patterns.

Most scholars who have compared labor relations in the United States and Great Britain have emphasized a cultural interpretation of the differences. The United States, they suggest, has a much more individualistic tradition; in American labor and industry, therefore, workers are seen more as individuals than as organized groups. The more traditional and less individualistic culture of Great Britain, they suppose, is a more hospitable environment for organized labor. But Haydu had a major problem with this interpretation. As he looked carefully at labor-management relations at about the turn of the century, he found essentially the same patterns in both Britain and the United States. In neither country were the patterns the same from industry to industry; both countries showed a lot of variation. And this variation, in both countries, included a great deal of ambivalence about organized labor. Leaders of industry were apparently testing the waters to see what their attitude should be toward labor unions. Within one or two decades, however, the British moved in the direction of accepting organized labor as a part of the way business was conducted, while American industrialists developed an almost completely united front to oppose the unions.

We cannot say that the cultural backgrounds of the two countries had no influence upon the different directions labor-management relations took. But Haydu believes that the primary reasons lay elsewhere: in changing technologies and their associated working conditions. He points to how nineteenth century craft organizations helped to create a high degree of work discipline in both countries. However, the new industrial technology of mass production was changing all of this, making particular skills less important for the way workers functioned on the job. A key difference between Britain and America was generally the speed with which the new technologies of mass production were adopted. They came faster and earlier in the United States—before craft unions were able to adapt to the new industrial order. As Haydu summarizes the differences:

> The greater progress of technological change made craft restrictions (e.g., the insistence that certain jobs be performed only by skilled men) more irksome and decreased American manufacturers' reliance on skilled unionists. As a result, U.S. employers had both greater interest in attacking union controls at work and found it easier to do so—less experienced workers could be trained quickly to take the place of striking craftsmen.[9]

The prevailing attitude of U.S. business and industry soon became strongly anti-union, with labor unions seen as having a clearly negative impact on industrial efficiency. In Britain the unions had more time to adapt to the new modes of industry, and industrialists there were more likely to see workers' organizations as a means for helping to manage the strains of the workplace.

Such is an explanation offered to help understand a period of American history when extremely bitter conflict accompanied labor's attempts to organize. It does not apply so much to the last two-thirds of the twentieth century; but even now, some of the patterns developed in the early years of the century help to set the tone with which labor-management conflicts are expressed.

Searching for Worldwide Variations

The study we have just discussed goes beyond American borders to give insight into patterns of conflict in the United States. Other studies may take the whole world as a subject for study. An example of such research can be seen in the cross-cultural study of interpersonal violence conducted by Carol and Melvin Ember.[10]

The amount and kind of interpersonal violence shows great variation from society to society. Are there some general worldwide patterns to help us understand this variation? Such is the basic question behind the research conducted by the Embers.

One of the important leads for answering this question comes from previous studies that point to a clear correlation between warfare and interpersonal violence. Those societies that have frequent warfare also tend to have more interpersonal violence, as expressed in such things as rates of homicide or assault. Although this is not particularly surprising, it immediately raises the further question of the nature of this linkage. What makes societies with more interpersonal violence also have more war? Are there some important mediating variables that need to be identified?

In order to answer these questions, the Embers made use of the Human Relations Area Files. These carefully compiled files include basic descriptive data regarding several hundred different cultures of the world. They are based primarily on anthropologists' reports, and they seek to broadly represent all parts of the world and types of culture. A total of 186 societies were included in the Embers' data base, though for some of their analyses (because of limited information available for some cultures on some variables) they had to use a much smaller number of societies.

In beginning their research, Ember and Ember looked at a great variety of socialization variables, for they believed that the linkage between war and interpersonal violence would especially involve the varied socialization patterns found from culture to culture. The main kinds of socialization features examined included socialization for aggression, the severity of punishment during childhood, low need satisfaction of children, low parental warmth, and special factors that might make it more difficult for boys to develop an adult male sense of identity. More specific variables were examined for each of the general variables of socialization, and research assistants laboriously sought to measure them. More than forty specific variables were used in all, and the assistants followed a carefully designed protocol for coding a rating for each socialization variable for each culture that had suitable data. In addition, they made measurements of the amount of interpersonal violence (such as in homicide or assault) and the frequency with which warfare might be experienced. The research assistants made these ratings without knowing the hypotheses that the Embers were seeking to test, lest that knowledge might influence the ratings they would give.

Once the ratings of all of these variables had been made, the Embers could examine the socialization variables for correlations with both the frequency of warfare and the amount of interpersonal violence. Not surprisingly, war and interpersonal violence were found to be positively correlated in their sample of cultures. Of more specific interest, both of these variables were definitely linked to socialization variables. They found an especially strong linkage of both to socialization for aggression, especially for socialization involving boys in late childhood.

Next the Embers used a series of statistical procedures to identify what patterns of other variables could best predict a society's amount of interpersonal violence. Using methods of multiple regression and path analysis, they were able to confirm that the socialization for aggression of boys was the strongest predictor of interpersonal violence. That is, those societies that placed the strongest emphasis upon making boys aggressive were also those with the most interpersonal violence. But how does war frequency relate to these key variables? Through a series of further analyses, the Embers concluded that socialization for aggression was more a result of war frequency than of levels of interpersonal violence. In other words, having wars encourages socialization for aggression more strongly than does having high levels of interpersonal violence. The direct linkage of war and interpersonal violence is not nearly as strong as that which is mediated by socialization for aggression.

The most remarkable piece of the analysis of Ember and Ember is the direction of causality they suggest: from war, to socialization for aggression, to interpersonal violence, and not the other way around. This differs from what most of us would intuitively expect. This leads the Embers to conclude:

> The various kinds of statistical evidence presented here are consistent with the theory that socialization for aggression is likely to be a consequence (not a cause) of war, that people will want their

sons to be aggressive when they have a lot of war and they need to produce courageous warriors.

They hasten to add that they do not believe parents deliberately have this in mind when they socialize their sons for aggression. Rather, these are unintended results of living in a society with a high frequency of wars. Stated briefly, "Once you learn to kill an enemy, you may find it easier to hurt or kill anyone."[11]

Studying How People Talk

Although the study just summarized focused on interpersonal violence, there was no examination of actual interpersonal relations. The data were highly indirect—they were what research assistants had coded from culture-to-culture comparisons on the basis of descriptions provided earlier by anthropologists. Some research is more direct in observing interpersonal interaction. The research of Savin-Williams mentioned at the beginning of this chapter is one example. Another example may be seen in some work done by Angela Garcia.[12]

Garcia sought to understand how interaction in mediation sessions differs from that in other situations, especially those in which attempts are made to resolve disputes in some other way. In order to do this, she made videotapes of all small-claims mediation sessions carried out during a six-month period in the program of one California county. The tapes were then transcribed very laboriously into printed texts, which included symbols to record inflections, pauses, and so forth. The texts were then carefully studied to understand how the interpersonal communication was organized.

Garcia drew upon previous studies to identify main patterns for the organization of ordinary conversation. This included norms for turn taking, for promoting agreement, and for handling disputes. Turn taking typically involves brief segments of speech that can be easily interrupted. There is a general assumption that agreement is to be promoted, but when disagreement occurs it can easily grow into a dispute. Disputes involve speech expressed directly between opponents, using forms of communication that magnify their differences.

The primary purpose of Garcia's research was, again, to understand how interaction in mediation may be different from that in ordinary conversation. In particular, she was interested in how the dialogues of disputes varied between the two forms.

One of the first things she noticed and documented was that turn taking in mediation was quite different from that in ordinary conversation. People in mediation have longer periods of speech, and the norms do not favor sharp interruptions. The mediator sets the stage for this, and most of the speaking is to the mediator and not directly between the disputants. By organizing the flow of communication in this way, the mediator assures that both parties in the dispute will have adequate time to express themselves fully, without immediate contradiction from an opponent.

The mediator organizes much of the discussion during mediation in terms of questions and answers, as the mediator promotes an understanding of particular aspects of the problem. Discussion can follow in a given line for an extended period, with the mediator primarily in charge of directing the subjects discussed and setting the tone for the discussion. This is different from the usual flow of conversation, especially when people are arguing with each other. When parties do start to argue directly with one another in mediation, the mediator seeks to assert command in the sense of again becoming the one to whom the parties address their comments. This is frequently followed also by a change in the focus of the discussion, at the initiative of the mediator.

These mediation procedures tend to neutralize disputing in a number of ways. For one, accusations and denials are usually not expressed immediately one after the other, thus they are not as sharply focused as in most arguments. Furthermore, with both accusations and denials addressed primarily to the mediator, who poses questions for clarification, they do not so clearly emerge as disagreements. They can be softened through a more selective response as the discussion is filtered through mediation. Finally, the norms that govern mediation sessions hold that arguments are to be expressed in a controlled fashion. Although displays of anger may be permitted, they are treated as outside the framework of problem solving that the mediation is supposed to promote.

All of these points are illustrated in great detail by Garcia, using segments of recorded mediation sessions. In moving toward her conclusion she then states:

> To discover how mediation works as a technique for conflict resolution, the interactional process of mediation hearings must be examined.

And she concludes:

> The advantages of mediation over other types of dispute resolution (e.g., trials, counseling, arguing) may lie not in characteristics of mediators or the difficulty of the dispute, but in the interactional organization of mediation itself.[13]

Main Methods of Research

The six research studies presented so far in this chapter have been selected to illustrate the main methods of conflict resolution research. These methods include: (1) observational studies, (2) survey research, (3) experiments, (4) historical studies, (5) archival research, and (6) content analysis. Each of these methods is illustrated by one of the studies described above.

Observational studies involve the direct observation of behavior. Sometimes this takes the form of "participant observation," as the researcher seeks to become a part of the situation being studied to better understand the meanings people attach to their own behavior. Sometimes observations are made in an almost mechanical way of recording very specific features of behavior. The research of Savin-Williams on dominance hierarchies was somewhere in between. As with participant observation, the research team made the attempt to be a part, as unobtrusively as possible, of the situation being studied. However, very definite forms of behavior were selected for observation, and these were measured quite precisely.

In survey research, a questionnaire is developed and presented to a sample of respondents. Sometimes the questionnaire is fairly general in the way it elicits information; the open-ended interviewing used by Gelles in his studies of family violence is an example of this. In other cases, all the items in the questionnaire are precisely standardized. Sometimes the sample is carefully drawn to represent a truly random selection of cases from a defined population. At other times the sampling is less formally organized, though it still needs to be planned in a systematic way, as was the case in Gelles' research.

In experiments, one or more variables (the independent variables) are carefully manipulated to study the effects they may have on variables measured later (the dependent variables). The key elements of an experiment are the systematic manipulation of one or more independent variables, the careful measurement of a dependent variable, and a random assignment of subjects to treatment groups. The study by Walker and associates manipulated the kind of conflict resolution attempted (adversarial or inquisitional) and studied the effects this (and other controlled variables included in the design) might have upon the level of satisfaction with the outcome. Sometimes we divide experiments between (*a*) laboratory experiments, done under completely artificial conditions; and (*b*) field experiments, done under more natural conditions, though still successfully manipulating the key variable(s). The study of Walker and associates had aspects of both of these—it was actually done under completely contrived conditions, and thus technically a laboratory study, but it had much in common with a field experiment in a business setting.

Researchers using the historical studies method seek understanding from what happened in the past. They may do this by using original sources (such as old documents) to help develop an interpretation of past events. Or they may use reports by others who have studied the past. The study by Haydu was a clear example of the latter kind—using the work of others as a description of the past. What Haydu attempted was to combine these reports of others into a new general interpretation of American labor-management relations during the opening decades of the twentieth century.

Archival studies involve data previously gathered, data either routinely accumulated or obtained for some other investigation. In either case, the investigator works with "old" data; he or she does not actually gather any data. Our example of such archival research was the cross-cultural study of Ember and Ember. They used the Human Relations Area Files as the source of their data; they did not themselves go out into the field to do anthropological studies of any of the cultures. They applied careful measures to the previously recorded descriptions of cultures in order to uncover the relationships among war, socialization for aggression, and interpersonal violence, as these might be expressed comparatively from society to society. (Incidentally, the term *archival* suggests that such research makes use of formal collections of data, such as may be found in the archives of organizations. In social research, the term is given a broader meaning, to include any kind of data previously collected and stored for possible further use.)

The method of content analysis studies the particular content of mass media or of social interaction in order to make summary statements about whatever is being observed. From such analysis more general inferences may be made about the phenomena under consideration. Content analysis may sample the frequency of certain themes in the mass media, or it may be applied to recorded samples of interaction. In Garcia's work, the videotaped interaction of mediation sessions was the source of data. The researcher studied the verbal content of these interactions as a means of making inferences about how mediation works.

Further Studies

Combinations

We have illustrated the main research methods used in conflict studies, and in so doing have also illustrated the wide range of subjects relevant to this broad field. What we have not yet sought to illustrate is the combination of methods often used in a particular study. We do that in this final section.

A Study of Community Justice

Some studies are identified as instances of "evaluation research," especially when they seek to give evidence of the effectiveness of a particular program or agency. Such research almost always involves a combination of research methods—including inspection of organizational records (archival research), development and use of a questionnaire (survey research), and the use of firsthand observations of activities (observational studies). Research for program evaluations typically arranges the results to show the extent to which the goals of the program are successfully achieved.

Some broader studies of programs are not explicitly labeled as instances of evaluation research, but may still have much in common with this type of research. An example may be seen in a study conducted by Christine Harrington.[14]

Harrington had two main purposes in her work. The first was to understand better how new means of nonadversarial dispute resolution (usually called "alternative dispute resolution" or "ADR," and giving emphasis to such techniques as mediation) were generally functioning in relation to the traditional court system. The second was more specific—to see how a typical ADR agency actually functioned, and with what consequences for the legal system. For the first purpose, Harrington reviewed the history of ADR in America, including previous studies. For the second purpose, she selected the study of a particular program that had been suggested as something of a model for ADR applications. This specific program was the Kansas City Neighborhood Justice Center.

Part of Harrington's research was an historical study—seeking to understand the growth and popularity of ADR approaches in the recent history of the United States. The other part of her work, that dealing specifically with the Kansas City agency, included historical studies, survey research, observational studies, and archival research. She focused especially on a study of 591 cases handled during a ten-month period. A statistical analysis of these cases provided a major part of her evidence on the way the center was functioning.

Harrington found that the cases coming to the Neighborhood Justice Center were mostly small disruptions of the public order, usually referred by the criminal justice system as an alternative to regular court processing. Although most cases were successfully settled by the Center, Harrington did not find notable differences between the effectiveness with which the center handled cases compared with the way the traditional court system worked. She therefore sees this center (and others like it) functioning largely as an extension of the criminal justice system, to handle some cases more informally than it chooses to handle others. Most mediations conducted by the center are successfully completed, but Harrington attributes much of this to the implied coercion represented by the possibility of more formal prosecution. She therefore describes such agencies as operating in the "shadow" of the criminal justice system.

The Civil Litigation Research Project

There were many more specific results in Harrington's study that we have not included here, for our interest is primarily in showing some of the varieties of conflict resolution research. Clearly her study used a combination of research methods. Another study that illustrates a variety of conflict resolution research methods is that of the Civil Litigation Research Project carried out in 1978 through 1980. This study sought to sample cases of ordinary litigation to see what main patterns might be observed.[15]

The Civil Litigation Research Project was carried out cooperatively by several institutions, including the University of Wisconsin at Madison and the University of Southern California. The project included an attempt to obtain a random sampling of cases in the courts of five federal judicial districts that together represent all major regions of the United States. Separate samples were made of cases in state courts and those in federal courts. A total of 1,649 cases were selected for analysis, and court documents for all of these cases were studied. In addition, for 1,423 of these cases there were follow-up telephone interviews with litigants and/or their attorneys. Such interviews generally were of about an hour in length.

We will leave for a later chapter (Chapter 9, on adjudication) a discussion of the findings of the Civil Litigation Research Project. In the present context we simply use it to illustrate the combination of archival research (court records) and survey research (telephone interviews) that were used in one rather notable research project.

What Makes People Compromise?

Another form of research is illustrated by some recent work by Daniel Druckman. The research we have in mind uses primarily experimental data, but Druckman himself did not gather the empirical data directl. Rather, he used what others (and himself, in earlier research) had previously reported. Still, this was not one of the common "library research" projects, where one simply analyzes and discusses what previous books and articles show. Rather, it was a quantitative study of previous work, using what has become known as "meta-analysis."[16]

The subject of investigation was that of what factors in negotiations are primarily responsible for encouraging the parties to compromise. Previous research had uncovered a wide variety of factors, and some reviews had suggested an especially strong role for the way negotiators may serve as group representatives. That is, when one negotiates on behalf of a group, rather than for oneself, a negotiator is *less* apt to compromise. While accepting that this might be a factor, Druckman had himself investigated a number of other factors in his previous research. His present purpose was to bring these studies (his previous research and that of a large number of other investigators) all together in a meta-analysis, to determine what factors most strongly influence the tendency to compromise.

Druckman looked for studies that had investigated one or more of the following factors: whether or how parties in negotiation served as group representatives, their prenegotiation experience and/or orientations before coming into negotiations, the visibility of the negotiations to others, the strategy of the opponent, time pressure, and the degree to which interests are clearly opposed. In each of these areas he attempted to measure just how strong were the influences studied upon the willingness to compromise. All in all, he used well over fifty studies for his analysis.

Meta-analysis is an approach for doing a secondary analysis of a large number of studies, summarizing their findings in terms of statistics that can be compared across studies. Correlations between the (various) independent variables and the dependent variable (willingness to compromise) were estimated by Druckman on the basis of statistics previously reported. For this, data often had to be transformed to provide statistics that could be compared; many studies had to be left out of the analysis because their data were too crudely reported for such a transformation. From the calculated correlations Druckman derived further measures of the "proportionate reduction of error," or just how much of the change in the dependent variable can be predicted on the basis of a change in the independent variable. This produced a measure of "effect size," which could be compared across studies.

The key question for Druckman then became: What variables have the strongest effect size in influencing the tendency to compromise? The detailed results here were quite complicated, but we can summarize them by reporting the mean effect size for those variables proving to be most predictive. These effect size results are (with the number of studies involved for each comparison shown in parentheses):

Negotiator's orientation (9 studies)	.42
Prenegotiation experience (14)	.37
Time pressure (6)	.37
Initial position distance (10)	.35
Opponent's strategy (11)	.32
Group representation (11)	.30

In other words, negotiator's orientation, prenegotiation experience, and time pressure are, on the average, the variables with the strongest effects. Other variables may also be important (including some not listed above), but their average impact is somewhat less.

Many criticisms can be made regarding meta-analysis procedures, and these can all be applied to Druckman's research. We will not here go into the finer points of this kind of research methodology. Our purpose has been more simple: to illustrate another form of conflict resolution research. Meta-analysis is a means of using previously obtained data (in this sense, similar to archival research) from well-designed studies (usually experiments, but sampled in a manner similar to survey research), in order to provide new empirical findings—but without gathering any new data. It is a form of research that has only been added to the literature of social science quite recently.

Resolving the "Prisoner's Dilemma"

Our last research example will show how empirical conflict resolution research can be conducted that uses *none* of the main research methods presented earlier in this chapter. The study we wish to use was done by Robert Axelrod, and it concerns a situation that has become known as the "prisoner's dilemma."

The prisoner's dilemma is a particular type of situation defined by the theory of games. It gets its name from one of the stories told by an early game theorist to illustrate this type of situation. In the story, two prisoners, in separate locations, are given a choice by the district attorney to either confess to their crime or remain silent. The situation is such that their self-interest leads both to confess—though both would be better off if neither would do so. What is generally known as the prisoner's dilemma is defined more abstractly within game theory. It is what is known as a 2 x 2 game (that is, two players with just two options each) which presents, in highly abstract form, the choice between responding selfishly or cooperatively. We do not here need to go into the technical description that game theory gives to this situation; suffice it to say that each choice of each player offers the dilemma of limited self-interest versus a movement toward cooperation with the other.

The prisoner's dilemma has been used by behavioral scientists in literally hundreds of studies. It gives a simple measure of what can be interpreted as a tendency to cooperate, and this in turn can be used to study effects of personality variables, initial orientations of players, specific features of the social situation within which the game is played, or a large number of different procedures that may be built into the game itself. To illustrate such varied procedures, the prisoner's dilemma is sometimes played as a 'one-shot' exercise (that is, there is only one chance for each player to make a choice), and in other experiments it is presented in "iterated" form (with a large number of trials that continuously use the same game structure). Not surprisingly, cooperation scores are much higher when the game is played in iterated form than when it is a one-shot exercise.

One of the fascinating things about the prisoner's dilemma is that game theorists cannot logically deduce any single mathematical solution for the way it should be played. There are different definitions of mathematical solutions which, when applied to the prisoner's dilemma, produce different results. This adds to the interest in what people actually do when faced with a prisoner's dilemma. What 'solutions' do they actually use to guide their behaviors within the game?

Robert Axelrod had been interested in game theory for some time before he did the research that we summarize here. He was concerned with trying to understand what makes one or another strategy more effective for playing the prisoner's dilemma. Of course, for any limited series of choices, it all depends on the strategy of the other party. But can we not generalize beyond this—what type of strategy will, in the long run and against a variety of other parties, be most likely to serve an individual's interests? Can this be either logically or experimentally identified?[17]

Axelrod developed a very original, though simple, idea for studying the effectiveness of different prisoner's dilemma strategies. He decided to hold a tournament. He invited game theorists and other behavioral scientists to submit computer programs representing how they would propose a player should deal with the prisoner's dilemma. The tournament rules provided for an iterated prisoner's dilemma game, with two hundred trials per contest. It would be conducted as a round robin competition, with each entry pitted against every other program. In addition, each entry would be placed in a contest against itself (that is, with both players playing the same strategy) and against a purely random strategy. The winning entry would be the computer program that won the most points in all the interactions (which involved more than one hundred thousand moves in all exercises of the tournament).

Fourteen people responded to Axelrod's first tournament. They included scholars from such different fields as economics, mathematics, political science, psychology, and sociology. Some of the programs presented were quite complex, building all sorts of conditions based on the previous plays of the other party, while others were quite simple. The simplest program was that submitted by Anatol Rapoport, a mathematical psychologist and leading game theorist. Rapoport's program, *Tit for Tat,* had just four instructions. Its strategy was simply to be cooperative on the first move, then proceed to match precisely on each next move the other party's cooperation or noncooperation.

Surprisingly, Rapoport's *Tit for Tat* program won the tournament. As Axelrod and others reflected on the results, the strategy of simple reciprocation seemed much more powerful than they had realized. They set to work to devise new programs, and Axelrod announced a second tournament. This second tournament would allow other computer programs that could take advantage of what had been learned in the first tournament. It would also allow a wider variety of participants. More than sixty programs were submitted for this second tournament, held again as a round robin, though with a few differences in detailed procedures. The winning program—the set of instructions that proved most able to make points in relation to all the other ways the other party might be programmed—was again Rapoport's *Tit for Tat.*

Axelrod saw some quite profound implications in the results of his two tournaments. He generalized broadly to all kinds of conditions in which we might try to build cooperative relationships. He applied his analysis to a wide range of subjects, including such diverse topics as military strategy and theories of biological evolution. We will not here try to follow these more general ideas; readers will find them well expressed in Axelrod's book, *The Evolution of Cooperation.* Our present purpose is more methodological than theoretical; and in this regard the main point of interest is Axelrod's method of research. Did he do a survey, compile historical records, or make direct observations of human behavior? No, none of these. Was this then a case of archival research or content analysis? No. An experiment, then; it must be considered a laboratory experiment? In a way, Axelrod's study was a laboratory experiment. But it was very different from most laboratory experiments. He used no human subjects. The "behaviors" he studied were simply products of computer programs!

An Endless Variety

One scholar has characterized the scientific pursuit as simply doing the utmost we can with our minds—no holds barred.[18] This suggests that a wide variety of methods of investigation should be open to those pursuing the science of conflict. In this chapter have suggested something of the range of methods that might be found in conflict resolution research. But there is an endless variety possible, as people seek to use their creative imaginations in asking questions that may be answered through research.

Summary and Conclusions

Summary

There are six primary methods of research in the study of conflict and its resolution. They are (1) observational studies, (2) survey research, (3) experiments, (4) historical studies, (5) archival research, and (6) content analysis. Each of these methods was illustrated by a concrete example of empirical research. The examples also showed something of the variety of topics that might be pursued in the systematic study of conflict resolution. They included interaction of young people at summer camps, domestic violence, arrangements for court proceedings, changing patterns of labor-management relations, cross-cultural analysis of the socialization of aggression, and interaction within mediation sessions.

Several other studies showed how a given piece of research may reflect multiple methods, and how some important research may not fit easily into any of the main categories of research usually mentioned.

Conclusions

The main conclusion for this chapter was stated just before our chapter summary, and we repeat it here. It is that there is an almost endless variety of research methods possible for our present field of study—as people seek to use their creative imaginations in asking questions that may be answered through research.

II

THEORY

Individual Characteristics Theories

Dr. Einstein Sends a Letter

A Special Project

Albert Einstein (1879–1955) was near the peak of his career when, in 1932, he was approached to participate in a special project under the general auspices of the League of Nations. No longer was he a clerk in a Swiss patent office, as he had been in 1905 when he first published a paper on his theory of relativity. He was now a professor at Berlin's prestigious Prussian Academy of Sciences as well as Director of the Kaiser Wilhelm Institute for Theoretical Physics. He had distinguished himself in theoretical physics to such an extent that his name was a household word—as a symbol of genius—in much of the world.

The project about which Einstein was approached was being sponsored by the particular body then known as the International Institute of Intellectual Cooperation, a rough equivalent of what has since become known as UNESCO (the United Nations Educational, Scientific and Cultural Organization). The idea was to publish a series of exchanges of letters between leading intellectuals of the world, and Einstein was one of the first persons invited to take part. He was free to choose anyone he wanted, and any topic, for this exchange of letters. He chose Sigmund Freud, and, as the subject of the exchange, the causes and control of war.[1]

Sigmund Freud (1856–1939) was then well recognized as the leader of psychoanalysis. At this mature point in his career, he too was widely known and probably more famous than any other psychologist. Freud agreed, though without enthusiasm, to participate in the project; and so the ground was prepared for the exchange of ideas between two of the greatest leaders of twentieth century thought.

Einstein and Freud were not well acquainted. They had met only once, and this would be their first exchange of letters. This was therefore to be more a public expression of views than a matter of private correspondence.

The Question

In his fairly short initiating letter, Einstein focused on the question, "Is there any way of delivering mankind from the menace of war?" He expressed some of his own views on the need for world government, but he also noticed how strong the resistance was to such a movement away from unlimited national sovereignty. Why is there such resistence, and why are masses of people so ready to sacrifice themselves (and with "such wild enthusiasm") during war? Einstein saw only one general answer for this question: "Because man has within him a lust for hatred and destruction." But here he recognized his own limitations, as a physical scientist, for providing much further clarification; he therefore invited Freud as much more of a specialist in such matters to give his views. The final question for which Einstein especially sought an answer was: "Is it possible to control man's mental evolution so as to make him proof against the psychoses of hate and destructiveness?"

The Reply

Freud began his reply quite modestly. He expressed surprise at the topic Einstein had chosen and doubt that his answer would be of any great use. Nevertheless, he proceeded with his analysis.

The first main point Freud makes is that violence has always been the final arbiter for human conflicts. This is rooted in our basic natures as animals, and it is only slightly controlled by our advanced civilization. True, there have been important developments toward the control of violence through the rule of law, but these are secondary refinements of more basic means of struggle. Legal control in civil society rests partly on the underlying power of coercion by the rulers, and partly on the recognition among the ruled of a community of interests in avoiding violent confrontations. Freud summarized these two factors as "violent compulsion" and "ties of sentiment" (between persons who share a common group identity).

The general conclusion to which these considerations pointed was, in Freud's view, a pessimistic one. He asserted that "the attempt to replace actual force by the force of ideas seems at present to be doomed to failure."

Freud does not stop at this point, but proceeds to a further analysis of the psychological roots of human aggression. We are, he asserts, fundamentally governed by instincts, which are of two basic kinds: the sexual and the destructive. Such instincts never operate separately or in isolation; they are always blended so that opposite tendencies within our natures may be expressed at the same time. Complex behavior typically includes many complex variations of these basic instincts. For example, Freud says that during war, people

may have a whole number of motives for assenting—some noble and some base, some which are openly declared and others which are never mentioned. There is no need to enumerate them all. A lust for aggression and destruction is certainly among them; the countless cruelties in history and in our everyday lives vouch for

> its existence and its strength. The satisfaction of these destructive
> impulses is of course facilitated by their admixture with others of
> an erotic and idealistic kind.

Often, continues Freud, though ideal motives may occupy the foreground of consciousness, they nevertheless obtain their strength from the destructive instincts submerged in the unconscious.

In concluding his analysis of the way life and death instincts function in human nature, Freud asserts that "there is no question of getting rid entirely of human aggressive impulses." However, it is possible to emphasize the positive sentiments that bind humans to one another. These are of two basic kinds: loving one another, and developing a common identification with each other. These reflect, respectively, our (usually sublimated) sexuality and our emerging sense of community (on which "the structure of society is to a large extent based"). Can this sense of community be nurtured to create a true world of peace? No, says Freud, for it is always modified by a hierarchy of authority. Further, he asserts that the tendency for persons "to fall into the two classes of leaders and followers" is an "instance of the innate and ineradicable inequality of men." True, we can try to cultivate greater wisdom among our rulers and more thoughtful consideration of their actions on the part of the ruled, but this does not change the basic nature of society, at least not in any forseeable future.

Before ending his letter, Freud poses and tries to answer a question Einstein had not raised. It is this: Given the persistence and inevitability of violent conflict, why is it that people like us continue to seek peace? "Why do you and I and so many other people rebel so violently against war? Why do we not accept it as another of the many painful calamities of life?" We so hate war, he answers, because we have this veneer of civilization which makes us seek higher purposes than simply the expression of our impulses. This is a part of our long-term growth of culture (which, in turn, Freud believes, ultimately becomes part of our organic nature) which seeks "progressive displacement of instinctual aims and a restriction of instinctual impulses." This is a very long-term (and painful, since it requires a modification of our basic instincts) process, and its ultimate results are uncertain. Nevertheless, therein lies at least some small hope for a reduction of war, especially when combined with the recognition of the dreadful destruction that can come in modern wars.

We do not know precisely what Einstein thought when he read Freud's letter. Freud himself apparently anticipated some disappointment; his final sentence begins: "I trust you will forgive me if what I have said has disappointed you."

Following this exchange of letters, Einstein soon found himself with more immediate and more personal issues than the general elimination of war. A few months after getting Freud's response (and before publication of the letters),

Adolph Hitler came to power as Germany's new Chancellor. Einstein then promptly resigned from his academic positions in Berlin, renounced his German citizenship, and went into exile. A statement he issued at this time (indeed, in the same month as his exchange with Freud appeared in print) said, in part: "As long as I have any choice, I will stay only in a country where political liberty, toleration, and equality of all citizens before the law are the rule."[2]

Natural Selection and the Killer Instinct

An Instinct?

Sigmund Freud obviously approached social conflict as an expression of forces deeply ingrained within the individual. So deeply ingrained are they that it is common to refer to them as basic instincts. For Freud, human conflict fed on the innate aggressive drive lying within us all.

What support for this idea of an aggressive drive or instinct can we find elsewhere in the biological and behavioral sciences? This is the question to which we now turn.[3]

First, in the biological sciences, there are several theories or theoretical approaches that one may see as supporting Freud's position, directly or indirectly. We will briefly discuss three: (1) nineteenth century Darwinism, (2) ethology, and (3) sociobiology.

Darwin's Contribution

The central theme in the explanation for biological change that Charles Darwin (1809–1882) set forth in his *Origin of Species* was the idea of natural selection. Many more individuals of a species are born than can possibly survive, so only those best adapted to their environment will live to reproduce. In a similar fashion, some species slowly die out, and others thrive; it is all a matter of successful adaptation to the particular environment in which each lives. Thus, through a very slow process, biological evolution gradually takes place.[4]

Darwin himself had little to say about how such biological competition applies to human society. In the few passages of his works that related to human society, he showed himself to be critical of social policies that tried to minimize the competitive forces within human nature. Other writers in the last half of the nineteenth century, however, were less reluctant to deal with the role of biological evolution in human society. Darwin's friend Herbert Spencer, one of the pioneers for the new science of sociology, used the concept of 'the survival of the fittest' as a general theme for both biological and sociological analyses. Other so-called 'social Darwinists' discussed at great length the central role that competition and conflict (between individuals, between different specific social practices, between social institutions, between groups, and, ultimately, between societies or nations) play for all forms of human society. That humans had an inborn tendency toward aggression was generally accepted as part of the universal struggle for survival.[5]

Although Darwin's theories continued to be central for biology in the twentieth century, there have been some recent qualifications. Darwin did not know about the role of mutations, or how biological change might occur through a fairly rapid transformation of genetic material. Also, he did not realize that species can continue for a very long time with little change; in other words, species are not always so sensitively adapted to particular environments as Darwin had assumed. In the late twentieth century we hear much more about theories of 'punctuated equilibrium' (assuming fairly brief periods of rapid evolutionary change interspersed with much longer periods of very little change). A more important qualification of the Darwinian perspective has occurred in the social sciences. The anthropologists and sociologists of the twentieth century have been far less inclined to see any instincts as residing in humans than had been their nineteenth century counterparts. Instead of tracing human behavior to biological roots, they see it as much more the product of human culture—as what we create through our groups and pass on through social learning.[6]

New Currents

So, as we approach the end of the twentieth century, can we forget about the implications of a Darwinian struggle to survive, at least for our understanding of human behavior? At mid-century this was indeed how the intellectual winds were blowing. But in the final decade of the century, it is not so clear. Two new theoretical perspectives have arisen in recent decades under the names of "ethology" and "sociobiology," and both of these provide a renewed emphasis on the genetic inheritance of social behaviors. Both imply that an aggressive tendency may be part of the genetic endowment that humans, among other species, express.

Ethology is the scientific study of animal behavior based on the painstaking study of animals in their natural settings. Not all biologists involved in such a study call themselves ethologists (the term itself has been applied more to European biologists, especially those placing a strong emphasis on the genetic basis of behavior, than to American zoologists); but those that do have been especially influential in the last half of the twentieth century. Through their careful studies they have mapped out many important behavior patterns of various species which seem to show a strong inherited base. Some of the most important insights about the inherited predispositions to social behavior (such as forming strong social bonds at rather specific early ages) have come from the work of ethologists. (Incidentally, ethology is not to be confused with "ethnology," the study of human cultures.)

Sociobiology is the scientific study of the social organization(s) of animals. Those zoologists who call themselves sociobiologists usually place a strong emphasis on population genetics as a basis for social organization. That is, the social organization of any species (or subpopulation thereof) is seen as largely determined by the frequency distribution of determinants of behavioral patterns within their gene pool. The term *sociobiology* was first used by Edward O. Wilson in his very influential book on the subject published in 1975; Wilson there sought to give the outline of a new biological science of social organization.[7]

What do the ethologists and sociobiologists have to say about the idea of a human instinct for aggression? Most ethologists do see aggression within any species as strongly rooted in genetic inheritance, and humans are in no way excepted from such genetic determinants of behavior. A highly influential statement of this position may be found in Konrad Lorenz's book *On Aggression*, in which he is quite clear in his view (similar to what was said earlier by Sigmund Freud) that humans do indeed have a strong instinct for aggression. Other ethologists are less convinced that aggression is a strong human trait, and they point to inherited patterns in humans that may help us avoid violent conflict. For example, Irenaus Eibl-Eibesfeldt suggests the presence of a biologically based norm among humans against killing one another, and he also suggests that innate gestures of submission (universal in all human societies) may be another means to control human aggression.[8]

Sociobiologists too see animal aggression as largely genetically based, but they emphasize its variability from species to species and from one pattern of social organization to another. They also frequently distinguish between different kinds of aggression (predatory aggression, inter-male aggression, maternal defensive aggression, fear-induced aggression, irritable aggression, and so on), each with its distinctive biological basis. In humans, sociobiologists are apt to see aggression as less simply produced than among other animals, and much more overlaid by human cultural learning. They suggest that strong patterns of aggression within a species are more apt to develop under conditions of population concentration than where populations are more spread out. This appears consistent with the observation that people in some of the most dispersed forms of human society (such as among such hunting and gathering peoples as the North American Eskimos or the Australian aborigines) engaged in very little violence before contact with Western culture, and had no clear conception of warfare.

Both ethologists and sociobiologists believe, with other biologists of the Darwinian tradition, that human nature has been profoundly shaped by the competitive conditions under which it emerged as the present species. They don't all see this as producing a general human instinct for aggression; but they do see mankind as faced with a wide range of conditions for which aggression may be a very natural response.

What does this brief overview of Darwinism, ethology, and sociobiology suggest about Freud's assumption of a basic drive or instinct for aggression among humans? Certainly humans have an inheritance from their past which includes strong tendencies toward aggressive responses. But is this in the form of an inner drive constantly pushing for expression? At this point the most we can say for such an idea is: not proven.

Other Biological and Psychological Considerations

Genetics

But what about the ever growing evidence about genetics and behavior? Every year researchers find new genetic links for some form of disease or an aspect of human behavior. Do these not include aggressive behaviors?

Some human diseases have been linked to rather specific conditions of our chromosomes. These diseases include Huntington's disease, cystic fibrosis, and at least some forms of Alzheimer's disease. Some research has suggested chromosomal links with more general diseases, such as alcoholism, schizophrenia, and manic depression; however, the findings are not yet conclusive in these areas, as mixed evidence accumulates. Manic depression provides an interesting example. Early studies, very carefully done, indicated a highly significant correlation of manic depression with conditions on chromosome 11 of the human genome; however, subsequent work has failed to replicate these findings (first published in 1987) and has pointed to significant methodological problems in the earlier research.[9]

There have been some suggestions of chromosomal links to aggressive behavior, but these have so far been even more elusive than those related to manic depression. In 1965 some evidence suggested that especially high levels of aggression were associated with an extra Y chromosome in some men. Although it has been confirmed that certain differences in behavior follow from having this extra chromosome, there has been a general backing off from the assumption that this includes anything so general as aggression. At most, it appears likely that the lower average intelligence of persons with this extra chromosome may be associated with higher rates of apprehension for criminal behavior. Much more recent, in 1993, were reports of a rare mutation involving the X chromosome which seems tied to aggressive behavior (or at least to such crimes as arson and attempted rape). But as the work goes on toward replication of these findings, we should not hold our breath. Not much of the wide range of aggressive behavior is apt to be explained by a very rare genetic condition.[10]

While specific chromosomes may not yet be implicated, many forms of complex human behaviors have been demonstrated to have strong genetic linkages. Schizophrenia, manic depression, and alcoholism all appear, on the basis of statistical evidence, to have strong genetic associations. Such is also the case with whatever is measured by IQ tests. However, the wide range of behaviors referred to as aggression is probably not so easily related to genetic factors.[11]

Twin studies have offered one of the most revealing approaches to understand gross genetic linkages with complex forms of human behavior. Identical and nonidentical twins, reared either together or apart, provide one of the best markers of degrees of both genetic and environmental similarity. With studies of behavior related to degrees of genetic similarity (such as between parents and children or among siblings, as compared to more distant relatives), researchers may measure the extent of "heritability" of different patterns of behavior. Such studies suggest that personality patterns do have a strong relationship to heredity—with between one-third and one-half of the variation in most measures of personality tied to genetic inheritance.[12]

A tendency toward friendliness or hostility toward others is one of the dimensions of personality often included in twin studies. This would appear at least close to the variable of aggression. Research does indicate some genetic basis for this friendliness-hostility dimension, though it appears less strong than for some other personality variables.

Whatever may be the ultimate findings on the influence of genes upon aggressive behavior, three points need emphasis: (1) aggression is an extremely complex form of human behavior, and it would be unlikely to find all its forms having the same determinants, genetic or otherwise; (2) what we know about genetic influences upon complex human behavior still answers very few of the basic questions for such research; and (3) even if there are genetic linkages, these must be expressed through other physiological and behavioral mechanisms.

This last point is especially important. To find genetic associations with certain types of behavior should not lead us to minimize the role of environmental experience—which may in part depend on what we are genetically programmed to seek out. There is no sharp dividing line between nature and nurture among the determinants of behavior. Further, the genes must express themselves through activities within the human body. Among the physiological processes that have received special attention in relation to aggressive behavior are neurological connections and endocrine secretions.

The Brain

Research has identified several parts of the brain as likely to be heavily involved with some forms of aggression (especially angry aggression and fear-induced aggression). These include areas in the lower central parts of the brain, especially the amygdala and the hypothalamus. The amygdala appears (through animal studies and some human studies) to be centrally involved in the expression of emotions. The hypothalamus appears to work with other parts of the brain (especially the temporal lobe and the midbrain) in triggering fighting behaviors. This has been clearly shown in animal studies, and human studies (mostly involving brain lesions in specific areas) seem to give similar evidence.[13]

Electrical stimulation of certain points in the brain appears to have direct effects on the expression of aggressive behaviors. This research, of course, has been mostly done with animals other than humans (though occasionally, electrical stimulation is part of the diagnosis or treatment for neurological disorders among humans). Kenneth Moyer describes an example of such a study with rhesus monkeys. The experimenters placed an electrode in the anterior hypothalamus of a male and observed his behavior. When alone he showed no tendencies toward aggressive behavior—no hitting at walls or things of that sort. But then he was placed in a cage with two other monkeys: one a female and the other a dominant male. When stimulated now, the subject animal immediately attacked the dominant male. This he did repeatedly and so intensely that soon the subject monkey replaced his opponent as the dominant male. Aggression in this situation appeared to be highly selective, for the subject animal showed no aggression toward the female. Moyer, in commenting on the implications of this study, says:

> This experiment shows first that the particular brain stimulation used resulted in one specific kind of aggression, which I have called "intermale," that is, the specific tendency for one male animal to attack another. Second, this experiment demonstrates that aggressive behavior is stimulus-bound. That is, even though the neural system specific to a particular kind of aggression is well-activated, the behavior does not occur unless an appropriate target is available.

What this further implies is that brain centers do not automatically initiate aggression all by themselves, but that specific forms of aggression occur only under certain stimulus conditions. The neurological and behavioral interactions are quite complex—even for animals other than humans.[14]

The Endocrine System

Endocrine levels are another important area of study for understanding the physiology of aggression. There are some rather clear patterns (both in other animals and in humans) of relationships between endocrine levels in the blood with tendencies toward aggressive behavior. This may be seen in seasonal variations in aggression (associated with endocrine levels), in relationships that change over the age span, and with differences in aggression between males and females. Of particular importance is the predominantly male hormone of testosterone. Higher levels or testosterone are associated with higher levels of aggression or violent behavior. However, most of the evidence from human studies fails to specify the precise forms of aggression that may be involved or whether high testosterone levels are more a result of, rather than the cause of, more violent or aggressive life styles.

Given the complexities of the human mind and the intricate relationships of the mind with the body, we must be careful not to claim too much for our knowledge of the physiological foundations of aggressive behavior. Especially important is the fact that what we consider as aggressive behavior may be at least as much determined by the consequences of acts as by the acts themselves. This suggests that the meanings we carry in our minds may be as important as the specific mechanisms of our bodies in creating aggressive behaviors.

Not only among humans, but also among other animals, aggression is not simply created from within. The internal determinants are themselves affected by perceptions of external events. In concluding a discussion of the physiology of aggression, a leading student of animal behavior has made this critical point:

> The important fact is that the chain of causation in every case eventually traces back to the outside. There is no physiological evidence of any spontaneous stimulation for fighting arising within the body.[15]

Although specific physiological mechanisms of aggression, and their relationship to psychological conditions, are still not very well known, we have not waited for extensive knowledge of such subjects before developing treatments for human aggression. There are drugs which appear to have positive effects in reducing aggression for persons whose behavior poses particular problems for themselves and others. The avoidance of other drugs (such as alcohol) may also be very important in controlling the expression of aggression by some individuals.

Theories of Social Learning

Psychoanalytic Theory

Sigmund Freud's explanations for human aggression were far more complex than the outline given in the first section of this chapter. He not only saw aggression as based on innate forces, but he also saw it as developing in the individual through experiences with others. How this development takes place has a profound impact on how the individual comes to express and control aggressive impulses.

Chief among the factors shaping the human personality, in Freud's view, is that of early family experience. A child's relationships with parents provide the framework for personality development and for later relationships to others. Since these early relationships always demand some control of the child's natural impulses, there comes to be a differentiation between the child's more or less self-conscious organization of behavior (what Freud called the "ego") from the more blindly driving impulses (called the "id"). But the requirements of parents extend further to include some specifically moral prohibitions, especially regarding the control of sex and aggression. These ultimately result, after a period of uncertainty and conflict, in identification with the parent of the same sex—to, in Freud's words, "mold a person's own ego after the fashion of the one that has been taken as a 'model'." With this, the child develops a new area of personality (what Freud called the "superego") to internalize the various moral imperatives that society, through the parents, imposes; the control of sex and aggression are central features of these moral imperatives.[16]

Of course, people differ in their distinctive experiences in such early socialization, even as they tend to have a common basic pattern. So in psychoanalytic theory we have not only an explanation for basic ingredients of personality, which nearly everybody has in common, but also a framework for examining individual differences in terms of distinctive experiences of early socialization.

According to Freud's theories, one never achieves real harmony between the mainly unconscious impulses and the more conscious forces of self-control. There is always ambivalence and internal conflict. Impulses toward sex and aggression might be controlled, but they also must be expressed in some way or another, if only through a ruthless repression to keep them unconscious. As a result of such forces, there is frequently greater unhappiness among persons who most represent the cultural ideal than among other persons. For example, in Freud's words: "The more righteous a man is, the stricter and more suspicious will his conscience be, so that ultimately it is precisely those people who have carried holiness furthest who reproach themselves with deepest sinfulness."[17]

The Authoritarian Personality

Freud's theory of social learning, which we have just outlined, has been applied by a number of social scientists in analyzing the dynamics of the control and expression of aggression. Of these applications, none was more famous, at least for a time, than the study of the 'authoritarian personality.' The basic assumption here was that a particular type of child rearing—one with strongly mixed signals on the part of parents regarding their children but with a determined drive toward respectability—was most likely to produce a pattern of personality that was strongly authoritarian. A part of this complex of patterns was often a strong tendency to look for scapegoats in other persons to blame for one's problems, as well as a high level of prejudice and hostility toward any groups considered as "outsiders" (that is, those not of one's own kind, however defined).[18]

Theodor Adorno and associates developed a questionnaire to measure the degree of authoritarianism in persons. They called this the "F scale," because they believed that it represented a susceptibility to fascist ideology. They reported findings of significant patterns of association between F-scale scores, conditions of early child rearing, and patterns of social attitudes. Although this work was initially hailed as among the most important contributions to social psychology, methodological problems soon led to strong criticisms. Ultimately, this work was treated as a suggestive exploration, but not one that met the increasingly demanding standards of good social science. Attention then shifted from authoritarianism to other underlying variables of personality that might represent some of the same kinds of personal rigidity. Openness to new experience became more commonly used as a key personality variable to measure central features of what previously had been seen as the authoritarian-democratic dimension. This research appeared more successful in identifying a central personality trait, and it continues to be one of the half dozen or so traits most commonly studied by personality research.[19]

The story of the change from 'authoritarianism' to 'openness' measures of personality has a rather unexpected ending. It started with a search for early childhood variables, especially within the family, that might be seen as creating certain kinds of personality patterns. As the research on openness accumulated, however, this variable became increasingly seen as not so much affected by early socialization as by genetics. At least in twin studies, the amount of variation in personality variables like openness that could be explained in terms of common family backgrounds of siblings was only a small fraction of what could be explained by genetic similarity. It would of course be too simple to say that a good part of the authoritarian personality is genetically determined—personality patterns and their associated attitudes are always complex in the way they reflect combinations of genes and experience. But these recent findings do give a strange twist to the theories originally set forth by Freud. His view that there is an innate basis of behavior is supported, but his views as to the role of early family relationships are not. After years during which many social psychologists decried Freud's emphasis on innate bases of behavior but accepted his theories as at least providing important insights on early socialization, we now have some reason to reverse our emphasis on these two aspects of Freudian theory.[20]

Aggressive Catharsis?

As Freud saw it, impulses for aggression must be either expressed or suppressed. If expressed, they may not always be expressed directly. Cultural learning leads humans to express their needs in a great variety of ways; and if there is a basic need for aggression, it can be expressed in many ways and toward a variety of targets. Also, we can try to suppress such a need altogether, by repressing all thoughts associated with the common expressions of the need. But such suppression can never be complete, as Freud saw it. There are always ways that the truth of one's basic desires for sex and aggression will show themselves: through dreams and slips of the tongue if not through other actions that indirectly express such motives. Indeed, indirect expressions are seen as the way civilized persons handle their aggressions, for if they try to inhibit them too much it may be debilitating. The general functioning of the individual may be seriously impaired, and a suppressed need may build up to such a point that it must finally—and perhaps explosively—be expressed. This is the thinking behind the idea, which Freud supported, of a 'catharsis' of aggression: that there must be a cleaning out of the psychic system to release the tension when a basic need is too strongly inhibited.

The basic idea of the need for an aggressive catharsis has become part of the popular way most of us talk about aggression building up within us and needing an outlet. It has also, in a more sophisticated form, found application in some of the more technical social psychological literature. For example, this idea is included in what has come to be known as "frustration-aggression" theory.

Frustration and Aggression

In a highly influential book based on careful scholarship, John Dollard and his Yale associates presented in 1939 a set of basic propositions about the relationship between frustration and aggression. As they saw it, frustration (that is, any blocking of action toward a goal) may not always lead to direct aggression, but it always increases the 'instigation to aggression.' That is, it increases the probability of aggressive acts and/or makes them more strongly expressed. Also, in the original formulation of the theory (though this was later qualified) frustration was seen as the basic source for all aggressive behavior. Thus we have the frustration-aggression connection set forth as a key to understanding a wide variety of human behavior.[21]

However, direct aggression is not always the result of frustration. There may be inhibitions against expressing aggression, especially toward persons most directly associated with our frustrations. For example, one may not find it prudent to explode against the boss associated with frustrations on the job; one may instead inhibit such aggression and seek a secondary target, such as one's spouse or the dog. But frustration—so goes the theory—always leads to an increased tendency toward aggression of some sort toward someone or something. The more directly the target of our aggression is associated with the frustration, the more effectively is the tension released. Here is again the idea of 'catharsis of aggression'; the release of aggression is seen as reducing the pent-up aggression.

Some basic facts support the frustration-aggression hypothesis. Most importantly, we can all reflect on times when we have been aroused to anger by some frustration, and how then our own aggressive behavior followed. Also, animal as well as human studies point to a close relationship between pain and aggression; indeed, 'pain-induced aggression' is one of the basic types identified by biologists who study aggressive behaviors. While not theoretically the same as frustration, pain and physical stress are clearly factors that may be closely associated with aggressive behaviors.[22]

Problems with the frustration-aggression hypothesis arise from the assumption that a basic drive is involved, from the indirect nature of much aggression, and from the implications that aggression has cathartic value. Many scholars dispute the utility of conceptualizing aggression as a drive. They prefer to see it as a classification for a wide range of behaviors that may be related to a great variety of motives. The indirect nature of much aggression leads to the question: If aggression is not expressed directly, how can we be sure it is linked to the original frustration? As a result of such considerations (doubts as to the drive status of aggression, and difficulties of verifying indirect links between frustration and aggression) most later frustration-aggression theorists consider cognitive associations as critical. Now emphasized as key issues are such factors as how we interpret certain events as frustrating, how we identify appropriate targets, and what we believe might be the consequences of aggressive actions. Finally, the idea of a 'catharsis of aggression' has received little empirical support. Most often studies have found that the expression of aggression does little to reduce its future potential. Indeed, the findings are generally in the other direction, with the expression of aggression leading to increased aggressive behavior later.[23]

A Rational Response?

Very different from a basic drive approach is that which sees aggression as primarily a rational response to given conditions. Instead of unconscious urges, such an approach emphasizes conscious objectives. Thus the playground bully learns to beat up on other kids because he finds that this gives him power over them (and perhaps even some extra lunch money). The general orders an attack because he sees this as part of the way his nation must uphold its vital interests. Or a wife angrily scolds her husband because she has found that this is the best way to ensure that certain repairs around the house will be attended to.

Conditioning

Those who question the drive status of aggression are likely to emphasize the learned nature of aggressive behavior. Aggression becomes part of the person only insofar as certain behaviors that are generally called aggressive have become learned. The nature of social situations and how one learns to cope with them are, in this view, the key elements for understanding an individual's aggressive behavior.

That classic forms of learning can be applied to the development of aggressive responses is well documented in the scientific literature. These include classical conditioning (based on the association of stimuli, which allows a transfer of a response from one stimulus situation to another) and instrumental, or operant, conditioning (based on the probability of a behavior being increased by its previous consequences).[24]

The positive and negative associations we make with other persons and their characteristics are strongly influenced by processes of classical conditioning. Further, the stimuli available in a particular situation may strongly condition what response we make. For example, if we have a gun in our house, we are more likely to fire upon a presumed intruder (who may turn out to be a friend playing a practical joke) than if we didn't have it. The further association of guns with violence may lead us to give a more aggressive response in any situation where guns are mentioned. Some experimental studies have suggested that just having a gun lying around in the room when an experiment is conducted will lead to increased aggression in the behavior of subjects. This leads us to question whether the "trigger" (that is, any stimulus associated with violence or aggression) may not pull the person, as well as the other way around.[25]

Even more apparent is the role of operant conditioning in learning aggressive responses. When we are rewarded by behaving aggressively, we will continue to show similar behavior in the future. The more rewarded, the stronger will become such behavior. If the reward is removed, the behavior will become less aggressive. The attention that rewards much youthful aggression is no doubt a frequent factor in its continued strength. Some programs of working with aggressive youth have found rather dramatic results in reducing aggressive behavior by the systematic application of principles of operant conditioning.[26]

Many people believe that complex human behaviors cannot be reduced to matters of simple conditioning. They suggest that something other than 'rat psychology' needs to apply to humans. Such a view must ignore a vast array of scientific evidence that principles of classical and instrumental conditioning do apply to humans. But there is also validity in the thought that the simple studies of conditioning do not capture some of the learning processes that are most distinctively human.

Observational Learning

Much of what we as humans do we learn from one another. We are cultural beings as well as animals, and human culture is totally learned through contact with others. Because we possess the power of language, we learn from what we are told by the words of other people. Even more importantly, we learn by what we observe in the actions of others.

The role of observational learning in the development of aggressive behavior has been especially emphasized by what has come to be most generally known as "social learning theory." A leader in this field has been Albert Bandura, and he and his associates have clarified many important issues regarding learning through observing others. They have demonstrated that we can learn through purely observational processes—that a new form of behavior may occur without any practice on the part of the individual, but only because it is observed in others. This is sometimes called "no-trial learning," in contrast with the more traditionally recognized forms of conditioning based on accumulated experience. The social learning theorists have also demonstrated that observing others being reinforced for aggression will increase one's own behavior of a similar sort. This, of course, has enormous implications for our age of television, with such frequent instances of justified violence shown on our TV sets. Also demonstrated by social learning theorists are the ways that the observation of others may serve to instigate certain responses on certain occasions and to inhibit similar responses at other times.[27]

Beyond the Individual

When studying such processes as classical conditioning, instrumental conditioning, or observational learning, it is not difficult to move one's attention beyond the individual. Much of our behavior showing aggression, is learned together with other persons. And observational learning directly involves someone else to be observed. While the focus may be on the individual's behavior and the conditions under which certain patterns become clear, it is easy to see that social processes involving other people are also occurring. In Chapter 4, we will build on this occurrence as we pursue the family of theories about social conflict that give primary attention to interaction between persons, rather than to the individual as such. These we will identify as "social process" theories.

Summary and Conclusions

Summary

We have used the theories of Sigmund Freud as a point of departure for examining those theoretical frameworks that give primary attention to our natures as individuals. Freud saw social conflict primarily in terms of individual behaviors. Thus the problem of war became, for him, largely a matter of the expression of aggressive impulses. While he also had theories about how basic drives may be modified through social influences, he still always focused on the behavior of individuals.

Of course, our attention has not been limited to Freudian theories. We used Freud's theories of innate aggression, and his views on the importance of early social learning in changing the expression of our basic drives, largely to lead into some of the other main theories that place emphasis on forces within the individual:

1. We considered the biology of aggression, in the sense that our aggressive impulses may have the heritage of many past generations of natural selection. This we viewed first in terms of the original views of Darwinism (including social Darwinism as well as the views of Darwin himself), and then in terms of the more recent developments of ethology and sociobiology. This survey leaves us with mixed signals on an inherited basis of aggression as a central part of human nature. We concluded that the idea of an instinct for aggression is not clearly demonstrated by the available evidence of human evolution.

2. We next examined the biology of aggression in terms of specific genetic evidence and key physiological processes that may often be involved in aggressive behavior. In this we found many interesting patterns. There may be some genetic base for predispositions toward certain forms of aggressive behavior; but our ability to locate specific genes for any forms have so far not been fruitful. More promising is the knowledge that certain parts of the brain are heavily involved in aggressive behaviors and that endocrine levels are also significantly related to aggression.

3. We examined the role of aggression as a possible personality trait. Here our findings were also inconclusive. Because there are so many different kinds of behavior that may be called "aggression," it is unlikely that they can all be correlated with any general pattern of personality. Nevertheless, we did find some basis for seeing certain personality traits as leading to higher probabilities of aggression, and we increased our appreciation for the extent to which such traits may be based on genetic factors.

4. We examined the theories that aggression builds up within the individual until it may be released upon some target. These included not only Freud's theory of displaced aggression, but also the general frustration-aggression hypothesis and certain related viewpoints. These theories may be seen as in some respects well founded (there does often appear to be a link between frustration and aggression), but there are other aspects where the evidence is not very supportive; for example, the idea of a 'catharsis of aggression' does not often lead to well-confirmed predictions.

5. Finally, we looked at various kinds of learning theory. These appear to be especially helpful for understanding how aggressive behaviors (as well as any other kind of response) might be formed. The three main theoretical approaches to learning that we examined—classical conditioning, operant conditioning, and observational learning—have considerable value for understanding a wide range of aggressive behaviors.

Conclusions

All of the theories we have examined primarily focus on understanding aggression within the individual. Social conflict between individuals or groups has not been our theme; we have looked only at factors of individual behavior that may be involved in such conflicts. Nevertheless, there are some fairly clear implications for conflict resolution. To the extent that social conflicts are based on the aggression of individuals, we might expect that such conflicts could be reduced by changing the individuals. In particular, the following conclusions are suggested.

a. To the extent that aggression is a basic drive of the human species, founded on our past history of natural selection, there's not much we can do about it in the near future. We can try to repress and control our aggressive impulses, but this gives us only limited kinds of resolution. Fundamental conflict remains both between us and within us.

b. To the extent to that certain aggressive behaviors are tied to specific patterns of genes, there is little we can do at present to use that knowledge. For humans, at least, any hope to resolve conflicts by changing our genes is not on anyone's current agenda. That kind of genetic engineering remains a highly speculative project for the future. However, the control of certain physiological processes involved in the more violent forms of personal aggression is more promising. At present, there are drugs that can be used to dampen the likelihood that our brains will trigger angry aggression, and there are other means of changing endocrine balances associated with aggressive behaviors. Such medical means may help toward the resolution of some, but surely not most, social conflicts.

c. To the extent that aggression is rooted in fairly long-term personality patterns, there is only a limited opportunity for reducing conflict. The most relevant application of this approach would be to see that our most aggressive personalities are not given positions of political leadership. Psychotherapy may sometimes be used to change personalities, and thereby tendencies to engage in conflict, but this approach toward conflict resolution is uncertain in its results, as well as costly.

d. To the extent that we see aggression building up in the individual as a result of the accumulation of frustrations, we do at least have a clear direction for seeking reductions in conflict: Try to reduce the frustrations of those engaged in conflict. This, of course, is much easier to say than to do. Still, it gives us an agenda to pursue in trying to reduce some of our most severe conflicts.

e. To the extent that aggression is a product of social learning, the conflict resolution agenda becomes that of changing the conditions of human learning. Providing new associations of stimuli, reducing the rewards for aggressive behavior, providing new examples for others to observe—by all such means we may change the probability of aggressive behaviors, thus providing a better base for conflict resolution.

4

Social Process Theories

Mr. Smith Returns from France

Adam Smith

When he returned to his home town in Scotland in 1767, Adam Smith was in an unusually fortunate position. Though only in his mid-forties, Smith was assured a satisfactory income for the rest of his life without regular work. He also was widely recognized for his wisdom, with most of the leading intellectuals of Europe (and Benjamin Franklin in America) pleased to know him. What more could he need? He could settle down in Kirkcaldy, the town of his birth, and live there in peace for the rest of his days.

Adam Smith wanted to live in peace. He was not one who craved constant excitement. He could enjoy the company of others, but much more did he enjoy reading the books in his library. Although he was a generally congenial person, others were sometimes exasperated by his frequent absentmindedness. He was so preoccupied with his own ideas that he frequently lost track of where he was or what he was supposed to be doing. But in Kirkcaldy, where he was well known, his eccentricities would not be much of a problem. He could settle down there to live with his mother and a maiden cousin.

Despite several friendships with women (especially during his recent sojourn in Paris), Smith never came close to marrying. However, he was devoted to his family, especially his mother (his father having died shortly before his birth). He also had numerous friends, with fellow philosopher David Hume among the closest of these.

He had had a distinguished career as a scholar in Edinburgh and Glasgow, serving in the chair of moral philosophy at the University of Glasgow until early 1764. At that time, his plans changed quite suddenly. His book, *The Theory of Moral Sentiments,* had won wide approval after its publication in 1759, and one of those much impressed by it was Charles Townshend, who moved in the highest social and political circles of Great Britain. Townshend wanted to reward the writer of such an outstanding book; he also had a stepson, the young Duke of Buccleuch, who needed a little more educational guidance before being launched into the adult world (in which Townshend had high hopes of a political career for him). So Townshend made Smith an offer he couldn't refuse: Smith would have a comfortable income assured for the rest of his life, and in return would serve as primary tutor of the young Duke for a few years.

Smith and his young charge left for France—the center of so much intellectual ferment at the time—early in 1764. They stayed at Toulouse and Paris until late 1966, when the unexpected death of the Duke's brother (who had joined them in France) led to their return to England. Shortly thereafter the Duke became occupied with matrimonial plans, an area in which Smith had little to offer. Smith then returned to Scotland. In June of 1767 he could describe his present situation (in a letter to a friend) as follows:

> My Business here is Study in which I have been very deeply engaged for about a Month past. My Amusements are long, solitary walks by the Sea side. You may judge how I spend my time. I feel myself, however, extremely happy, comfortable, and contented. I never was, perhaps, more so in all my life.[1]

Previous Work

Those who knew Smith well would not be surprised that he, in his new opportunities for leisure, would be devoting himself to study. Most, however, had only a vague idea of what kind of study he was pursuing. After all, he had already distinguished himself in a wide variety of fields at the University of Glasgow during the period that this relatively young man served as a faculty member. (He was still in his twenties when first appointed to a chair there and only forty when he left.) He had taught in the fields of logic, rhetoric, theology, ethics, jurisprudence, and political economy.

Smith at the time was most noted for his work on ethics. His point of view in this field, as set forth primarily in *The Theory of Moral Sentiments,* provided one of the fresh, new views of the eighteenth century. Standards of right and wrong, according to Smith, were not given in some absolute way from above. Instead they were developed through experience. It was primarily through social experience that these standards emerged. Out of a process of interaction with others we gradually learn what is considered right and wrong. "The general maxims of morality are formed," said Smith, "from experience and induction. We observe in a great variety of particular cases what pleases or displeases our moral faculties, what these approve or disapprove of, and, by induction from this experience, we establish those general rules."[2]

In developing our general principles, we are guided not only by what is taught in our society but also by an inner voice. This inner voice, what Smith called the "impartial spectator" or the "man within the breast," is formed out of our interaction with others. It is an internal representation of the reactions of others, gradually becoming more organized as our social experience accumulates. Because of its source in social interaction, it is natural that this inner voice is closely tied to an emotion of empathy or "fellow feeling" with others. At the heart of all moral sentiments is therefore this empathy rooted in social interaction.

Not only general ethical principles but also the very nature of the self arises out of a process of social interaction. If it were possible to imagine a person in complete isolation he would have no definitely formed character. However, said Smith, "bring him into society, and he is immediately provided with the mirror which he wanted before. It is placed in the countenance and behavior of those he lives with." This "mirror" of other people provides the framework into which a person forms self-consciousness; for without any communication with others one could "no more think of his own character, or the propriety or demerit of his own sentiments and conduct, of the beauty or deformity of his own mind, than the beauty or deformity of his own face." We thus, through interaction with others, become not just physical beings but moral and ethical beings as well.[3]

New Work

In 1767 Smith still held such views as to the foundations of ethical judgment. But it was in a different direction that he now turned his attention. Smith was concerned with the larger world of political and economic affairs. This world lacked a good intellectual framework that would allow its comprehensive study. He would like to supply that framework, and in so doing also provide many insightful comments about the public affairs of his time. He had already started working on this project during spare moments while in France, and now back home at Kirkcaldy he could work on it in earnest. A new book was clearly in the works. However, it would take another nine years of work before this book, *An Inquiry into the Nature and Causes of the Wealth of Nations,* would make its appearance.[4]

The Wonderful World of Markets

Key Themes

The Wealth of Nations is of course the book that we now consider Adam Smith's great contribution. Therefore, today we mainly know Smith as the father of economics and not as a moral philosopher. We associate him with the ideology of capitalism and its profit motive rather than as a philosopher stressing the importance of fellow feeling and sympathy. These two sides of Adam Smith's work (if we even hear of his moral philosophy) seem discordant. Nevertheless, we have no reason to believe that Smith saw any inconsistency between his two great books. One was concerned with the personal side of experience, and the other was concerned with public affairs. Both had similar themes in two key aspects: (1) both placed central attention upon the human individual, and (2) both took a social process view of their primary subject matter.

In his *Theory of Moral Sentiments,* Smith had given special attention to the virtue of prudence. Virtue? Yes, said Smith; along with beneficence toward others and justice in one's relationships must come the virtue of a circumspect life. Smith recognized that prudence is not the most endearing of virtues; at most, he admitted, it "commands a certain cold esteem." Still, we must give it close attention because "every man is, no doubt, by nature, first and principally recommended to his own care" and, Smith was convinced, "is fitter to take care of himself than of any other person."[5]

There is, in such passages, a strong spirit of individualism. This individualism, characteristic of his era (and ours), is also clearly manifest in *The Wealth of Nations,* with its central emphasis on self-interest. It is out of the self-interests of individuals that the vast panoply of economic relationships are formed. One of Smith's most famous quotations presents this clearly:

> It is not from the benevolence of the butcher, the brewer, or the baker that we expect our dinner, but from their regard to their own interest. We address ourselves, not to their humanity but to their self-love, and never talk to them of our own necessities but of their advantages. Nobody but a beggar chooses to depend chiefly upon the benevolence of his fellow citizens.[6]

The Theory of Moral Sentiments and *The Wealth of Nations* were also similar in the centrality of a social process perspective. In Smith's first book, a social process view is used to develop the basic principles of an individual's ethical framework; in his second, the broader institutions of society are seen as products of a similar process of interaction between individuals—albeit now in their primary roles of workers, producers, or consumers. Political and economic institutions are developed not so much by the fiat of rulers or the moral expressions of more common people as by the actual relationships worked out through the give and take of the real world. This real world is seen fundamentally as a product of market relationships.

The Market

For Smith, the market continually balanced the self-interests of individuals. On one side of the market was the supply of goods or services: how much was available at a particular time and place. On the other side was the demand: how much people wanted of that form of goods or services. Supply and demand always worked together as a general process that determined prices. Reduce the supply, and prices will rise. Or increase the demand, and the result is similar. Increased supplies or decreased demand will both lower prices. And it is this determination of price in a free, competitive market that allows other economic forces to function effectively.

How much are workers to get for their labor? Since in a basic way they create the value of a product (for Smith, as well as Marx after him, espoused a labor theory of value), they need to be paid generously. But not too generously—for if other workers are available, they should also be considered as potential employees; and this added supply of labor helps to control its price.

How do we decide what to produce? We seek to go into the production of those goods and services that appear to be greatly in demand. Therefore, a society's most urgent needs are most likely to receive attention, as production flows to whatever shows the greatest market demand. And the amount produced is likewise a function of the demand; for when more is produced than people need or want, the price falls and the incentive is then provided to get into some other line of production.

How do we decide where a product is to go to be consumed? By wherever the demand is greatest. Distribution and consumption, as well as production, follow the laws of the market. Where there are greatest demands for a product, there will it be sent and there will it be consumed. "Consumption," Smith said, "is the sole end and purpose of all production; and the interest of the producer ought to be attended to only so far as it may be necessary for promoting that of the consumer."[7]

Thus, in Smith's view, market mechanisms control the basic economic processes of a society. They control who works for whom, what is produced, the price at which it is sold, and where it is consumed. All of these processes occur without any general dictation of society or governmental planning. They just naturally occur. Even the individuals involved are only vaguely conscious of how the market works. Each individual, said Smith, in one of his most famous passages, "intends only his own gain, and he is in this, as in many other cases, led by an invisible hand to promote an end which was not part of his intention." In addition, he suggests that "by pursuing his own interest he frequently promotes that of the society more effectively than when he really intends to promote it."

The Role of Government

Smith saw a limited (but important) governmental role in all this. Governments must uphold a system of public order and justice, for "no social intercourse can take place among men who do not generally abstain from injuring one another." There are also some special needs of the public that require governmental action; Smith here explicitly recognized projects such as roads and harbors, a postal system, public education, and even some assistance to religious institutions. But most important is the need for governments to limit their role in economic affairs, allowing what Smith called "the obvious and simple system of natural liberty" to become established "of its own accord."[8]

If we can just promote such an "obvious and simple system," believed Smith, a steady stream of progress would be the result. The economic efficiency of markets would be a spur for improved goods and services. Moreover, with an increasing division of labor and a growth in population, economic growth could continue indefinitely. Such was the progress that could come from a system in which individuals were free to pursue—within the law and within generally approved moral guidelines—their own self-interests.

Competition and Conflict

A Conflict Theorist?

If conflict theory deals with the way persons confront one another in anger, Adam Smith was not a conflict theorist. He gave little attention to the more aggressive and violent aspects of human behavior, other than to recognize their existence. But he did emphasize the presence of conflict in the sense of conflicts of interest. They were, in his view, all around us as an inevitable condition of life. It was his understanding of how we deal with interest conflicts, especially indirectly, which is at the heart of Smith's contribution.

Much more clearly than a conflict theorist, Adam Smith was a theorist of conflict resolution. His focus was on how interest conflicts get resolved through the impersonal mechanisms of the market. Of course, this is not quite the same as what some people emphasize when they speak of conflict resolution. He did not analyze in detail the haggling that could go on between buyer and seller, or how management and labor representatives could engage in many hours of hard bargaining before reaching a final agreement. He was concerned with conflict resolution in a more fundamental sense: how we can resolve our everyday conflicts of interest automatically and without particularly trying to, through the impersonal processes of the marketplace.

Park and Burgess

In Chapter 1 we defined social conflict broadly, as including not only direct confrontations but also competitive pressures. Other scholars have emphasized more of a distinction between competition and conflict. Robert E. Park and Ernest W. Burgess made such a distinction, in what was perhaps the most influential textbook in the history of sociology. They distinguished four great types of human interaction: competition, conflict, accommodation, and assimilation. Of these, they saw competition as the most "elementary, universal and fundamental" process; it is "universal in the world of living things." But competition does not require direct contact between persons; it is rather an underlying struggle. When the struggle becomes more conscious and direct, it becomes considered "conflict." Out of the social processes of competition and conflict come the basic resolutions of accommodation and assimilation. Accommodation involves persons making adjustments to situations of competition and conflict, but without resolving the fundamental issues; "antagonistic cooperation" is how it has sometimes been characterized. In contrast, when persons overcome their differences, we may speak of assimilation. Such are the key concepts in the approach of Park and Burgess to the science of society—one that is often called a "social process" approach, in contrast to the social structural perspective of other sociologists.[9]

Simmel

While in America sociologists were distinguishing between competition and conflict as fundamental social forms, in Europe some scholars were emphasizing the continuity between conflict and other social processes. The outstanding example of this is Georg Simmel, an early-twentieth-century German philosopher and sociologist. In his richly insightful essay, "Conflict," Simmel emphasizes how all social organization rests on an intertwining of cooperation and conflict. Said Simmel: "A certain amount of discord, inner divergence and outer controversy, is organically tied up with the very elements that ultimately hold the group together," and antagonism "is an element almost never absent" in human association. Simmel saw competition as a major form of conflict, and he described in rich detail how both hostile confrontations and more indirect forms of conflict may affect human relationships.[10]

Coser

Nearly a half century after Simmel first wrote on the subject of conflict, Lewis Coser attempted to give a more formal presentation of the same basic ideas. This he did in the form of sixteen propositions in his book, *The Functions of Social Conflict.* While acknowledging a direct debt to Simmel for his basic ideas, Coser also provided a rich commentary of his own on the way conflict may be observed throughout human relationships. Something of the central character of his (and Simmel's) work can be seen in a selection of Coser's propositions. Let us note a few of the summary statements of these ideas.

- Conflict serves to establish and maintain the identity and boundary lines of societies and groups.
- Conflict is not always dysfunctional for the relationship within which it occurs; often conflict is necessary to maintain such a relationship.

- Antagonism is usually involved as an element in intimate relationships.
- A conflict is more passionate and more radical when it arises out of close relationships.
- Conflict with another group leads to the mobilization of the energies of group members and hence to increased cohesion of the group.
- Groups engaged in continued struggle with the outside tend to be intolerant within.
- Conflict, rather than being disruptive and dissociating, may indeed be a means of balancing and hence maintaining a society as a going concern.[11]

Thus, in the 1950s, at a time when conflict seemed to be avoided as a central concept in American sociology, Lewis Coser reminded his fellow social scientists of the key role that conflict always plays for society. His book was highly influential in reminding sociologists of ideas that had been central earlier in the century (in writings such as those of Park and Burgess and of Simmel), thus setting the stage for a remarkable rise in sociological attention to conflict in the period since then.

The Termination of Conflict

Among the authors that we have considered so far in this chapter (Smith, Park and Burgess, Simmel, and Coser), Simmel most explicitly discusses the topic of conflict resolution. First of all, suggests Simmel, we must recognize that the transition from conflict to peace is more problematic than that from peace to conflict. "The ending of a conflict is a specific enterprise," says Simmel. "It belongs neither to war nor to peace, just as a bridge is different from either bank it connects." The termination of a conflict is therefore a distinctive activity, and it deserves special sociological attention.[12]

Among the motives for conflict resolution, Simmel specifically mentions a generalized desire for peace, the need for contrasts in the rhythm of life (sometimes people "need discord in order to preserve the relationship" and to enjoy the fruits of ending conflict), the exhaustion of one's energies through conflict, and changes in the interests each party pursues (sometimes persons may find "the issue of the fight has merely lost its interest, and they only want to free their energies for other purposes").

Simmel recognizes five main types of patterns in the termination of conflict: (1) disappearance of the object of conflict, (2) victory for one of the parties, (3) compromise, (4) conciliation, and (5) irreconcilability.

Issues of dispute sometimes do go away by changes of one or the other party, or even by accident. Simmel gives several examples of how outside forces may lead to the end of a conflict: "a rivalry where the person or party decides in favor of a third party; a fight over a booty which in the meantime is taken by somebody else; or a theoretical controversy where the problem is unexpectedly solved by a higher intelligence and both conflicting positions are shown to have been wrong."[13]

Sometimes conflicts end in the victory of one party. This may be because of the superior power of one of them, or it may be because of the willingness to give in on the part of the other. Regarding this last possibility, Simmel makes an interesting point about how in some personal conflicts, yielding may even be a way of demonstrating superiority; he asserts that sometimes "the yielding of a party before the other has conclusively made its case, is felt by the more powerful one as a sort of offense; it is as if it actually were the weaker of the two and the other had for some reason yielded without having had to."

Very different from victory is compromise, especially applicable when there is some way to quantify and divide the objects of conflict. Simmel suggests that this tendency to compromise, especially in matters of economic exchange, "is one of mankind's greatest inventions." He further asserts that "all exchange of things is a compromise" which is based on the development of a common standard of value for what is at issue and some explicit agreement on that basis which serves the interests of both parties.[14]

Conciliation is sometimes the subjective side of a compromise. At other times, conciliation (especially in its more religious forms) may take place by itself, as parties move from enmity to forgiveness and acceptance. Sometimes when parties move through conflict to conciliation they have a stronger relationship than one that is untested. As Simmel points out, sometimes "the breach has created a background against which all values . . . of the union now stand out more consciously and clearly."[15]

Finally, there may be an acceptance by the parties of irreconcilability, which Simmel identifies as "the negative extreme of reconcilability." The active phase of the conflict may pass with the fundamental issues still unresolved; or out of the conflict may have grown such a degree of hostility that it cannot be removed. In intimate personal relationships it is often the case that irreconcilability can coexist with love and affection; Simmel here points to how we may continue to harbor a grievance, but "it is localized, as it were, it is taken, as one factor, into the total relationship, whose central intensity does not necessarily suffer therefrom."

Interactionist Perspectives

Smith as an Interactionist

Adam Smith's basic perspective can be described as "interactionist." The emergence of a sense of right and wrong in the individual comes primarily, he believed, through interaction with others. We continue with an internalized summary of that interaction to guide our further actions, even when not directly in the company of others. Likewise, his view of economic relationships can be described as interactionist, for it is out of the interactions of exchange between individuals that economic institutions emerge.

Symbolic Interactionism

Among twentieth century movements of thought that may broadly be considered interactionist perspectives, none has a more direct relationship to Smith's thinking than what has come to be known as "symbolic interactionism." From the writings of William James, John Dewey, George H. Mead, and Charles H. Cooley emerged a common approach which later (in 1937 by Herbert Blumer, to be exact) came to be identified as "symbolic interactionism." When he formulated the key ideas of symbolic interactionism, Blumer paid special attention to the earlier work of Mead (his former teacher) in stating the following as the basic premises: (1) "that human beings act toward things on the basis of the meanings that the things have for them"; (2) "that the meaning of such things is derived from, or rises out of, the social interaction that one has with one's fellows"; and (3) "that these meanings are handled in, and modified through, an interpretive process used by the person in dealing with the things he encounters." Although others have defined symbolic interactionism in other ways, all have emphasized that behavior can be fully understood only if we take into account its subjective or reflective character, and that the meanings we use to guide our behavior grow primarily out of our interaction with others.[16]

In becoming a main framework for social psychology, especially for those social psychologists with a background in sociology, symbolic interactionism came to be widely applied to all aspects of human behavior. These naturally include the study of social conflicts. However, in general, symbolic interactionists have been more interested in studying how humans cooperate—how, through interaction, they form the bonds that tie them together—than how they come into conflict. They have examined conflicts and their resolution primarily in order to consider the underlying positive relationships among people. There is therefore no distinctive conflict theory coming out of symbolic interactionism, except when it is combined with other approaches, such as Marxism.

In his work on negotiation, Anselm Strauss gives a good example of how symbolic interactionists may deal with the subject matter of conflict. He views negotiations not as specific processes occurring between individuals and groups, but rather as representing a fundamental process by which society is formed and constantly remade. His approach to society is often called the "negotiated order" approach, suggesting that human institutions are not simply transmitted from the past or determined by some present authority, but that they grow from innumerable workings out of the interests of people with one another—in other words, through a process of negotiation. With this very broad view of negotiations, Strauss then turns to a review of the social science theories that he sees as most relevant, followed by an examination of particular case studies. The case studies include relations within an industrial firm, negotiations between insurance companies and claimants, courtroom behavior, relations between ethnic groups, bride-price negotiations, relations on geriatric hospital wards, and international diplomacy.[17]

Among the key factors Strauss examines in his study of negotiations are the following:

- The number of negotiators, their relative experience in negotiating, and whom they represent
- Whether the negotiations are one-shot, repeated, sequential, serial, multiple, or linked
- The relative balance of power exhibited by the respective parties in the negotiation itself
- The nature of their respective stakes in the negotiation
- The visibility of the transactions to others
- The number and complexity of the issues negotiated
- The options available if negotiations are avoided or discontinued

These factors occur in what Strauss calls the direct social context of negotiations. Behind such considerations is the larger context of social institutions which provide the framework for negotiations. Strauss, as a sociologist, is especially interested in examining these larger conditions of social organization within which negotiations take place.

As one strongly influenced by the traditions of symbolic interactionism, Strauss has a special concern for understanding how negotiators themselves see their negotiations. What they carry around in their heads about the meanings of what they are doing, Strauss believes, has a profound impact on negotiation behavior. These ideas may partly grow out of their past experiences, but they emerge only in the context of their present social relationships. In any case, they are very important for the social scientist to try to understand.

Field Theory

If we use the term broadly, much of contemporary social psychology (not just the work of those who call themselves symbolic interactionists) can be seen as following an interactionist perspective. That is, most social psychologists see social interaction as the ground upon which they study the social thought and behavior of their subjects. The variables found in interaction are often the key variables manipulated in their experiments.

This is especially true for those who follow in the tradition associated with Kurt Lewin. Lewin, coming out of a background of gestalt psychology (the gestaltists emphasized that perception and behavior always come in organized patterns, never as isolated stimuli or responses), gave the name of "field theory" to his approach. Behavior, he said, is always the result of a field of forces, never a matter of specific traits in the individual or specific conditions of the environment. The way these forces come together determines the behavior of the individuals involved.

Although this is hardly an adequate description of Lewinian field theory, it at least gives an initial characterization. Field theory has been extremely influential upon the work of social psychologists (especially those trained in psychology departments) since Lewin's time. Indeed, many of the leading social psychologists in the last half of the twentieth century were directly influenced by Lewin. Although the specific formulations of Lewin's field theory (especially the mainly geometric forms he used to describe various fields) are no longer much used, the general legacy of Lewin remains strong.

As a field theorist, Lewin considered not only the fields that helped us understand the behavior of individuals; he also applied his field theory to the group level. He, more than anyone else, was the founder of what is usually called "group dynamics"—the study of groups as fields of forces in their own right. For Lewin, the interaction between individuals in their groups always was a central aspect of their behavior. In early experimental work on the social climates of groups, Lewin and his students sought to show how different styles of adult leadership (they examined especially what they called authoritarian, democratic, and laissez-faire styles) may affect the behavior of children toward each other. This, and many other examples of Lewin's scholarly work in social science, were reprinted in two books that appeared shortly after his death, *Resolving Social Conflicts* and *Field Theory in Social Science.*[18]

Among Lewin's colleagues and students, Morton Deutsch has probably focused more clearly on social conflict and its resolution than anyone else. In 1949 he published an influential theoretical paper analyzing the concepts of cooperation and competition. His analysis focused especially on the basic goals of the parties involved and the kinds of interaction likely to come from the way these goals were kept separate or combined. His theoretical statement was followed closely by empirical work, exploring the conditions under which cooperation might emerge out of competitive situations. Some of this work involved highly abstract formulations of two-person interaction, which showed that the extent and form of communication was critical for the emergence of cooperation. Other research (especially that carried out with Robert M. Krauss) dealt with simulations of more realistic situations, and this seemed to show that the presence and use of threats (that is, communications suggesting that one has the power to act against the other) is a key factor affecting whether cooperative resolutions can occur.[19]

Based on both his theory and research, as well as suggestions found in the work of others, Deutsch has given us a general statement of the conditions for effective conflict resolution. He first notes the characteristics of destructive conflicts and their typical patterns of escalation. For a conflict to move into a destructive spiral, he suggests, three main factors are necessary, each of which he discusses in detail: (1) competitive processes lead to the idea that the conflict might be "won"; (2) misperception and selective information accentuate the contrast of oneself with the other side; and (3) pressures toward cognitive and societal consistency heighten one's commitment to engage in the conflict. When such processes act on both sides of a conflict at the same time, a mutually destructive spiral easily ensues. But conflicts need not have such a pattern. There is also the pattern Deutsch calls "productive conflict." The parties here too have different interests or attitudes. However, they resist the temptations to escalate the conflict and, instead, focus on such factors as: (a) creative thinking about their problem(s), (b) searching for possibilities for mutual problem solving, (c) giving one's opponent the benefit of the doubt in regard to the interpretation of motives, and (d) seeking to negotiate cooperative commitments.

What determines whether a conflict is to move in the destructive direction rather than become a productive conflict? Among the factors Deutsch emphasizes are the presence of honest communication, a prior relationship between the parties that is not antagonistic, an issue that is relatively small and/or well focused, an avoidance of rigidity in regard to the issue, and a conscious focus on the more objective aspects of the conflict. Of course, some of these may be present only in moderate degree. That may be enough to prevent the conflict from moving into a destructive spiral but still may leave the basic conflict unresolved. This then leads Deutsch to the subject of conflict regulation.

Effective conflict regulation requires the development of certain rules that both sides will agree to follow, even while continuing their conflict. Such rules will be most likely to be developed when the following conditions are present:

1. Each party must be coherently organized to allow its actions to be effectively coordinated.
2. Each party must be willing to recognize the legitimacy of the other.
3. Both sides to the conflict see themselves as part of a larger community.

Systems Theory

Similar to, and overlapping with, symbolic interactionism and field theory is an approach that has come to be known as "systems theory." A "system" is a unity of interacting parts, but with inputs from the surrounding environment. There are many variants of systems theory, for it has been used as a perspective for many fields, from engineering to biology to the social sciences. The conceptualization of a physical system in relationship to its environment has been applied to such diverse subjects as movements of the solar system and the operation of computers. The language of a systems approach has been especially applied to the design of computers, with the resulting popularity of such terms as *input, output,* and *system configuration.* Biology also has treated individual organisms as living systems functioning in a larger environment, with internal systems in turn functioning as parts of the organism. In the social sciences there is frequent discussion of organizations as systems, or even of society itself as a system. Finally, there has been the attempt to bring all these kinds of phenomena together in what has become known as "general systems theory."

A pioneer in general systems theory was Ludwig von Bertalanffy, who pointed to "concepts like those of organization, wholeness, directiveness, teleology and differentiation" as "indispensable for dealing with living organisms or social groups." He sought therefore to develop a general method of analysis which could apply to the study of processes of organization, wherever they may be found.[20]

A systems theory approach does not generally emphasize concepts such as conflict or conflict resolution. The emphasis is placed on how things work together, not how they fall apart. Nevertheless, there have been some forms of systems theory that do provide for perspectives on social conflict. We have already mentioned field theory, which may be seen as one form of systems theory. Other forms of systems thinking include sociological functionalism, the study of formal organizations as systems, and family systems theory. Each of these provides a somewhat different way of conceptualizing conflict, but all have in common a consideration that the parts of a system may not always nicely harmonize. In other words, all have had to make some room for the study of conflict and its resolution.

Those sociological theorists who are generally known as functionalists (such as Talcott Parsons and Robert K. Merton) emphasize how the parts of a social system work together. Following the lead of Emile Durkheim (the French sociological pioneer), they see social institutions as parts of some larger whole, and specific social practices constantly show the signs of their integration into the larger societal framework. But not only must we analyze "functions" (ways the specific parts fit into larger wholes); we must also allow for "dysfunctions," instances where the parts do not work together in complete harmony. This gives a handle for concepts like social conflict and its resolution. They are examined in somewhat the same manner that illness might be viewed in the study of biological organisms—that is, as disruptions of an otherwise stable system.[21]

A systems approach has also been applied to the study of formal organizations. The organization is seen as a unity of interrelated parts functioning within a larger environment (with inputs for, and outputs from, the organization providing the central explanation for how it functions). Within the organization there are always points of conflict, for the parts are never perfectly unified. These points of strain (such as between different authority lines) may then be examined as instances of social conflict. Of course, most organizational theorists view conflict as a secondary aspect of organizations, not a primary feature.

A systems approach has been applied to more personal forms of human interaction as well. A leading example of this is known as "family systems theory." Family systems theory focuses on the family as a system of interaction built by mutual expectations regarding one another's behavior. These expectations are in turn based on past behaviors. Family members come to count on one another to continue these patterns of behavior—and this includes both healthy and unhealthy relationships. Behavior of persons in families is thus seen as the product of 'circular causality' through interaction, rather than the result of individual experience. Many family counseling professionals emphasize a family systems approach, which means that they see themselves as treating the whole family and not primarily individual clients. Of course, they need to be attentive to sources of strain in the family's patterns of interaction. In this way family systems theory provides a distinctive way of thinking about family conflict and its resolution.

Social Exchange Theory

Homans

Adam Smith's contributions to economics provided a base for what has come to be known among sociologists and social psychologists as "social exchange" theory. Social exchange theory is essentially an attempt to apply the framework of market analysis to such phenomena as informal interaction and the emergence of group patterns.

Although with elements dating back to Aristotle as well as to Adam Smith, modern social exchange theory was first given clear formulation in a 1958 essay by the sociologist George C. Homans. In this essay, entitled "Social Behavior as Exchange," Homans treats social interaction generally as an exchange of "goods"—with goods considered to be not just material benefits but also social benefits people provide for each other. He analyzes interaction in terms of the rewards and costs experienced by the individuals involved. Each person tends to change his or her behavior when profit (that is, rewards in relation to costs) is low, and to maintain behavior that proves profitable. With such terms, we may analyze how and why groups emerge and what the primary patterns of interaction may be within them.[22]

Others

There have been a number of important variations on social exchange theory. Some theorists emphasize a direct tie to behavioral psychology in the way they formulate social rewards and costs. Homans, for example, uses individual psychology as a base for his attempt to formulate basic laws of social interaction. Others, such as Peter Blau, put the emphasis more on social frameworks that may not be reducible to the behaviors of individuals. Still others view social exchange theory not so much as a general theory of social behavior as an approach that may usefully apply to certain questions about human interaction.[23]

One subject within exchange theory with a direct relationship to social conflict is that of equity theory. Homans included the concern for distributive justice—how all persons involved are to get their just desserts—as one of the key questions for understanding group interaction. Others have pursued the subject from more psychological standpoints, trying to understand why certain individuals perceive certain arrangements as being just or unjust. In any case, those conditions in which people fail to achieve outcomes they consider to be equitable are conditions apt to be marked by social conflict. The conflict is especially intense when persons see themselves committed to a social relationship that is inequitable, for often one cannot easily leave such relationships. Of course, here the analogy to economic markets seems to break down; one is always free to leave the marketplace. However, on second thought, it is the absence of freedom to leave (thus creating conditions of 'imperfect competition') that sometimes prevents the market from serving its basic role as the automatic regulator of human economic self-interests.[24]

Exchange theory has moved in many new directions in the closing decades of the twentieth century, with an increasing sophistication in both research and theory. While much of the early work was on interaction within two-person relationships, it is now being applied mostly to patterns of relationships beyond the dyad. It is increasingly applied to such subjects as the structure of power and influence and the analysis of social networks. Although questions of conflict and its regulation become part of this research, it is seldom the central theme for attention.[25]

Other Social Process Theories

Boulding

Some of the important theories of conflict cannot be easily placed within the categories previously used in this chapter, yet they remain predominantly social process approaches. We mention here in particular the work of Kenneth E. Boulding.

Boulding was a distinguished economist as well as a general leader in conflict studies. Much of his conflict work drew heavily on economic models. In fact, he suggested, with ideas directly continuous with those of Adam Smith, that much conflict, especially in matters of economic interests, is regulated by markets. "The more perfect the competition becomes," he said, "the less economic conflict there is." This leads him to make an interesting observation regarding economic conflict:

> We notice the occasions when the market breaks down, but we do not notice the occasions when it operates successfully. Hence, we tend to attribute to the institution itself phenomena which are essentially associated with its breakdown.[26]

Boulding also takes specific ideas from economics and applies them to more general social conflict processes. An example is his projection of the theory of the firm to key issues of national defense. Given transportation costs and other considerations of location, an individual firm will have a stronger place in the market the closer it is to its home base. One can therefore chart out the firm's market potential as a gradient of influence. The same idea can be applied to the influence of nations in world politics and their capacity to defend themselves. "The closer, the stronger" seems to be the general rule here; and this idea (called by Boulding the theory of viability) helps us understand a wide range of conflict processes.[27]

But, of course, economics deals primarily with what might be called positive exchange. Conflict often involves negative exchanges—exchanges of "bads" rather than "goods." In recognizing this, Boulding attempts to formulate some of the general ways exchanges of rewards and promises of reward differ from exchanges of punishments and threats to harm one another. Negative exchanges, for example, may often not have points of equilibrium (such as those that determine price in economic markets) in the same way as do positive exchanges. Boulding also studies one-way transfers of goods or services and how such unilateral actions may relate to the more common forms of exchange.[28]

Pruitt and Rubin

Among the social conflict topics of special interest to Boulding were patterns of equilibrium and escalation (or what he called the "conflict spiral"). Among other students of such phenomena, we may mention Dean Pruitt and Jeffrey Rubin, two social psychologists who also have a general interest in social conflict. In their book, *Social Conflict: Escalation, Stalemate, and Settlement,* Pruitt and Rubin identify five basic strategies for dealing with conflict: (1) contending, (2) yielding, (3) problem solving, (4) withdrawing, and (5) inaction. Conflict escalation is likely to occur when both parties adopt a contending strategy. This is in turn most likely under conditions where each party perceives itself as powerful and has high aspirations for the future, but there is little perception of interests in common. On the other hand, escalation may be resisted by such forces as

- fear of escalation;
- bonds between potential antagonists;
- bonds to other parties who oppose conflict;
- conflict-limiting norms and institutions; and
- the existence of a balance of power.[29]

Kriesberg and Colleagues

Studies of escalation lead us also to recognize that some conflicts seem never to get resolved. They just go on and on and on. These have been called "intractable conflicts," and Louis Kriesberg and his colleagues have made important contributions toward their understanding. In his study of historical examples of intractable conflicts, Kriesberg points out that the elements that make one conflict seem incapable of resolution and another more easy to resolve are not always clear in advance. For example, he describes how the status of Berlin was for many years an intractable conflict between East and West; then, suddenly, the conflict vanished with broader changes in the international system. On the other hand, the status of the Palestinians in relation to the early state of Israel did not at first appear a very difficult problem; but a combination of factors over the years have made it one of the most intractable of recent world conflicts. This uncertainty about the future intensity of a conflict suggests that at times there is almost nothing that can be done to resolve it; however, it also suggests that we can never be sure that the present is not an appropriate time for an apparently intractable conflict to be moved toward some kind of resolution (witness, for example, some recent diplomatic events in the Middle East).[30]

Terrell Northrup, an associate of Kriesberg's, has formulated a general theory about the intractability of conflicts. She places a strong emphasis on the formation of personal and social identities, suggesting that intractable conflicts are usually those in which the pattern of opposition becomes strongly imbedded in a party's (whether of a person or a group) central sense of identity. This suggests that a rational discussion of interests—in terms of objective criteria—often does not get at what is really at stake in a very bitter conflict. Rather, the complexity of the conflict and the way it touches central identities may make it almost impossible to resolve. This, she suggests, tends to happen through a series of stages, which may be summarized as (1) a strong sense of threat to a group's (or person's) central commitments, (2) the distortion of one another's positions because of the sense of threat, (3) a hardening of positions so that central assumptions about the conflict become fixed for both parties, and (4) the development of fixed patterns of response which assume the conflict as a central and ongoing fact. Once a conflict reaches this final stage, it is extremely difficult for the parties to reach an agreement of any kind. Perhaps the best that can be hoped for is some success with conflict management, seeking to guard against a further escalation of the conflict. Ultimately, conflict resolution rests on a reduction of the sense of threat and of the misperceptions that are caused by it—and this often requires a changed sense of identity for one or both parties. This is, of course, much easier to analyze than to apply, once conflicts have become apparently intractable.[31]

Summary and Conclusions

Summary

A social process view of conflict and its resolution does not try to reduce conflict to some quality residing in the individual, nor does it see it as primarily given by the structure of society. Rather, conflict is a process that deserves study in its own right, and the resolution of conflict is seen in process terms.

We used the work of Adam Smith as a starting point for examining social process theories. Smith was both a socially sensitive philosopher of ethics and the modern world's first great economist. We drew on both of these areas of Smith's work. His work in moral philosophy helps us to see how, out of the fabric of social relationships, may emerge the principles we try to apply to conflict resolution. His work in economics helps us to see how the natural functioning of markets is one of the great resolvers of human conflicts.

In proceeding to twentieth-century theories, we especially noted the following:

1. How the concept of conflict has been related to competition (such as in the writings of Park and Burgess or of Simmel).
2. How processes of conflict are interwoven into the positive functions of social institutions (especially in writings of Simmel and Coser).
3. How systems of interaction form the basis for examining how conflicts get resolved and "negotiated order" is established (in the work of the symbolic interactionists, especially Strauss).
4. How a view of conflict and its resolution as products of a field of forces or a system of relationships can be helpful in understanding the dynamics of conflict and for developing effective conflict management (in the work of field theorists such as Lewin or Deutsch or in various formulations and applications of systems theory).
5. How principles of exchange in economic markets can be extended to matters of noneconomic exchange, thereby clarifying patterns of conflict and its resolution (in social exchange theories and in works of such authors as Boulding).
6. How escalation may occur and patterns of intractability develop (such as is summarized in works by Pruitt and Rubin or by Kriesberg and his associates).

Conclusions

The reader may draw numerous conclusions from this survey of social process theories. The writer draws the following main conclusions about social conflicts and their resolution:

a. Many potential conflicts are resolved automatically through impersonal forces of economic and social markets. The market is a great resolver for many interest conflicts, including those in intimate relationships, if we can see the laws of supply and demand extending to such matters as social communication, personal recognition, and informal influence.

b. Market mechanisms, however, do not operate in a vacuum. They are related to other social patterns, and they are limited by both general notions of equity and by preexisting power relationships.

c. Conflict is closely interwoven with cooperation in most social relationships, and the products of conflict may be positive as well as negative.

d. Explicit attempts at conflict resolution are more likely to be successful when they take into account the full dynamics of a particular situation. This requires more than an attempt to apply simple ideas about conflict in general or observations about conflict resolution in other settings.

e. Not all conflicts can be resolved. Escalation and intractability may develop in many kinds of relationships making conflict management (rather than resolution) sometimes the best that can be obtained.

f. Finally, however, we never can be sure when resolutions are impossible or when situations are only challenging opportunities. Even when mutual deadlock seems to exist, there may be ways of moving in a more productive direction—if one is sensitive to the full range of social processes operating in the particular situation.

5

Social Structural Theories

A Revolutionary Discovers the British Museum

Marx Comes to London

A destitute refugee from struggles on the continent, Karl Marx arrived in England in August of 1849. His wife and three children came the next month, and their fourth child was born shortly thereafter. Marx had no steady source of income, but good friends such as Friedrich Engels helped out, and he and his family somehow survived. The Marx family had no intention of making London their permanent home; but what started out as a temporary expedient became Marx's city of residence for the remaining 33 years of his life.

Marx would have preferred some other city. Paris, with its cosmopolitan atmosphere, was a particular favorite; Brussels was another suitable city; and he had also felt more at home during his stay at Cologne, in his native area of western Prussia. But Marx was no longer welcome in any of these places, so he sought refuge in England.

It was Marx's well-known career as a revolutionary that led to his banishment from France, Belgium, and Germany. When the German newspaper he edited was closed by Prussian authorities in 1843, he happily moved to Paris to start a new journalistic venture. But two years later he was expelled from France. Since a warrant for his arrest had been issued in Prussia, he then chose to live in Brussels, Belgium. It was there that he and Engels wrote a tract for a small group of radicals (officially named the "League of the Just" but generally known as the "Communist League"), which was issued in 1848 as the famous *Communist Manifesto*. The year of 1848 was a great year for revolutions; they broke out all over Europe and led directly to greater official suppression of dissidents almost everywhere. Marx was officially given just twenty-four hours to leave Belgium. Then he went back to Germany to help with revolutionary activity there, but that soon fizzled out. Fleeing again to Paris in 1849, he was soon ordered once more to leave France. This led him to cross the channel and take up "temporary" residence in England.

Within a few months Marx was seriously considering emigration to the United States, a country whose dynamic change fascinated him. That never came to be, though he did send articles across the Atlantic for Horace Greeley's *New York Tribune* (one of his few sources of income during the 1850s). The Marx family settled down to stay in London.[1]

The Museum

One of London's greatest attractions for Marx was the British Museum. He obtained a ticket for regular access to the museum's reading room in June of 1850, and spent long hours there reading and taking notes on almost all subjects under the sun. He especially focused on the subjects of history, economics, and current social conditions in Great Britain.

Marx continued to provide leadership for radical political movements— in particular, the International Working Men's Association, which he helped to found and later to reorganize. However, despite some brief periods when he saw hope for political revolution here or there, he focused his energies more upon revolution in the fundamental sense of basic social and economic change. This required serious study and understanding rather than an emotional call to the barricades. Marx's long hours in the museum and in his own study at home came to be applied more and more to a monumental work in history and economics, which he undertook in 1851. He then expected his fundamental economic analyses could be completed in a few months. At the time, he wrote to a friend:

> I am so far advanced that in five weeks I will be through with the whole economic shit. And that done, I will work over my Economics at home and throw myself into another science in the Museum.

This estimate of his future activities proved to be very wide of the mark for Karl Marx. He never really completed his economic analyses, for they continued to grow into his great project, *Capital* (with the subtitle, *Critique of Political Economy*). And of this work, only the first of four projected volumes was published before his death in 1883. His friend Engels worked with Marx's manuscripts and notes to bring out two more volumes after Marx's death. The projected fourth volume was never written.[2]

The Dynamics of Class Conflict

The Class Struggle

Following their introductory comments, Marx and Engels opened the main body of the *Communist Manifesto* with the assertion that "The history of all hitherto existing society is the history of class struggles." This theme is then developed at some length, and it is a central thread throughout Marx's writings. Class conflict is the central factor in historical and social change, Marx held, and it is the key to understanding contemporary society.[3]

Throughout history (or at least since the time of early simple societies) humanity has been divided into classes. These classes, for Marx, always have an economic base, for it is the material conditions of life that are crucial for understanding social relationships. In particular, Marx held that property ownership was the basis on which classes may be distinguished. Some people live primarily by owning property, while some exist by giving their labor for the benefit of others. In past ages when society was primarily agricultural, land was the key to understanding social classes. Some people owned landed estates, others had to work for them; thus we have a dominant landed aristocracy (united to preserve their landed property rights) and a large but relatively powerless peasant group. As we move into the modern world, it is business and industrial property that increasingly becomes critical. We therefore have a general class of business people seeking dominance in society, with industrial workers more and more taking the place of peasants as the primary source of labor. For these two emerging main classes, Marx used the French terms *bourgeoisie* (for the business class) and *proletariat* (for the working class). Without property, workers are largely at the mercy of the economic system developed and managed by others. Meanwhile, as Marx saw it, the business class assumes dominance—largely at the expense of the previously dominant landed aristocracy—and seeks to protect and preserve their rights and privileges.

Marx viewed persons in different classes as having fundamentally different economic interests, even though they may not always be conscious of this. The interests of a worker are very different from those of a manager or owner. Managers, of course, try to gloss over such differences in order to keep a docile work force. And workers may often not be aware of the way their interests contrast with those of their employers; they may have a 'false consciousness' that sees themselves as similar to their masters. The key to understanding what is really going on, according to Marx, is not to look at the attitudes of individuals about their economic conditions, but rather to look at the forces of society more broadly. This must include the understanding that social classes are based on the general structure of economic relations, and that economic relations in turn are based on the material forces of producing goods and services. At one point, Marx expressed his thoughts as follows:

> In the social production which men carry on they enter into definite relations that are indispensable and independent of their will; these relations of production correspond to a definite stage

of development of their material powers of production. The sum total of these relations of production constitutes the economic structure of society—the real foundation, on which rise legal and political superstructures and to which correspond definite forms of social consciousness. The mode of production in material life determines the general character of the social, political and spiritual processes of life. It is not the consciousness of men that determines their existence, but, on the contrary, their social existence determines their consciousness.

Thus the economic foundations determine what we as individuals will do—or even the way we think. As Marx saw it, it isn't very useful to view society in terms of its individuals; rather, we must view individuals in terms of the larger social structure of which they are a part. This is expressed quite clearly when he says, in the preface to *Capital,* that in this book attention is placed on "the personifications of economic categories, embodiments of particular class-relations and class-interests." He continues:

My standpoint, from which the evolution of the economic formation of society is viewed as a process of natural history, can less than any other make the individual responsible for relations whose creature he socially remains, however much he may subjectively raise himself above them.[4]

Changing the System

Marx was bitterly opposed to idealists, including idealistic socialists, who believed that by preaching peace and goodwill we can change the structure of society. The basic structure of society has its own rules of development, he said. However, if we understand these forces of social development (and their economic base), we may be able to see where they are moving and make some small efforts to help them move more expeditiously. At the present stage of history, this means, for Marx, to see that the capitalistic structure of industrial society is something that cannot last. The very successes of capitalism will lead to its demise, for it will be, in a real sense, its own gravedigger. The competition between capitalists will lead to a concentration of capital into fewer and fewer hands. Meanwhile, as industrial enterprises become larger, workers will also be concentrated in larger numbers in fewer factories. Smaller businesses will be wiped out by larger concerns, and these small owners will then become part of the working class. Periodic crises of overproduction will create ever greater periods of economic chaos. At some point, all these forces will come together to create a fundamental change in the system. The kind of change that

Marx saw as inevitable was toward socialism, with social ownership and control of the main means of production. This would, of course, require the defeat of the capitalists, who would not voluntarily relinquish their economic and political power. Marx saw it as quite natural that political revolution would be part of this process.

Note that in his mature work, Marx is not so much advocating socialism or political revolution as seeing these as natural developments for the future. But let us not forget that he was also a committed revolutionary. He was a revolutionary against established ideas (especially those of religious thought) before he was a socialist or communist. And he was a political revolutionary before he embarked on his advanced analyses of economic forces. He never gave up hope that major political upheavals were just around the corner, and that the revolutionary socialist parties (such as those he tried to direct) would soon be successful in taking power in the more advanced capitalist nations. In the *Communist Manifesto,* Marx and Engels had been quite clear about their position on revolution. They closed this document with these words:

> The Communists disdain to conceal their views and aims. They openly declare that their ends can be attained only by the forcible overthrow of all existing social conditions. Let the ruling classes tremble at a Communist revolution. The proletarians have nothing to lose but their chains.
>
> Workingmen of all countries, unite!

Later Marx was much more cautious in his expressions of revolutionary views, for he became more and more aware that political revolutions could succeed only when conditions were fully ripe. But he never gave up. He continued to advise his colleagues on the fine art of revolution. The following passage indicates the kind of advice he gave:

> Firstly, never play with insurrection unless you are fully prepared to face the consequences of your play. Insurrection is a calculus with very indefinite magnitudes, the value of which may change every day; the forces opposed to you have all the advantage of organization, discipline, and habitual authority; unless you bring strong odds against them you are defeated and ruined. Secondly, the insurrectionary career once entered upon, act with the greatest determination, and on the offensive. The defensive is the death of every armed rising; it is lost before it measures itself with its enemies. Surprise your antagonists while their forces are scattering, prepare new successes, however small, but daily; keep up the moral

ascendancy which the first successful rising has given to you; rally those vacillating elements to your side which always follow the strongest impulse, and which always look out for the safer side; force your enemies to retreat before they can collect their strength against you; in the words of Danton, the greatest master of revolutionary policy yet known, *de l'audace, de l'audace, encore de l'audace!*[5]

After Marx

Weber

It is difficult to separate Marx the social analyst from Marx the revolutionary socialist, for in him these elements were so closely intertwined. However, others who came after him often did try more to separate their sociology from their political ideology. This clearly was the case with the distinguished German sociologist and historian, Max Weber.

Weber's analysis of relationships between economic forces and the rest of society was heavily influenced by Marx. Weber recognized many keen insights in Marx's analyses, but he also disagreed sharply with many of Marx's views. There are at least two key points at which Weber's analysis broadly followed that of Marx. One of these was that class conflict was a very important part of modern society. Another was that economic forces are often primary in setting the stage for social change. But on neither of these points did Weber agree precisely with Marx; and in other respects there were larger differences.[6]

First, for Weber class conflict was important, but it was only part of the total picture of conflict within society. Where Marx had seen just one base for social stratification (economic property and power), Weber suggested that there were three main bases. These were (1) economic wealth or power, which formed the basis of classes, (2) social reputation and prestige, which formed the basis of status groups, and (3) political power, which formed the basis of political parties and interest groups. Only in the first area (economic class) did Weber's analysis show a strong similarity to that of Marx, and even here Weber saw, much more than did Marx, the importance of matters other than simple property ownership. More important, though, was the weight Weber gave to noneconomic factors, emphasizing their potential independence from economic criteria. True, there tends to be some correlation between economic power, social status, and political power, but none, in Weber's view, is the basis for the others. All are important aspects of the stratification systems of modern societies.

Just as Weber did not give economic forces the priority that Marx did, so Weber also did not see the forces of production as the sole foundation of social change. Weber saw the forces of production and exchange as extremely important, and he supported many of Marx's insights here; but he also saw ideas as having an independent influence upon human history. In fact, one of Weber's most famous works, *The Protestant Ethic and the Spirit of Capitalism,* is usually viewed as refuting the Marxian interpretation of history. Here Weber attempts to show that distinctively religious views were probably crucial, at one stage of Western history, in building a base for modern capitalism. This is sometimes seen as turning Marx's analysis upside down (ideas in society affect material forces, rather than material forces shaping the ideas), though this is far too simple a statement of Weber's position. What Weber tried to show was that a number of key social institutions, including economic institutions, had many complex interrelationships in providing the framework for social change.[7]

Weber, like Marx, believed that much social change grew out of social conflict. Unlike Marx, however, he emphasized how society can function in spite of its severe underlying conflicts. Weber held that power in society seldom comes from brute force. Rather, it becomes generally accepted or given legitimacy by a variety of processes. Here, too, Weber had a three-fold classification of the bases of legitimate authority. There are, he suggested, (1) legal authority, (2) traditional authority, and (3) charismatic authority. Legal authority is based on formal norms and the established offices that carry out these norms or rules. A bureaucrat is a good example of legal authority. Traditional authority is based on traditional usage and ideas from the past. A Roman Catholic priest is an example of a role that depends largely on traditional authority. Charismatic authority is based on the personal appeal of a leader. Examples here might include a television evangelist, a movie actress, or an inspiring political leader. Power in society, in Weber's view, grows from authority; and authority, in turn, grows from the acceptance and regard generally granted by society. There are many factors involved in this acceptance and regard, including legal rationality, the impact of tradition, and the emotional appeal of particular leaders.

Dahrendorf

A leading sociologist in the last half of the twentieth century who continued on in the long shadow of Marx has been Ralf Dahrendorf. Dahrendorf was, like Marx, a German who took up residence in England, there to pursue more fully his studies in social science. Dahrendorf is, indeed, often called a "neo-Marxist," but not because of any similarity to Marx's politics. Dahrendorf has been active in politics, but as a reformer who largely accepts the principles of what Marx would call "bourgeois capitalism." Dahrendorf is appalled at the thought of urging a violent revolution, and he is not a socialist. But as a social scientist, Dahrendorf owes a great debt to Marx. He has called Marx "the greatest theorist of social change," for more than anyone else, according to Dahrendorf, Marx laid bare the importance of conflict in shaping society. Marx also helped us look at society in structural terms, rather than just as the product of actions by individuals, and this, Dahrendorf believes, has been a major contribution to modern sociology.[8]

Social change, for both Dahrendorf and Marx, grows out of social structure. The way society is structured affects the lines of conflict, and conflict in turn is the primary engine for social change. Dahrendorf, like Marx, saw social classes as a key basis of structural conflict; however, he looked at structural conflict in more general terms than did Marx. Any groups in society can serve as the basis for social conflict, not just those based on economic foundations; and Dahrendorf also saw the potential for conflict within any group. There are always differences in power that can serve as a basis of conflict—either between or within groups. Such power differences are structurally based; that is, they are products of the way society is arranged. Economic considerations may be an important influence, but Dahrendorf saw the key as being power, not wealth or property. For him, conflict in society is more directly a matter of political than economic forces.

In his explanation of how conflicting groups arise from the structure of society, Dahrendorf starts with the assumption that there will be, in any form of social organization, power differentials. These tend to form into the subgroups of those who dominate or lead and those who are led. Such subgroups always have different interests, though they may not always recognize that their interests are in conflict. In such cases Dahrendorf calls them "quasi groups," in the sense that their shared and diverse interests are not made explicit. However, when conditions call attention to conflicting interests, such quasi groups become interest groups and form self-conscious organizations to promote their interests.

Dahrendorf sees many different forms of social conflict, depending on the particular kinds of organization involved. He has classified the types of social units having superordinate-subordinate conflict as (1) roles, (2) groups, (3) sectors of society, (4) societies, and (5) suprasocietal relations. The middle three of these types can be viewed as having what Dahrendorf broadly calls class conflict. Dahrendorf has made his distinctive sociological contribution to the study of such conflicts and the development of theoretical generalizations about them. His book *Class and Class Conflict in Industrial Society* summarizes this work.[9]

Some conflicts are resolved, but Dahrendorf (contrary to Marx) believed that class conflicts never are. Class conflicts can only be regulated, not resolved, because the structural basis of conflict is never eliminated. The conditions under which class conflicts can be most effectively regulated occur when those involved recognize the nature of the conflict, are systematically organized, and accept certain rules for the manner in which they will pursue their opposed interests. Examples of such conflict regulation may be found in the forms of labor-management relations practiced in Western nations.

To think that class conflicts can be resolved through some form of violent struggle is, for Dahrendorf, an illusion. Such struggles may change those who have temporary positions of power, but their general effect is to exacerbate the conflict and make it more difficult to manage—not to resolve it.

Critical Theory

Another twentieth century scholar who was profoundly influenced by Marx was Max Horkheimer. Horkheimer, along with colleagues such as Herbert Marcuse and Theodor Adorno, developed the approach that has come to be known as "critical theory." It was said to be "critical" in the sense that these writers tried to encourage self-conscious thought about society, even though the basic social forms were seen as objectively determined. Since Horkheimer and most of his early associates were affiliated with the Institute of Social Research in Frankfurt, Germany, this group is also sometimes referred to as the "Frankfurt school."[10]

Critical theory began with a Marxist theory of history. The historical process, in the view of these theorists, clearly has a materialist base. They also emphasize the class basis of society, as had Marx, though they are not identified with a revolutionary agenda to the extent that Marx was. Indeed, the critical theorists have not been a cohesive movement in terms of politics. What has held them together is (1) agreement on a basically Marxist theory of history, (2) an attempt to provide an interdisciplinary bridge between social philosophy and the social sciences, and (3) a special concern with the cultural effects of capitalism.

This last point deserves further comment. The inspiration from Marx for the critical theorists came less from *Capital* than from some of his earlier writings, in which Marx discusses the alienation of modern man. Developing such themes, the critical theorists saw many ways that modern culture—particularly under advanced capitalism—is in conflict with the basic requirements of human freedom and dignity. Criticism of mass culture is an especially favorite subject of the critical theorists, for they see popular culture and the mass media as generally opposed to our most fundamental and humane interests.

Other Marxists

Although Weber, Dahrendorf, and Horkheimer were all strongly influenced by Marx, none of these was a simple follower of Marxian ideas. Other scholars since Marx have been more faithful to his original ideas. These include, of course, the philosophers and social scientists who have represented the recommended ideology in officially socialist states, such as in China or the former Soviet Union. But they also may be found in other parts of the world—in Latin American and other developing countries, and in some of the leading universities of Western Europe and the United States. Marx's materialistic conception of society, his view of the class struggle, and his advocacy of revolutionary social change are all themes that are still very much alive.

However, the influence of Marx has sometimes been less in those who claim to be his ideological heirs than in other students of society who disclaim Marxism. Even while they reject much of Marx's ideology, there are two key features of Marxian thought that are widely shared by contemporary social scientists. One of these is the idea that social change comes largely through social conflict. The other is that social conflict is an inevitable part of the way society is structured.

The structures of society are not created by our wishes, most social scientists now agree, but by the objective conditions of our common life. Whatever else may be his contributions or errors, Marx at least raised our consciousness about the way material conditions may lead to conflict between key segments of society—especially between social classes.

Before Marx

Plato

We should not think of a social structural perspective on human conflict as something that first surfaced in Western thought in the middle of the nineteenth century. Although expressed more commonly in religious or philosophical terms than in those of modern social science, ideas about the structural basis of conflicts in society have a long history. An example can be seen in Plato, that great philosopher of ancient Greece who wrote nearly twenty-four centuries ago.

In Plato's view, a human person is composed of three main elements: (1) the senses or appetites, (2) the spirit or will, and (3) intelligence or reason. Although all of these are important, the chief role for personal integration must be performed by intelligence or reason. Similarly, society is composed of three main groups: (a) those who devote themselves to sensual gratification, (b) those who live for honor and prestige, and (c) those who mainly pursue reason and truth.

Plato did not see a differentiation of classes in society as necessarily present from the beginning, but rather as something that developed out of an increasing division of labor. It is true that, for Plato, the basic groups in society are based on fundamental differences of human nature, but it was also necessary for society to develop some degree of complexity before these various divisions could show themselves in such groups as (1) peasants and artisans, who deal primarily with physical and sensory matters; (2) soldiers and military officers, who strive for honor and prestige; and (3) intellectuals, who pursue reason and truth.

Plato believed it natural for tensions to form within society and that some conflict is therefore inevitable. However, he felt that if a proper balance of the parts could be obtained, social conflict would be at a minimum. Each segment of society must know the part it must play and be guided in such a fashion that all segments work together in harmony. Only with proper leadership can such a balance be secured, and this means that persons of the highest quality should be identified and trained for political leadership.

For Plato, the ultimate reality, for us as individuals or as members of a society, is not in our senses or our physical attributes as humans. The ultimate reality is a product of the human mind, and can only be recognized by trained minds. This means that reason and the search for truth must be the central part of the education of all who would seek to guide a society to realize its highest potential. Such truth, furthermore, is not to be seen in purely mundane or physical matters, but rather in the realm of abstract ideas. The clear implication of this line of reasoning is that we must have trained philosophers in the highest positions of responsibility. Plato expressed this most strongly in asserting that societies will always be plagued with conflict and misrule until either philosophers become kings or kings become philosophers. Only in this way can political greatness and wisdom meet in the same persons—a necessity for wise political leadership.[11]

In *The Republic,* Plato describes the kind of education he sees as appropriate for the production of such 'philosopher kings.' It is a very rigorous regime of instruction for both the mind and the body. One of the features of special note is the denial of private property for those who are to become the guardians of society. They must be interested in the whole of society, not in any narrowly personal interests. Only if the ruling groups practiced a form of communism would this be possible. So Plato, with the opposite kind of general philosophy (idealism rather than materialism) came to similar conclusions as did Marx on the issue of private property: The needs of society could best be realized if private property were eliminated—at least for those who would provide political leadership. For Plato, the basic need is for individuals who would be very wise in philosophical matters and would keep the interests of the total society in mind. They could not do this well if they were motivated by their private interests. He makes an analogy between the role of the political leader and that of a physician. He points out that a doctor, "insofar as he is a doctor, considers or commands not the doctor's advantage, but that of the sick man." He is "a ruler of bodies and not a money-maker." Likewise, with a sensitivity to the needs of the total society and an understanding of the basic ideal forms that need to be embodied in the social order, wise rulers can benefit the entire society. All groups have to be guided to keep in their proper spheres, thus promoting the general good. Such was Plato's prescription for how a society could best overcome the conflict of competing interests carried by different groups.[12]

America's Founding Fathers

Plato's social philosophy, although complex in its implications, did have a strong social structural component. Most Americans who look back with reverence at their founding fathers do not recognize how much the framers of the U.S. *Constitution* were also motivated by structural considerations. True, like Plato, they believed in a moral order of the universe, and that certain features of society were given by "Nature and Nature's God," to use a phrase from the *Declaration of Independence.* But they also believed that the complexities of human society need to be wisely considered in determining an appropriate political order. This thinking is present in the papers circulated as *The Federalist,* which promoted ratification of the *Constitution.* This is probably most clearly spelled out by paper number 10, written by James Madison in 1787.[13]

Madison saw that political factions provide an especially great problem for governments of democratic or republican forms (the founding fathers tended to prefer the "republican" label, given the associations of "democracy" with mob rule). All successful political forms must, in Madison's words, "break and control the violence of faction." Further, said Madison:

> By a faction, I understand a number of citizens, whether amounting to a majority or minority of the whole, who are united and actuated by some common impulse of passion, or of interest, adverse to the rights of other citizens, or to the permanent and aggregate interests of the community.[14]

Popular forms of government have been especially prone to divide into factions. Said Madison:

> The instability, injustice and confusion introduced into the public councils, have, in truth, been the mortal diseases under which popular governments have everywhere perished; as they continue to be the favorite and fruitful topics from which the adversaries of liberty derive their most specious declamations.

Although such factions (or "interest groups," as we have since come to call them) may have many different foundations, property interests are generally the most powerful. In Madison's words, "The most common and durable source of factions has been the various and unequal distribution of property." He continues by asserting that

> A landed interest, a manufacturing interest, a mercantile interest, moneyed interest, with many lesser interests, grow up of necessity in civilized nations, and divide them into different classes, actuated by different sentiments and views. The regulation of these various and interfering interests forms the principal task of modern legislation, and involves the spirit of party in the necessary and ordinary operations of the government.[15]

After examining further the nature and consequences of factions, Madison concludes that they must play a significant part in public life. Factions are inevitable, and they can only be suppressed by tyranny. But even if we cannot remove the causes of factions, we can, Madison held, do something about their effects. What we can do is develop a system that controls these effects. What kind of a system would do this? The answer, for Madison, is clear: the kind of system being proposed in the U.S. *Constitution.* By a system of checks and balances no single faction is likely to be able to exert undue control upon the rest of society. This may be furthered by the doctrine of limited government, a separation of powers between a federal government and those of the constituent states, and a separation of powers between executive, legislative, and judicial functions—all clearly embodied in the *Constitution.* With such agencies to control the desire for domination by one faction or another, the entire social order can function more freely, and republican forms can survive.

Clearly, factors of social structure were central in Madison's thinking as he wrote this paper for *The Federalist.* And clearly, he felt, the different interests embodied in the structure of society must be allowed for—but also they must be controlled in their effects. Madison believed that they could best be controlled by a political structure that checked the power of any one faction.

It is interesting to note that most of the framers of the *Constitution* hoped to avoid the presence of political parties in American government. By controlling the influence of factions, they thought, we could keep from having continuing political parties; thus, the *Constitution* makes no mention of parties. It is a bit ironic that Madison himself, along with his friend Thomas Jefferson, helped to organize the first recognizable political party. This was during the administration of John Adams, when opponents, Jefferson and Madison among them, wanted to appeal to the populace for a fundamental change of direction. The party they founded has continued ever since to be a leading force of the American political system. Though generally not dominated by a single faction, this Democratic Party (as it is now called) does provide a cleavage in

American political life which is quite different from what Madison had in mind when he wrote paper number 10 for *The Federalist.*

Other Structural Bases of Conflict

Religious, Racial, and Ethnic Differences

The term *ethnic group* is popularly used with various meanings; and even scholars do not always use the same terminology when referring to racial, religious, or nationality group divisions in society. We will here use the concept of 'ethnicity' broadly to include all racial, religious, and nationality group identifications that become recognized divisions in a society's social structure. In this we will be following the usage most common among sociologists, which has been expressed as follows:

> An ethnic group is a collection of people whose membership is largely determined by ancestry and which regards its place in society as affected by its ethnicity. Thus the test of differences in physical appearance (frequently referred to as racial), national origin, or religion is not the difference per se, but whether this difference is considered socially significant. Some societies will disregard a rather wide range of differences in physical appearance, while others will relate social privileges to rather minute types of variations. Likewise, some societies will be greatly concerned about the national (or tribal) origins of the people in a given territory, while, to other societies, this will be a matter of indifference. . . . What matters is not the nature of the difference, but the intensity of feeling about the importance of the difference, and the way in which this difference is associated with economic stratification, political power, and other elements of social structure.[16]

Note that this usage emphasizes the relation of ethnicity to social structure, as well as the great variation possible from society to society.

Racial and ethnic relations may be seen in terms of social psychological factors: as patterns of prejudice, the socialization of stereotyped images, or tendencies of interpersonal association. Our present discussion is not meant to belittle such approaches to the study of ethnic relations. However, here we want to emphasize the way ethnic groups become part of the social structure. These groupings are not just features of individual behavior, but rather are recognized as key groups within the social structure. It might be useful here to understand clearly how ethnic as well as economic and political divisions may be involved in social structure. In the words of one sociologist:

> By the social structure of a society we mean the set of crystallized social relationships which its members have with each other which places them in groups, large or small, permanent or temporary, formally organized or unorganized, and which relates them to the major institutional activities of the society, such as economic and occupational life, religion, marriage and the family, education, government, and recreation.[17]

Note the emphasis here on "crystallized social relationships." Certain patterns of relationships become generally recognized and expected. Even when they might not be universally followed (for example, in regard to marriage choice), they still provide a basic framework for how persons tend to relate to each other.

Of course, what is recognized and expected is vastly different from society to society. Even societies that are neighbors to one another may have widely different patterns of ethnicity. In Canada, for example, the language used (French or English) becomes a key dividing line, with all kinds of associations (especially national origin and religion) made on the basis of this difference. In the United States the markers are more matters of physical appearance, with race at the center of attention. In Mexico the racial blend leads away from racial categorization, but groups are still divided in ways that combine ethnicity with region. If we continue further down the North American continent, we find still other patterns—such as in Guatemala (where "indigena" and "latino" make fundamental racial divisions between people whom outsiders would consider very similar in appearance), in Belize (with a rich variety of ethnic groups but with none clearly dominant), or in El Salvador (where social class and economic divisions tend to take precedence over ethnic identity). Elsewhere in the world, the variation continues in other directions. In spite of the ethnocentric tendencies that we all have, we must recognize that other societies really and truly are different in the ways that they categorize and give meaning to ethnic divisions.

Still, every society has some recognized ethnic divisions. Even in Japan, surely one of the world's most homogeneous countries racially and culturally, there is a recognition of some minority groups (such as Koreans or overseas Japanese) as being different from (and usually less worthy than) the majority Japanese. In most other countries the ethnic divisions are much more obvious.

Whenever ethnic groups come into contact, there is always some degree of conflict. The more the contact, the greater is the likelihood of conflict and confrontation—unless all concerned are able to set aside their ethnic identities, which is usually asking more than is realistic.

Theorists of comparative ethnic relations have usually avoided a general explanatory theory which would apply to all societies. Instead, they point to the important effects of historical backgrounds, population composition, patterns of location, rural-urban differences, occupational patterns, political leadership, and so forth; and each society is different from all others in regard to some of these factors. There are, however, a few general patterns we can see as we compare different societies. One of these is that the overall pattern of ethnic relations in a society tends to move in one of three directions. Chester Hunt and Lewis Walker, in their survey of ethnic relations around the world, have identified these basic directions as (1) segregation, (2) cultural pluralism, and (3) integration. Each of these represents a theoretically distinct way of trying to deal with ethnic conflict.[18]

In segregated societies, contacts between various groups are limited by law or custom. This creates a strong sense of identity and division. Group differences are assumed to be permanent, and they strongly affect the lives (and life chances) of the various groups. Usually segregated societies have a dominant majority group which seeks to maintain its privileges and to create an ideology that will justify its dominance. The historical backgrounds of segregated societies tend to show strong patterns of dominance on the basis of ethnicity, which carries over to many different spheres of social life.

In culturally plural societies, a variety of different ethnic groups are recognized, but no one group is viewed as dominant. Each is seen as having its own special characteristics, but all are viewed as parts of the nation or larger society. Such a system is especially likely to develop when a political system includes a wide variety of ethnic groups, each perhaps dominant within limited territories (but still not strongly set off from each other geographically), but in which none has recognized dominance over the entire society.

In integration, the thrust is to cast ethnic differences aside. Persons are viewed as individuals, families, or occupational groups with little regard to their ethnic identities. The emphasis is on rights for the individual, not on group privileges. Persons are expected to downplay their ethnic identities in the interests of all sharing in the common culture. Such a system is apt to develop in a rapidly changing society which provides extensive opportunity for social and economic betterment, and which also has a strong ideology of democratic egalitarianism.

Of course, these three are not the only patterns. Hunt and Walker also recognize "temporary accommodation" as a common pattern, though they do not consider it to be a stable, long-term system of relationships. Also, we must recognize the theoretical possibilities of large-scale expulsion (such as Spain's resolution of ethnic conflicts between Christians and people of other religions in 1492), or genocide (as pursued within Turkey early in this century, by Nazi Germany a few decades later, or by a dominant group in Rwanda in 1994). The three patterns of segregation, cultural pluralism, and integration represent relatively permanent systems of ongoing ethnic relations.

How individuals (or small groups) react to a dominant pattern can vary widely. Still, they must recognize that their society tends to deal with ethnic relations according to a primary pattern. Also, the primary pattern may be different for different forms of ethnicity. For example, in the first half of the twentieth century, American race relations generally embodied a pattern of segregation, religious contacts could be characterized by cultural pluralism, while many nationality groups moved strongly toward integration. This has changed significantly in the last half of the century, as race relations have ambiguously moved toward both cultural pluralism and integration at the same time—but with strong pockets of segregation still remaining.

Age and Gender Differences

Every society must recognize age and gender differences in some way, though the meanings attached to these basic biological differences can vary a great deal, between as well as within societies.

Few social scientists have a systematic theory about age differences. These are taken for granted as fundamental parts of the social structure. It is also recognized that privileges are often correlated with one's age level. However, not often has there formed the strong cleavage on the basis of age as has been manifest in regard to race, religion, nationality, or gender. This is in part related to the fact that one's age status is always temporary. If a child feels unduly denied privileges on the basis of age, he or she can just wait a few years for this to change. Or if young people feel that the elderly demand more than their share of social benefits, they too can just wait. Of course, at the final period of the age span one can do little about changing one's age status without leaving the system altogether (an eventuality that most people seek to delay), though there still is an opportunity for most of the elderly to enjoy youth again through their grandchildren!

Nevertheless, there have been times when age is more clearly than at other times recognized as a dividing force in society. While there is always some degree of a generation gap, at times it becomes more acute and divisive. Such times are likely to be those of rapid social change, where established institutions lose some of their legitimacy, and/or where demographic changes yield a sharp growth in the proportion of young people. Add to this the possible effects of political decisions (such as the U.S. involvement in Vietnam and the continuation of the military draft) and it becomes understandable why a generational cleavage was very strong in the United States in the 1960s.

Gender differences also vary over time in the way they are regarded in society. Of course, they are always important for individuals in their informal relationships; but what regard society at large imposes on gender differences is subject to wide variation. When a society is undergoing rapid social change, gender roles may also be expected to change, increasing the likelihood that gender issues will become more salient. For example, in the 1970s there was a rapid increase of female participation in the American work force, including many occupational areas that had previously been considered male domains. Along with this was a significant change in household technology, making homemaker role specialization less needed. Add to this a significant leveling off of economic growth—making a family's economic prosperity more and more uncertain and increasingly requiring two wage earners to maintain expected standards of living. With all of these conditions obtaining in the 1970s, it is not surprising that gender conflict would become an increasingly prominent theme of American society.

Recent decades have seen a resurgence of feminism in the United States and Western Europe. Along with this has been the rise of 'feminist theory,' an attempt to make a thorough-going analysis of life and society from a female point of view. Feminist theory includes many strands, some pointing toward a recognition of distinctive female qualities and some pointing toward a lowered regard for sex differences. Much feminist theory is focused on psychological and cultural issues that are only indirectly tied to a social structural approach. However, a great deal of feminist theory does take a structural approach, seeing the female sex as systematically disadvantaged by a male-dominated society. Insofar as this is viewed as an organized part of society (and not as just a biological or social psychological phenomenon), feminist theory becomes a social structural approach to understanding basic social conflict.

Among the more social structural versions of feminist theory is that contained in Jessie Bernard's *The Female World*. Bernard's view of feminism ranges widely over the intellectual landscape, including cultural and social psychological factors. However, there is a strong sociological base for her theoretical and empirical analyses. She broadly characterizes her approach as a social "system" view which sees femininity in its total social context. She says:

> The female world in this view is a sociological entity with a characteristic demographic structure (age, marital status, education, income, occupation), a status and class structure, and a group structure.

An example of Bernard's strong emphasis on the implications of a gender framework in social structure can be seen in her discussion of how, especially in the nineteenth century, women moved from being given a general station in society (clearly inferior to men) to being given a separate sphere of activities (theoretically equal, but still primarily justified by a male-centered ideology). The ideology supporting this traditional separation of sex roles included the belief that "although women were not intrinsically inferior to men, their sphere still had to be subordinated to that of men in the interest of national welfare." Also supporting this separate sphere was the belief that "the home, extended to include related moral and charitable activities, was the natural, normal, and only concern of women's spheres." Women thus were forced to work within the framework of such a sphere, and they developed something of a distinctive female culture in this way. As Bernard expresses it:

> Excluded from partnership in the management of the economy or the polity, cut off from shared companionship with men, they sought emotional sustenance from others in their sphere, and supplied it to them in return.[19]

International Differences and the World System

So far we have looked primarily at social structures within societies. We also must be alert to the structure of the larger system of societies and states over the entire world.

Central players in such structures are national states. States (at least in the modern world) claim a monopoly of legitimate physical force. This allows those with state power to have enormous power over citizens within a nation's territory. It also helps to create an international system in which physical power, in the form of military might, plays a central role—given that the national state remains fundamentally an independent and sovereign unit.

One important school of thought, generally identified as "political realism," has seriously tried to identify the basic interests of a state and its people as a basis for its international policies. Hans Morganthau, a leading exponent of such political realism, characterizes this view as follows:

> This being inherently a world of opposing interests and of conflict among them, moral principles can never be fully realized, but must at best be approximated through the ever temporary balancing of interests and the ever precarious settlement of conflicts. This school, then, sees in a system of checks and balances a universal principle for all pluralist societies. It appeals to historic precedent rather than to abstract principles, and aims at the realization of the lesser evil rather than the absolute good.[20]

Clearly this unsentimental approach to power among nations takes for granted that nations will have important power differences and that effective peace depends on obtaining a working balance of power among them.

A very different approach is represented by Johan Galtung, a European leader in the field of peace and conflict studies. Galtung believes strongly that equality should be the norm of all relations among humans. Not only does he promote democratic equality within a society, but also between societies. This leads him to note the tremendous disparity of wealth and power throughout the world, and to see in such differences systematic patterns of exploitation. In the international system, he especially points to the differences between the "Center" (the core nations for political and economic power) and the "Periphery" (the nations that become dependent on the Center nations and are largely manipulated for the benefit of people of the Center). This takes many forms, including economic imperialism, political neocolonialism, and social imperialism. Social imperialism is as serious a problem as economic and political penetration, for it tends to displace peripheral cultures in favor of the norms of dominant societies. For example, the English language is now becoming central for international contacts, largely because of the dominance of Anglo-American political and economic institutions.

Galtung believes that true peace can come only with justice, for he holds that "structural violence" (that is, the oppression, directly or indirectly expressed, of some people by others) is as serious a problem as is physical violence. This leads him to very ambitious proposals for reducing the forces of constraint and inequality within societies, as well as between societies throughout the world.[21]

Although less moral in tone, the world system approach of Immanuel Wallerstein shows some similarities to Galtung's perspective. Galtung and Wallerstein see enormous differences in political and economic power within the different parts of the world. Wallerstein differs, however, in being mainly concerned with the historical analysis of this state of affairs rather than proposing how it may be eliminated. Taking a thoroughly interdisciplinary approach, Wallerstein seeks to show how the entire Earth has come to be dominated by a world capitalist system which increasingly limits the autonomy of any of its parts. Although with centers of power in Europe, Japan, and North America, this system is really worldwide in its pattern of organization and its impact on the lives of people. No one can escape it—at least, not at this stage of human history.[22]

Hans Morganthau, Johan Galtung, and Immanuel Wallerstein are among the leading twentieth-century theorists who have examined social structures on a world scale. Although they differ greatly in their emphases, there is one point that all see as basic: Social structure applies not only to a society, but also to relations between societies. All three see the world structured as a system of national states with constant tensions and conflicts. Whatever else we may say in relation to such theories, we need to recognize that there are divisions of wealth and power in the world today that are enormous—even more obvious than those within most nations—and that these form a continuing basis for conflicts on a worldwide scale.

Solutions to Structural Conflict

Five Approaches

Once we see a structural basis for social conflict, there are a number of different attitudes we may take about it. Distinguished scholars, as well as more ordinary mortals, have varied greatly in their stance regarding solutions to such conflict. We may briefly characterize this range of reactions as those of (1) avoidance, (2) acceptance, (3) gradual reform, (4) nonviolent confrontation, and (5) violent confrontation.

It is always possible (even after it is recognized) to avoid dealing with a structural basis of social conflict. This does not mean that we do not acknowledge the presence of conflict or that we fail to do anything about it. Rather, we may attempt to deal with it in terms of its more immediate manifestations—as destructive processes or destructive persons. There is certainly much that can be done at these levels without dealing with sociological questions about the organization of society. Besides this, it is often believed that society at large is too big a thing to try to change, that we can only hope to be effective when dealing with conflicts in more specific and concrete ways. Many behavioral scientists are included among those who actively avoid consideration of structural bases of social conflict—typically in the interests of keeping their scientific work focused on more manageable topics.

Acceptance is the second possible response. This approach recognizes that conflict may be based on social structural foundations, but it sees the conflict as so basic a part of life that we can do little about it except study it. Some sociologists take this approach. One of the most distinguished sociologists of the nineteenth century, Ludwig Gumplowicz, saw racial and ethnic conflicts as fundamental to all forms of human society. However, he was so thorough a social determinist that he believed there was little anyone could do about such conflicts other than accept them. By understanding the basic laws that conflict follows in society, according to Gumplowicz, "sociology lays the foundations for the morals of reasonable resignation, morals higher than those resting on the imaginary freedom and self-determination of the individual."[23] Whether or not one recognizes resignation in the face of fundamental social conflict as a "higher morality," we can see it as an option that some scholars, as well as others, take.

A third possibility is that of gradual reform. The structure of society is too well established to try to do much about it, but it can be changed little by little by continuing to deal with the sources of social tension. Thus through an evolutionary kind of change, policies of social reform can achieve a restructuring of society. For example, if one is concerned with the gulf between the rich and the poor, one might see social welfare provisions and a graduated system of taxation as appropriate responses. Such policies do not eliminate social class divisions, but they may make them less immediate issues; and, in the long run, the social structure does change—not drastically, but significantly—as a result of such limited interventions. Many, perhaps most, social scientists have this kind of attitude toward structurally based conflict in society.

Nonviolent confrontation is the fourth approach. One may enlist directly in movements for fundamental social change, and seek to accomplish that change in the near future, but without violence. The stance of nonviolence is often seen as central, for if we can limit the violence of those opposed to a change (and use whatever strategies might weaken their resistance), the change may be more readily accepted. Also, the cost of change is much less if it can be accomplished without violence. The drive for Indian independence led by Mohandas K. Gandhi in the 1940s and the leadership of Martin Luther King, Jr., in the American civil rights movement of the 1960s provide leading examples of this kind of response to structural conflict. The Polish Solidarity movement represents a more recent example of a successful, though nonviolent, revolution. In all such cases, the conflict is joined in order to seek a fundamental change in the social order—in the near future, but without violence.

Finally, there is the possibility of violent confrontation. Keeping always present the possibility of violent tactics is seen by some as the most effective way to seek basic social change. Those who take this viewpoint hold that, after all, social change comes mostly through conflict; and success in conflict is most likely if one is willing to keep active all options, including that of a violent uprising. Fears of violence may be an important force toward partial changes in the system by those in charge—and sometimes a violent upheaval may be the only way to replace those in charge. In organizing the forces of confrontation, according to this viewpoint, we must assume that violence (however distasteful it may be personally) will be part of the process. Thus scholars and others may be led to see violent confrontation as an important option for dealing with structural conflict. This is the option chosen by Karl Marx, as well as by many since his time who have been strongly influenced by him.

Summary and Conclusions

Summary

A social structural view of conflict and its resolution places central attention on the way society is organized. The major divisions of society are seen as the underlying foundations for conflict; and conflict resolution is viewed as requiring some readjustment in these basic structures.

Karl Marx and his theories were our point of entry into a social structural way of thinking. Marx was a thoroughgoing structuralist in the way that he considered the structures of economic organization to provide the foundations for class conflict. His proposals for dealing with such conflict involved participating in groups seeking revolutionary change.

Using Marx as a starting point, we also noted several other theorists, since his work or before his time, who have seen the socioeconomic divisions of society as central forces in conflict. These included:

1. Weber, who had a more complex view of the relation of social conflict to social change, and who emphasized the role of legitimacy in social power.
2. Dahrendorf, who viewed class conflict in broader terms than Marx and emphasized political as well as economic factors, but who still saw conflict as the prime mover for social change.
3. Horkheimer and other critical theorists, who assumed, like Marx, a materialist basis for history and society, but who emphasized cultural consequences of contemporary class divisions.
4. Plato, who saw the main divisions of society growing out of an economic division of labor, and who believed that rational idealism provided a way to bridge these divisions in the interests of social harmony.
5. Madison, among the framers of the U.S. *Constitution,* who assumed the inevitability of some form of class conflict, but who believed that it could be effectively regulated through well constructed political institutions.

Moving beyond socioeconomic divisions, we examined how race and ethnic divisions may serve as the foundations of basic conflict, and the main ways that such conflict is managed (by segregation, cultural pluralism, and/or integration) in modern societies. Age and sex divisions were also examined as key elements always present in social structure, along with their potential for social conflict. Finally, we looked at international divisions as a basis of conflicts on a world scale, and we examined how several theorists (in particular, Morganthau, Galtung, and Wallerstein) have conceptualized conflict on a world scale.

With each of these areas covered in our examination of social conflict, we suggested how such conflicts might be resolved or managed. The same kind of conflict—even though analyzed in much the same way—may be seen by different theorists as having very different recipes for resolution. We identified the following basic approaches to dealing with structural conflict: (1) avoidance, (2) acceptance, (3) gradual reform, (4) nonviolent confrontation, and (5) violent confrontation.

Conclusions

From this survey of structural theories, the reader may form conclusions that differ from those suggested by the theorists we have examined; or that differ from those of the present author, which may be summarized as follows:

a. We live not just in a world of interacting individuals and groups, but these are also part of a broader society.

b. This broader society is structured into a distinctive organization of recognized parts, including divisions of power and class, of ethnicity, of age and gender, and of nationhood. These parts all carry the potential for fundamental social conflict.

c. There may be little correlation between the structural conflicts of which we are most aware, and those that are most important in shaping the future of our society. Awareness depends on popular discussion of issues and events regarding a basic division in society. The potential for affecting the future is often a result of how fully taken-for-granted a structural division may be, and therefore *not* an object of much popular attention.

d. Although the chapter may not have suggested it, this author believes that the most important structural feature today for producing conflict and affecting future generations lies in the way our national states are arranged. We are increasingly a world society in fact, but we have not yet forged the institutions that will effectively manage our world conflicts.

6

Formal Theories

An Ambulance Driver Ponders the Rhythms of War

A Quaker at War

Lewis F. Richardson was a Quaker, and as such was opposed in principle to war or the taking up of arms in national defense. But he was also a loyal British subject, and when World War I came he felt he had some duty to serve his country. More importantly, he wanted to lessen the suffering in this war, if he could do anything to help. His solution was to volunteer for noncombat duty in the British medical services. He was sent to France, where he spent much of his time driving an ambulance to bring the wounded from the front lines to medical facilities in the rear.

Though occasionally exciting, this job also had many slow periods. During these idle times, Richardson let his mind wander freely about the war around him and about the patterns of violent conflict that this war represented. He found the rhythms of war fascinating, with the frenzied activity during battles and the lulls between them. He began to observe such phenomena as having predictable patterns amid their apparent chaos. He wondered whether or not these patterns might be expressed in some kind of mathematical form.

After the War

Richardson had been trained in the physical sciences and had developed a special interest in the forces determining weather. After the war, he followed through with these interests and became one of the early leaders of the science of meteorology. He saw his interest in weather forecasting as akin to understanding the conditions of war between nations. Just as certain conditions in the physical atmosphere make violent weather likely, so do certain measurable conditions of the social atmosphere make group violence highly likely. Richardson asked himself, Can we identify these social conditions and use the power of mathematical logic to help us understand the basic processes of human conflict? Increasingly, he devoted himself to this central question.

After World War I, Richardson had pursued his work in physics and meteorology and was eventually elected a Fellow in the highly selective Royal

Society. At the same time, Richardson considered himself as much a social scientist as a physical scientist, though he had difficulty in getting anyone else to recognize this. His writings on social conflict went mostly unpublished, at least in his lifetime. When he privately published some of this work and gave copies to his friends, their reactions were not always supportive. As he later recalled: "Some of my friends thought it funny, but for me it was the beginning of the investigations on the causes of wars which now occupy me in my retirement."[1]

Richardson retired early from his work in physical science and educational administration in order to devote full time to studies in social conflict. One of the tasks that he took on was that of quantifying human violence. No one before him had attempted so complete a compilation of wars and other episodes of violence as Richardson now attempted. He gathered statistics on wars, and attempted to discern some underlying patterns in their occurrence. For example, his statistics suggested that wars might tend to have a cycle of intensity, with roughly a span of a generation occurring between peaks of international violence.

Richardson pursued his studies on conflict with the attitude of a natural scientist and mathematician. He attempted to get as complete a count as possible of what he called "deadly quarrels." These included not just international conflicts, but any episodes of violence resulting in the loss of human life. He was alert to mathematical order in his data. He found, for example, that the frequency of violent conflicts showed a very regular relationship to their magnitude; the higher the magnitude, the lower the frequency. And this relationship, moreover, could be expressed in terms of a fairly precise mathematical function. This shows a certain lawfulness in the apparently chaotic episodes of human violence. By understanding such lawfulness, are we not in a better position to deal intelligently with such phenomena as war?

The fact that we can identify quantitative relationships about our deadly quarrels does not mean that we have no choice in what happens. Richardson described his own view of the world of social conflict as having "characteristics intermediate between those of machine-like determinism and those of freely willed choice." There is a certain momentum of events that we must take account of, but there is also room for us to guide them in some way—and our very knowledge of the natural patterns of human conflict should enable us to guide them more effectively away from violence.[2]

Although some of his articles had appeared earlier, only in 1960, seven years after his death, were Richardson's two major books published. His manuscripts were edited by other scholars who believed that this work deserved greater recognition than had been given during his lifetime, and they were published with the titles of *Arms and Insecurity* and *Statistics of Deadly Quarrels*. They were soon to become classics in the mathematical study of human conflict. *Statistics of Deadly Quarrels* gives Richardson's general work on quantifying violent conflicts. *Arms and Insecurity* deals with the specific topic of arms races, which we will next explore more fully.[3]

A Mathematical Formulation of Arms Races

The Uses of Mathematics

The use of mathematics in measurement is well known. We learn to count and calculate very early in our education. Social scientists must develop further refinements to measure the particular kinds of data used for their studies. The use of mathematics for analyzing data is also relatively well known, even though many students have difficulty with learning the proper uses of such things as correlation coefficients and tests of significance. The social scientist finds it necessary to develop some competence in statistical reasoning for data analysis, as well as using elementary skills in quantitative measurement.

There is another use of mathematics for scientific work that is not as familiar to most social scientists as it is to physical scientists, though its practice is clearly increasing in the social and behavioral sciences. This is the use of mathematics for building theory. We can use mathematics as a tool for describing our world, for analyzing data about the world, and for organizing our thinking. In this last activity, we use formal logic and mathematics to assist us in the task of theorizing. It is in this area, above all, that Richardson made a contribution to the study of social conflict and its resolution. The work for which he is now best known is his mathematical formulations of arms races.[4]

Although Richardson focused on arms races, it is clear that his kind of mathematical reasoning can be applied to any subject where parties are highly dependent on each other's actions—to all kinds of fights, or, indeed, to falling in love.

Mathematical Models: First Steps

In this work Richardson went through several steps that are characteristic phases in the development of mathematical models. First, he identified key concepts to be used as the basic variables in the model. Next, he made some reasonable assumptions about how these concepts were related to each other. Third, he put these assumptions into mathematical form, most commonly using an equation to express the ideas. Fourth, he derived conclusions regarding the logical consequences of his formulation. After taking all of these steps, we are then ready to test the model in terms of some concrete data, which will give us a basis for revising or refining the model for further use.

What are the key concepts for conceiving how arms races work? Clearly, a key idea is that one nation feels threatened by the arms buildup of another. This leads us to such concepts as the amount of arms, changes in armament levels, and the costliness of arms production. We also need a key concept to express how quickly one side tends to react to the other, as well as some notion of the accumulated grievances.

What are some reasonable assumptions for how the key concepts are related? One would be that one side feels more threatened when the arms buildup of the other is most rapidly increasing. Another is that one side will increase its own armaments when it feels a sense of threat. Still another is that the more responsive one side is to the actions of another, the stronger will be the impact on one's own armaments of those of another. Costs of arms, however, will dampen this tendency, though an accumulation of grievances should in some way sharpen the sense of threat and, thus, the level of arms production.

The assumptions we have made seem very simple, yet they may become powerful when given a mathematical formulation. If we devise a set of equations, one to represent each side or nation, we can use mathematical analyses to give us the consequences of our assumptions. With these equations we may enter different quantities for our key variables, then see how this changes the outcomes.

Following Richardson, we may express the arms buildup of one side or nation, which we will call X-land, by the following equation:

$$dx/dt = ay - mx + g$$

What this says, literally, is that the change in armament levels of one nation *(dx)* over time *(dy)* is a function of three factors working together: the tendency to react strongly or weakly to the threat of the other *(ay)*, the tendency to be strongly or weakly influenced by the difficulties of producing arms *(mx)*, and the extent of accumulated grievances *(g)*.

Some special assumptions built into the above equation probably should be noted, since they affect the kind of mathematical analysis that may be given. One is that we are fundamentally trying to measure change—a difference in a quantity over time—which is slightly more complex than a simple measure of quantity (as in the usual "Let $x =$"). Another is that each of the first two terms on the right side of the equation has two measures: one a variable *(y or x)*, and one a constant *(a or m)*. The variable represents armament levels of the other *(y)* or oneself *(x)*, which will change at different points in an arms race; the constant represents a characteristic quality of the nation's reaction to the other (to be strongly reactive for *a*, or to be strongly sensitive to costs for *m*). Each of these two terms is expressed as a multiplicative relationship (indicating a close interaction of the two measures involved), while the combination of the three terms is additive (indicating a degree of independence of these terms from one another). All of these are quite straightforward mathematical expressions of the assumptions that Richardson started with for his analysis of arms races.

We can now formulate a similar equation to represent the changes of arms of the other side (nation or bloc), which we may call Y-land. This is represented by Richardson as:

$$dy/dt = bx - ny + h$$

where Y-land's change in armaments levels is also a function of three terms, each parallel to those we have identified for X-land. Here b takes the place of a, n takes the place of m, and h takes the place of g, all recognizing that the determinants affecting Y-land may be different from those of X-land (that is, they may not be just mirror images of each other, in spite of the parallel equations).

By bringing these two equations together for combined analysis, we can make use of well-established mathematical procedures for differential equations. We can then grind out the logical consequences of feeding different quantities into our equations. It is at this point that the power of mathematical reasoning becomes especially evident, for one can easily deduce what must follow from a great variety of starting points. The logic becomes inexorable and the conclusions certain—or at least following with certainty from whatever is put into the equations initially.

Predominant Patterns

The specific outcomes of Richardson's equations of arms races may be endlessly varied, but they fall into several primary patterns. There are basically four types of outcomes:

Type 1.
    Here the two sides move quickly to a stable equilibrium. This happens when, despite an accumulation of mutual grievances, the braking factors or cost considerations *(m* and *n)* together outweigh the strength of reactivity *(a* and *b)*.
Type 2.
    Here the two sides move quickly toward total disarmament. This happens when we start with an accumulation of goodwill outweighing grievances (that is, g and h tend to be negative), and the braking factors or cost considerations together outweigh the strength of reactivity.
Type 3.
    Here there is a runaway arms race. This happens when we start with an accumulation of mutual grievances *(g* and *h)*, and the strength of reactivity *(a* and *b)* outweighs the braking factors *(m* and *n)*.
Type 4.
    Here there is an interesting indeterminacy. The result could be *either* a runaway arms race *or* total disarmament, depending on the initial level of

armaments. This happens when the strength of reactivity outweighs the braking factors and there is an initial accumulation of goodwill. However, if we start at high levels of arms, this goodwill is overshadowed by the need to keep pace with the arms of the other. At low levels the opposite is the case, and mutual disarmament is the result. There is some point where these two patterns would be evenly balanced, but it is an unstable equilibrium. The tendency is clearly to move in one direction or the other.

Type 3 is, of course, the classic pattern of an arms race. Once the quantities are fed into the equations and develop into this type, there is no escaping the conclusion that the arms race will continue indefinitely—culminating naturally, Richardson assumed, in war.

Mathematics and Reality

Does Richardson's mathematical model fit well with events in the real world? Richardson himself took very seriously the possible implications of his mathematical reasoning, and he attempted to see how well they fit actual patterns of international relations. He looked in particular at the arms race that preceded World War I. He laboriously gathered statistics on armament levels and other factors applicable to the two main blocs of European nations in the years immediately before the war. What he found was a very close correspondence between his mathematical projections of year-to-year changes in armament levels and the actual production figures he obtained from his historical sources. The model, he concluded, was a workable one. Although a gross simplification of reality, it mirrored sufficiently well the dynamics of the real world that it could be used to make reasonable predictions.

Others who have followed Richardson have criticized some of the details of his work, including the facts and assumptions he used in testing his arms race model on European data. But the basic mathematics used by Richardson has not been questioned, nor his impact on further studies of arms races. True, the arms race scholars who came after Richardson tended to see the process as more complicated than Richardson had represented it, and the mathematical formulations have therefore become harder to follow in this area of study. But Richardson's role as a pioneer cannot be questioned.

Mathematical Inevitability?

The mathematical models that Richardson produced suggest an inevitability about the way conflicts develop. Given some initial conditions, it seems inevitable that certain outcomes will follow. This is what comes from using mathematical logic, for there can be no second thoughts about the results once the equations have been formulated in a particular way. But does this mean that there is no escape from a pattern that seems to lead in the direction of an arms race? Not quite, for Richardson viewed his mathematical formulations as showing only what will happen if people do not stop to think. By knowing with mathematical certainty what follows from certain assumptions, we may be persuaded to behave in a manner that creates a different outcome. Richardson expressed this in the form of a dialogue with an imaginary critic as follows:

Critic: I still don't like the fatalistic look of your mathematics. The worst disservice that anyone can do to the world is to spread the notion that the drift toward war is fated and uncontrollable.

Author: With that I agree entirely. But before a situation can be controlled, it must be understood. If you steer a boat on the theory that it ought to go toward the side to which you move the tiller, the boat will seem uncontrollable. "If we threaten," says the militarist, "they will become docile." Actually, they become angry and threaten reprisals. He has put the tiller to the wrong side. Or, to express it mathematically, he has mistaken the sign of the defense coefficient.[5]

The Mathematical Formulation of Interests

Money Isn't Everything

When we think of a quantitative measure of what people value, the first thing we usually think about is money. Money serves not only as a medium of exchange and as a store of value, but in serving these functions it also serves as a measure of value. Generally, we value more the things we pay more for. However, there are some problems with money as a measure of value. Some things do not cost us much money, yet they are of enormous value for our continued existence. Air to breathe and water to drink are some obvious examples. Just because they are present in relatively abundant supply, they cost us little. But the fact that we are asked little in exchange for such vital necessities does not reduce their basic value to us—unless we want to define values solely in terms of market prices.

Then there are those things we need that never enter into market transactions at all. Only in a most indirect way can we see friendship and esteem as matters of market exchange. In fact, much of the confirmation of our commitment to close friends and family members comes in avoiding any close calculation of exchange values in our dealings with them. We give and take without regard (or at least with a lowered regard) for profits and costs with those who are closest to us.

Even when we feel justified in using money as a measure of our values, there is a problem with seeing the gradations of our satisfaction as precisely reflecting monetary units. Maybe we would like more money better than less money. But can we say with confidence that the second million a wealthy tycoon might make is equal in value to the first? Or that a hungry beggar values the money needed to buy a good meal precisely twice as much as half that sum of money, which could buy a smaller but still nutritious meal?

It has been more than 250 years since this difference between monetary values and satisfaction values was clearly identified. In 1738, Daniel Bernoulli published a paper on this subject and suggested his solution. Satisfaction value (or what Bernoulli called "moral worth") increases with money values, he suggested, but at a lower rate of increase. Thus real values should be counted as a function of their money values, but not in any one-to-one relationship.[6]

During the nineteenth century, philosophers and economists began to talk about 'utility' as the measure of subjective value. Utility was held to be a measure of one's fundamental interests, but both its psychological and mathematical foundations remained fuzzy.

It was not until about the middle of the twentieth century that a theoretically sophisticated theory about the foundations of utility became generally accepted. This was largely a product of the work of John von Neumann and Oskar Morgenstern.[7]

A Theoretical Derivation of Utility

Von Neumann and Morgenstern approached the problem of the measurement of utility in terms of relative preferences. When faced with a choice, what do we prefer? This question gives us the basic framework for deriving measures of utility. There is another basic assumption behind the conception they proposed: that individuals have a basic consistency in the way they make their preferences known. Starting with these two basic assumptions (of utility seen in terms of expressed preferences, and preferences seen as generally consistent), von Neumann and Morgenstern erected their simple but elegant theory of utility. They ended with a theory that can provide interval measures of utility, that is, allowing real numbers other than monetary units to be attached to the objects of our desires. It need not bother us unduly that it is seldom practical to actually do this; just the thought that it can be done theoretically is impressive.[8]

The idea of a lottery provides the basic tool for von Neumann and Morgenstern's derivation of utility measures. The lottery they conceived of combines percentages of success with different objects of our preference. For example, we might conceive of being given the option of choosing between

a. $50 for certain, or
b. a 50-50 chance of winning either $100 or nothing.

If the stated result is anything but indifference, we have a utility scale which will be different from a monetary scale. If *a* is the option (which most people would probably choose), it suggests that the utility of further units of money declines as we get richer—a pattern that Bernoulli observed long ago. On the other hand, if *b* is chosen, then we are dealing with a person with an unusual attraction to risk—the sort of person that official lotteries thrive on.

Of course, we would need to give more than one choice before we had a clear notion of the slope of a person's utility scale in relation to a monetary scale. After several hundred choices, though, a fairly clear picture could emerge. But why should we limit our thinking to monetary values? The lottery approach can be used for *any* kind of choice. For example, we might present this choice:

a.   the certainty of a piece of cherry pie, or
b.   going out for the football team with a one-in-ten chance of making it.

This, of course, would be a ridiculous choice to consider. But that we can in theory pose any kind of ridiculous choice only suggests the power of the lottery idea. It allows us to extend a quantitative approach for conceiving utility to, literally, all kinds of human preferences. Quantitative measures need not be limited to economic goods and services; they may apply to any and all objects of our desires.

What this approach leaves us with is a method of theoretically deriving utility measures on an interval scale. However, each person is seen as having his or her own scale. This approach does not allow for interpersonal comparisons of utility; utility, rather, is individualized. But is this a problem? Is it not a realistic way of representing the basic truth that different people have different values?[9]

We have only sketched the barest and most nonmathematical aspects of the approach von Neumann and Morgenstern used to derive units of utility. However, its mathematical sophistication greatly impressed most economists and others who worked in the area of quantitative decision making. It became a starting point for what came to be known as "decision theory." Soon—especially in the work of L. J. Savage—von Neumann and Morgenstern's contributions became the basis of a reformulation of the foundations of mathematics and statistics.[10]

Econometrics and Other Applications

Classical decision theory (based on the foundation of von Neumann and Morgenstern's utility theory) soon became the basic framework for economists studying interest conflicts as found in market phenomena. This was especially true for those economists who were most quantitatively oriented. Their field is generally called "econometrics," which is the study of economic data and theories as related to mathematics and statistics. Econometricians assume that economic phenomena can be expressed in mathematical form. Their characteristic mode of operation is to start with a mathematical model, then observe data viewed as samples of the universe defined by the model, and then revise the model to provide ever closer approximations to the empirical findings. This is the same general style we described earlier in discussing Richardson's models of arms races.

Although economics has become the most mathematically oriented of all the social sciences, persons in other fields have also increasingly used mathematical thinking in their theories. This is certainly true for both political science and sociology. Among the scholars in these fields are those who have turned their focus especially upon social conflict. Much of the work of Kenneth Boulding (discussed briefly in Chapter 4) would fit in the category of a mathematical approach to the study of social conflict. Walter Isard is another leader in conflict studies or peace science whose work is strongly grounded in mathematical reasoning. So, too, is much of the other work found in such publications as the *Journal of Conflict Resolution.*[11]

Among all areas of the application of mathematics to the social sciences, one stands out as most clearly directed to the analysis of social conflict. This is that area of mathematics usually known as "game theory." It is to this mathematical formulation of interest conflicts that we turn our attention for the remainder of this chapter.

The Theory of Games

Foundations of Game Theory

The theory of games originated with von Neumann and Morgenstern as a natural accompaniment to their utility theory. Or, more accurately, utility theory served as the base for their elucidation of the principles of game theory. In any event, their *Theory of Games and Economic Behavior* provided the starting point both for modern decision theory generally and for game theory in particular.[12]

Game theory starts with some basic assumptions regarding the way the interests of different individuals may be related to each other for mathematical analyses. In its classic form, game theory started with such assumptions as the following:

1. Games always involve two or more players, each with an opportunity to choose between alternatives.
2. Each available alternative is fully known to each player.
3. All possible outcomes that might occur to any player may be expressed in terms of numerical measures of utility.
4. Each player will make those choices that will provide the maximum expected utility.

With such basic assumptions, game theorists proceed to a mathematical analysis of the way interest conflicts may be resolved for all kinds of situations. Most of the work has been devoted to two-person games, that is, situations with just two parties (whether real persons, or groups, or nations—it makes no difference so far as the mathematics is concerned). Game theory has been especially successful in its analysis of situations of pure conflict between two parties, usually referred to as "zero-sum games."[13]

Zero-Sum Games and the Minimax Solution

Technically, a zero-sum game is any situation in which, for every outcome, the utilities of all the parties add up to zero. Put another way, any gains for one party must always be at the expense of another. This means that the game is one of clearly opposing interests. If we have two players, it means that they have a pure conflict-of-interest situation.

We will not here go into the details of mathematical analysis, but it turns out that there is a mathematically elegant way of solving all two-person zero-sum games. This mathematical solution for the pure conflict-of-interest situation was called the "minimax solution" by von Neumann and Morgenstern. This term indicated that, in the matrix formulation they tended to use to analyze joint decision making, the outcome would always be the minimum value in the row or column which in turn has the maximum minimal value. If the reader has difficulty in following this, he or she can relax a bit; others have said that this solution could better be called the "maximin solution," as the recommended strategy is always that of maximizing the minimum that one can be assured. Whatever term we use, the general idea is that one seeks out what we might call the "least worst." That is, when you face a wise opponent whose interests are diametrically opposed to yours, the best solution for you (and for your opponent) is to choose the option that gives the most that you can assure yourself. What this indicates (and von Neumann and Morgenstern proved it mathematically) is that all two-person zero-sum games have an equilibrium point where the parties will come together if they are both wisely following their best interests. By an analysis of coalitions, von Neumann and Morgenstern also applied the minimax solution to games with more than two players (or, in game theory parlance, "n-person games").

It should be pointed out that not all zero-sum games have a direct minimax solution. For some (in reality, most) situations, one must analyze various strategy mixes for both players before one can identify the mathematical equilibrium point for the game. That is, the solution turns out not to be a simple choice, but some mathematically derived combination of choices. But even here, there is always an identifiable mathematical solution, if one follows the assumptions of the theory of games.

Let us not neglect to admire the achievement of von Neumann and Morgenstern in developing their minimax theorem, which proves mathematically that all zero-sum games have an equilibrium solution. This suggests that even the most severe of conflicts, those in which interests are completely opposed, can be seen as having solutions—if we can only translate the interests involved into a mathematical formulation.

Non-zero-sum Games and Multiple Solutions

It would be nice to be able to report that all mathematical representations of conflict are susceptible to a common method of obtaining a solution. Alas, this is not to be. The minimax theorem provides a clear solution only for zero-sum games. When we consider other kinds of situations (and non-zero-sum games represent most of the conflicts in the real world), obtaining a solution is not so simple.

There are some non-zero-sum games of nearly complete conflict of interest for which the minimax solution seems to provide a reasonable solution. However, it is not clear just where the dividing line is between those games where a minimax solution applies and those where it does not.

To take the opposite extreme from the zero-sum game, we may consider games where there is a complete absence of interest conflicts. These are sometimes called "coordination" games, or games of pure cooperation. Obtaining a mathematical solution here is not much of a problem; however, when more than one outcome meets the criteria for a solution, there is often a problem of coordinating the actions of the players in order to obtain an outcome they both desire. This turns out not to be a mathematical problem, but a social psychological one. It requires mutual agreement to coordinate each player's moves, which usually is easy if there is opportunity for free communication.

In between pure-conflict (or zero-sum) games and no-conflict (or cooperation) games, we have a great variety of mixed-motive games. We call them this because of the combination of opposed interests and common interests that are present. Such a combination surely complicates the mathematical search for solutions or equilibrium conditions. Indeed, for many of them there may be equilibrium conditions that fail to meet some of the reasonable criteria for a solution. (One of the types of games for which this is true is the prisoner's dilemma, which we discussed briefly in Chapter 2.)

We do not wish to suggest that there are no general solutions for mixed-motive games. There have been several approaches suggested, with one by John Nash especially popular among mathematicians. However, there is always room for raising theoretical questions—questions that point out that a given approach never meets all the criteria we would like to see in a mathematically elegant solution.[14]

Summary and Conclusions

Summary

A formal theory of conflict or its resolution places primary emphasis on the logical and mathematical nature of its generalizations. While ordinary language may be used for part of the exposition of these theories, the central ideas are expressed in the language of mathematics. In such a framework, social conflict is seen primarily as a manifestation of quantitatively expressed relationships; and conflict resolution is seen in terms of positions of stability or equilibrium in the dynamics of such relationships.

We considered Lewis Richardson and his quantitative analysis of arms races as a way of introducing formal theory. Richardson tried to study social conflict in a thoroughly quantitative manner, and his work on arms races gives a good example of the formulation and use of mathematical models.

Among other theories of a formal nature, we considered especially the theory of utility as developed by von Neumann and Morgenstern. This theory allows us to represent human interests on an interval scale. This, in turn, was seen as especially useful for work in econometrics and game theory.

In our discussion of game theory, we saw how mathematical analyses of conflicts of interest can be used not only to evaluate the strategies of the players, but also to determine how they might best come together for a resolution of their conflict. However, criteria for a good mathematical solution for a conflict may be different for different kinds of games.

Conclusions

The most general conclusion following from the materials examined in this chapter is, at least in the author's view, that formal theory possesses an elegance and power not found in other kinds of theory. Formal theories are elegant in the sense that rather simple mathematical formulations may be developed which have a clear-cut, logical structure. They are powerful in the sense that their results flow relentlessly from the premises. They are powerful also in the sense that a wide range of phenomena may be covered by the same mathematical model.

Among the more specific conclusions suggested by this chapter are the following:

a. Arms races represent a highly dynamic phenomenon in which eventual results are strongly conditioned by the initial relationships. Slight differences in initial conditions can sometimes produce very different final outcomes.

b. Human interests may be expressed quantitatively in terms other than those of money. The theory of utility allows us to study systematically the processes of conflict and conflict resolution in quantitative terms other than those of simple monetary values.

c.   It is easier intellectually to deal with situations of pure conflict than those that embody mixtures of conflicting and common interests. The clarity of the opposition in zero-sum games makes them more susceptible to mathematical solution than is possible for most mixed-motive games.

We should also mention some problems that are especially evident in work with formal models. First, most of us are not as well trained and comfortable in the language of formal logic and mathematics as we are in ordinary language. We therefore find it strange to work through even rather simple mathematical models; that just isn't the way we normally think. Second, the primary subject matter used in formal theory is not that of the real world; it is that of the world of mathematics. True, we hope to make connections to the world of empirical reality, but that is not what occupies our primary attention. This makes it possible to work hard at a mathematical model without being sure that it mirrors anything beyond itself. For most of us, that is an uncomfortable situation. Finally, even when much of a mathematical model seems to be a good representation of reality, there are usually special assumptions made that represent gross simplifications of the observable world. Of course, this point may be made in regard to theories of any kind. However, the problem may be more serious in the case of formal theory; here the exactitude of the processes of inference may give us a false sense of security about the reasonableness of the primary assumptions.

III

PRACTICE

7

Coercion

Fighting over the Falklands

Conflicting Claims

Certain islands in the South Atlantic had been included in the portion of the world identified as Spanish by the Treaty of Utrecht in 1713. However, these islands, variously known as the Falklands or the Malvinas, were not settled till over fifty years later. The first settlers came from France, but Spanish sovereignty was recognized in 1767. The British had also furnished some early settlers, and these made claims on behalf of Great Britain. With Argentine independence from Spain, the Spanish claims were transferred from Madrid to Buenos Aires. A new government in Buenos Aires sought to assert its control over these islands, which they called the Malvinas. However, the British did not recognize this, and within a few years they sent two warships to take over the islands by force. The British then continued to treat this territory, which they called the Falkland Islands, as a colony of the British crown.[1]

Do these events sound familiar? Most readers will not have heard of them, despite knowing something about the Falkland Islands. What we recounted in the above paragraph were not twentieth-century events. Rather, we summarized the history of the Falklands only up to the early part of the nineteenth century. It was in 1833 that the British warships first sailed into the Falklands to assert British control. Thereafter, the inhabitants of the Falklands (varying up and down from a population of about 2,000) continued under British authority. As others left, people from England came to replace them, mostly involved with the economic activities of servicing ships and raising sheep.

Argentina continued to formally claim the Malvinas Islands, with verbal support from Latin American neighbors, but it did little to push its claims. At least, there was no sense of a major international dispute until the middle 1960s. Then, amid worldwide anticolonial pressures, the Argentines renewed their claims and were able to get a resolution through the United Nations General Assembly in 1965 which called for negotiations toward "a peaceful solution to the problem." The following year, bilateral negotiations began between Argentina and the United Kingdom.

Negotiations

Negotiations began secretly, and the early discussions appeared to assume an eventual transfer of the Falklands to Argentine sovereignty. In 1971 the two nations agreed to work jointly toward serving the needs of the islanders, but without resolving the question of sovereignty. As an interim response, Argentina was to provide a new shipping link with the islands, and Britain was to develop an airstrip, making possible regular air travel to and from the South American mainland. However, both parties found some difficulties in living up to this agreement, for both had higher-priority needs than those of the small population on these islands. Then in 1973, Juan Peron returned to power in Argentina, and Argentine sovereignty demands were soon renewed. When a new military coup gained control of the government in 1976, they did nothing to reduce the sovereignty issue. They renewed with even more vigor the Argentine claims in the South Atlantic, and they became more insistent in raising the sovereignty issue in negotiations with the British. When Margaret Thatcher became the British prime minister in 1979, the British also reconsidered their stand in regard to the Falklands. Gradually the idea of a 'leaseback' arrangement became the favored option to be pursued by the British negotiators; this arrangement would recognize Argentina's ultimate sovereignty, but would include an agreement for British administration over an extended period of time.

The lease-back possibility never seriously entered into Argentine-British negotiations. It was partly sidetracked by the Falkland Islanders themselves, who became energized—as negotiations became more publicized—by the thought that the British government might 'sell them out.' They wanted to remain British, and the government did not want to oppose the expressed interests of the islanders. In addition, Argentina became more insistent on resolving the sovereignty issue soon.

War

In 1981, a new military triumvirate seized power in Buenos Aires. They made recovery of the Malvinas a high priority, and they secretly developed a plan for their seizure. Although talks with the British were renewed, General Leopoldo Galtieri, the new Argentine leader, did not pursue them seriously. Instead, he used Argentine business interests in salvaging materials at another largely uninhabited island of the South Atlantic (South Georgia) as a means of enforcing their claims in that area. Then on April 2, 1982, there was a full-scale invasion of the Falklands by Argentine forces. Before that day was over, the small British garrison had surrendered, and Argentina had control over the Malvinas Islands. That evening the streets of Buenos Aires were filled with wild celebration. On that same day, the British began the formation of a special military task force designed to again assert the British claim over the Falklands.

A United Nations resolution sought Argentine withdrawal, to be followed by negotiations to settle the issue without the use of force. Argentina refused to withdraw, and considered negotiations (some of which were mediated by U.S. Secretary of State Alexander Haig) primarily as a means for getting their claims over the islands recognized. The British carrier group sailed from Portsmouth on April 5, and additional forces were added to the Falklands military task force from other areas. On April 25, an advance group recaptured South Georgia, and the next month the British were ready for a full-scale invasion of the Falklands. This began on May 21, and ended with the surrender of Port Stanley (the capital and main town) on June 14. This war included more than three weeks of bitter fighting, involving about 39,000 men in the forces of both sides (over islands which then had less than 2,000 inhabitants). The British reported 255 killed and 777 wounded, while Argentina reported 652 dead or missing. The naval and air aspects of the military confrontation were especially critical, with Argentina putting up a formidable challenge to the British in both of these areas. Although the Argentines sank six British ships, Great Britain ultimately asserted naval dominance. Likewise in the air, British superiority was not immediately apparent, though in the end the Argentine air force suffered more losses than the British (out of about 70 planes lost altogether).

Almost immediately after the final surrender at Port Stanley, the Galtieri government fell (its international disgrace the last straw when added to unpopular economic policies), and a new military group took over. Meanwhile, the British consolidated their power over the Falklands. The life of the islanders, however, did not soon return to normal, for their normal pursuits were now overshadowed by the large number of military personnel remaining to protect them.

Since 1982, Argentina has not sought to regain the Malvinas by force, and their diplomatic offensive has continued on a subdued level. The British remain in control, with the Falkland Islands continuing in the status of a crown colony.

Can Force Really Resolve Things?

Physical Force as Conflict Resolution

Was the conflict over the Falkland Islands resolved by force? The events recounted above seem to indicate clearly that military force was decisive regarding who would control the Falklands. But did this really resolve the problem? One leading analysis of the Falklands crisis ends with these comments:

After 149 years of claims and counterclaims, 17 years of fruitless negotiations, and a seventy-four-day war, the Falklands/Malvinas conflict is still unresolved. . . . Argentina was defeated and humiliated, and its military government fell in disgrace and dishonor. Britain recovered the islands but at a cost it can ill afford. And the sovereignty of the islands remains in dispute.[2]

Granted, not everyone was satisfied by the outcome of the Falklands war, and it did not end all Argentine claims for sovereignty. But it did at least settle, for the foreseeable future, the issue of which flag would fly over these islands and which nation would have responsibility for their administration.

To some, a military victory is the simplest and clearest form of conflict resolution. The issue is joined and dealt with in a most direct manner until one side (usually) emerges triumphant. But to others, force provides no resolution. Only, they hold, when parties come together and voluntarily agree is there a true resolution of a conflict—one that will eliminate the rancor and hostility that the parties feel toward one another.

Given the rather broad definition of conflict resolution we have chosen to use, we must accept force and coercion as among the ways that conflicts are in fact resolved. At least, a resort to force may provide an end to a conflict's most intense period and may determine who is to have the upper hand in consequent decisions. We therefore take seriously the idea that force and coercion may provide one form of conflict resolution.

A similar question may be raised about any major form of conflict resolution. Is a conflict ever completely resolved? Just because negotiators reach an agreement, is everybody happy? Often not. And does a court case really end a dispute? Often a decision is appealed, and even when not, one of the parties may feel it has been unfairly treated. Does mediation solve all issues in a dispute? Often not, even though an agreement may be reached, sometimes grudgingly, on major points. Likewise, arbitration may provide a decision without fully satisfying anyone. Indeed, arbitrators often consider the fact that both sides are unhappy with the outcome as evidence that a fair conclusion was reached.

So even though a resort to force may not end a bitter conflict forever, no other form of conflict resolution can always perfectly resolve issues either. Of course, the costs of a physical confrontation are often enormously high. Consider, for example, the costs to the British in their successful retaking of the Falkland Islands. They suffered almost a thousand casualties (dead and wounded), had six ships sunk and ten more badly damaged, lost nine planes, and had a financial cost estimated at about two billion pounds. All this in order to have the British flag wave over nearly unpopulated islands more than 8,000 miles from Great Britain.

Furthermore, a resort to force often does not resolve the conflict. It may only make it worse. Even if we admit physical force as a way conflicts may be resolved, we must recognize that force can play this role only under certain conditions.

Conditions of Forceful Resolution

To identify the conditions under which a resort to force may allow one of the parties to resolve a conflict (or at least to conclude its most active phase), we may point to four main considerations. These are capability, credibility, relevance, and legitimacy. In order to discuss how these might apply to effective conflict resolution, we will draw illustrations from several international conflicts with which most readers are likely to be familiar. In addition to the Falklands War, we will refer to the Cuban-American conflicts of 1961 and 1962, the struggle for South Vietnam during the period of 1963–75, and the Persian Gulf War of 1990 and 1991. Let us recount a few of the events of these conflicts to remind readers of their main outlines.

After Cuban revolutionaries, led by Fidel Castro, had taken control of Havana on January 1, 1959, there was a period during which Cuba's relations to other nations were unclear. However, as Castro dealt harshly with internal opposition and took an increasingly anti-American line in his speeches and policies, confiscating most American landholdings and other investments in Cuba, relations with the United States soured. The United States broke off diplomatic relations in January of 1961, and immediately Cuba forged an alliance with the Soviet Union and began its transformation into a Communist dictatorship. The U.S. government reacted by supporting, through its Central Intelligence Agency, a secret expeditionary force which prepared for an invasion of Cuba. The invasion came on April 17, 1961, when about two thousand men landed at the Bay of Pigs, along the southern coast of Cuba. They were quickly and easily defeated by Castro's forces. Thereafter, Cuba's military alliance with the Soviet Union became more open, and Russian military bases were established on the island. In the summer of 1962, a decision was made to establish intermediate-range missile launching sites in Cuba, which would have the capability of a direct nuclear attack on the United States. However, before these sites could become operational, they were discovered by U.S. intelligence; President John F. Kennedy then publicly demanded that the Soviet Union remove the missiles or face the full power of American military forces. A limited military blockade of Cuba was also put into effect. After a week of intense uncertainty, with the threat of nuclear war between the two superpowers a distinct possibility, Soviet Prime Minister Nikita Khrushchev, on October 28, 1963, ordered the missile sites dismantled and the missiles returned to the Soviet Union.

French colonial forces withdrew from Vietnam in 1954, and the country was then divided into two parts, with a Communist government recognized as ruling in North Vietnam. South Vietnam, under anticommunist leadership, became supported by the United States. The Viet Cong, an insurgent group allied with North Vietnam, challenged the government of South Vietnam, which passed in 1963 from the authoritarian rule of Ngo Dinh Diem to a series of generals who were increasingly dependent on American support. To prevent the collapse of the South Vietnamese government, U.S. military forces became involved, with about a half million U.S. troops there by the end of 1965. The war had by then become largely an American war against the Viet Cong and North Vietnam. Although initially the commitment of U.S. forces seemed sufficient to quash the rebellion, by 1968 it became apparent that the insurgents were as strong as ever, despite massive American operations in the South and heavy bombing by Americans of North Vietnam. Popular opinion in the United States had begun to turn away from pursuit of this war, and this contributed to a Republican victory in the presidential election held that year. The new administration of Richard M. Nixon sought both to continue to prosecute the war and to seek a diplomatic resolution with their enemies. Early in 1973 an agreement was announced which led to a withdrawal of American forces and a reduction of the opposing forces in South Vietnam. Two years after the Americans withdrew, the government of South Vietnam succumbed to a combination of rebel forces of the South and an armed invasion from the North. Saigon, the southern capital, fell on April 30, 1975, and soon thereafter the two parts of Vietnam were united under the dominance of North Vietnam.

Iraq still had not fully recovered from a bloody war with Iran, during 1980–88, when a dispute developed with another neighbor. The small kingdom of Kuwait had some of the richest oil fields in the world, and it had lands to which (like some in Iran) Iraq had long-standing claims. In fact, many in Iraq—and most especially its leader, President Saddam Hussein—viewed the origin of Kuwait as an arbitrary vestige of colonialism, carved out to allow further European influence in the Gulf area. Perhaps most important was Kuwait's wealth in oil, allowing the million and a half Kuwaitis a higher standard of living than that found in any neighboring country, higher even than in Saudi Arabia. Claiming that Kuwait was undermining efforts to restrict the sale of oil in world markets (Iraq was among those nations that sought to keep world prices up through restricting production), Iraq began diplomatic efforts in the summer of 1990 to dictate policies for its smaller neighbor. Territorial claims were also pursued in these high-pressure negotiations, and other Arab states became involved in seeking to mediate between Iraq and Kuwait. Then, suddenly, on August 2, Iraq launched a full-scale invasion which quickly conquered the smaller nation. Iraq then annexed Kuwait. The United Nations immediately condemned this action and sought Iraq's withdrawal from Kuwait; then a military and economic embargo was put into effect against Iraq. Despite intense diplomatic pressure, the Iraqis indicated their resolve to stay in Kuwait. A military force was then organized and led by the United States. With the general support of the world community of nations, including most Arab states, this force (known as "Desert Shield") sought to force the Iraqis to withdraw. Large-scale bombing of Iraq by Allied forces began in January of 1991, and the following month, Allied ground forces invaded Kuwait and Iraq through the campaign they called "Desert Storm." Iraq's forces were quickly subdued, the monarchy was restored in Kuwait, and Iraq was forced to accept heavy restrictions on its military policies as a condition for an uneasy peace.

Capability. One of the most obvious requirements for successfully resolving an international conflict by physical force is sufficient capability in military might. Without a full-scale British response, the Argentine invasion would have succeeded in making their Malvinas part of Argentina. Even with the full might of Great Britain brought into the conflict, the outcome was not clear for several weeks. Then, however, the superior capability of the British became apparent.

In its dispute with the United States, Cuba clearly was at a military disadvantage. However, its capability was sufficient to repulse an invasion that was not supported by the full power of the U.S. government. Some military analysts believe that the outcome of the Bay of Pigs invasion might have been different if the United States had provided direct air support—a part of the original CIA plan that President Kennedy and his advisors felt would be unnecessary, thus allowing the invasion to appear to be a purely Cuban affair. The following year, however, even the full support (for a time) of the Soviet Union could not counter the U.S. military advantage. A key element here was that the missiles in Cuba had not had time to become operational; therefore, their potential contribution to the balance of military capabilities was never realized. Given its lack of other forces in the Western Hemisphere, the Soviet Union could not persist with its missiles in Cuba without a worldwide military confrontation with the United States; a confrontation in the Western Hemisphere alone would be doomed to failure. The Soviet Union therefore chose to back down from its effort to install missiles in Cuba.

The United States also had a clear edge in military capability over either the Viet Cong insurgents in South Vietnam or their supporters from the North. Had the war been a conventional military contest, there would have been no doubt as to its outcome. The Americans could have established whatever government they wanted in the South. But American military forces were continually frustrated in their efforts to find the enemy, which seemed both to be everywhere and nowhere. When the insurgent forces finally came out to openly challenge the Americans in the Tet offensive of early 1968, they were clearly defeated in conventional military terms. However, the fact that such an offensive could be launched against the clearly superior American forces—and that such a capability remained to be exercised in the future—proved a major watershed in American public support for the war. From then on, the United States began to seek the means for a graceful withdrawal, and the Viet Cong and North Vietnamese had the patience to keep their forces in reserve until the final victory in 1975 was feasible.

In the Persian Gulf wars of 1990–91, Iraq's military was clearly sufficient to subdue Kuwait, if that were the only issue. However, when the full military power of the United States (along with the support of many other nations) was brought into the conflict, the outcome could not long be in doubt. It then became only a question of how united and determined the Allies would be in their efforts.

Credibility. Although military capability was of great importance for establishing the outcomes for each of the disputes we have examined, the significance of credibility in the use of force is also apparent. Even when force is used, the credibility of its future use may be more important in deciding the outcome than what has been done in the past. Furthermore, there is the frequent desire to use one's military power to restrain a potential opponent through threats without actually applying force. In such cases, credibility becomes the primary consideration in affecting the outcome.

Much of the world doubted the credibility of Argentina's claim over the Malvinas. Apparently, the only way their claim could be recognized was by means of military force, which they chose to use. Once established on the islands, they did not believe that the British would have the will to send sufficient forces to dislodge them, even if the British were theoretically capable of this. The invasion had established Argentina's credibility to hold the islands. Great Britain apparently could only establish its own credibility by launching superior forces against the Argentines. Before they organized their military task force, the British had given good reasons for the Argentines to believe that British resolve would be less than it was. During the years of recent diplomacy, the British had not been firm in claiming future sovereignty for the Falklands. They had been willing to consider forms of divided sovereignty, so long as the desires of the islanders themselves were included. Also, they had announced plans to retire the only British naval vessel regularly stationed in the South Atlantic. Even more to the point, when Britain established a more restrictive immigration policy in 1981, it avoided making a special exception for residents of the Falkland Islands (as it had pointedly done for those of Gibraltar). This could easily be interpreted as an indication that the British would not strongly resist an Argentine take-over. But this interpretation failed to the take into account the determination of Margaret Thatcher that Britain should not give in to such direct military action on the part of Argentina.

In the Cuban conflict of 1961, the Cubans doubted (correctly, as it turned out) that the full power of U.S. military forces would support the Bay of Pigs invasion. Their credibility to govern in Cuba was therefore increased by defeating the invading forces without significant defections from their own ranks (in which the invaders had had misplaced hopes). The next year, the Cuban desire to have Soviet missiles brought in would have helped to establish their own military credibility in resisting U.S. power, had they been successfully installed. After the Americans discovered the missiles, they made very clear their intention to force their removal—in one way or another. That Khrushchev believed the American threats would be carried out was the primary factor in his withdrawal of the missiles from Cuba.

The credibility of American power in the face of challenges from Communist forces was the basic factor behind the American involvement in the Vietnamese War. The United States had established an alliance with the anticommunist leaders of South Vietnam, and American leaders felt duty-bound to use whatever military force was necessary to preserve the Saigon government. The credibility of this commitment, however, became less impressive as American public opinion began to turn against the war. Ultimately, the decisive factor was the credibility of the Viet Cong and North Vietnamese to pursue the war, year after year after year, until their forces could emerge victorious. U.S. military leaders finally concluded that the costs would be too high to continue indefinitely to prosecute the war.

By the Iraqi invasion of Kuwait, Saddam Hussein made it quite clear that Iraq intended to dominate that oil-rich area. The credibility of his government toward that end was enhanced by a refusal to consider any proposals for withdrawal. From then on the issue became the credibility of Allied forces to apply sufficient force to dislodge the Iraqis. This may have been in some doubt, as internal debates in the United States and elsewhere included strong sentiment against an early resort to military force (often with the argument that the effect of economic sanctions against Iraq had not been adequately tested). But the resolve of U.S. President George Bush was clearly to proceed directly with military force; and once this had been decided, the ultimate result could not long remain in doubt.

Relevance. Even with military capability and credible claims to its use, sometimes force cannot succeed in resolving an international conflict. One important factor is relevance in the way force is threatened or applied. If used without a clear strategy to support national policies, the resort to force may be ineffective.

Both Argentina and Great Britain made their use of force clearly relevant to their claims to sovereignty over the islands in dispute. While relations were not good between them, both resisted any attempt to widen the war beyond the islands of the South Atlantic. This assisted both, in turn, to get recognition (albeit only temporarily for Argentina) for their military conquests.

The support of the United States for the Bay of Pigs invasion proved to be of little relevance either for promoting an internal uprising on the island or for winning Cuban respect for U.S. power. The following year, when the stakes were much higher during the Cuban Missile Crisis, the Americans very carefully chose the forms of military activity that would be most relevant to removal of the missiles. Although there was an imminent threat of extensive bombing and an invasion of Cuba, these alternatives were held in reserve while a military blockade was put into effect. This prevented further Soviet military supplies (including missiles, which had to be imported into Cuba) from reaching the island. Despite high tensions between them, both the United States and the Soviet Union resisted the temptation to use the Cuban crisis as a basis for increasing their conflict elsewhere in the world.

American power in Vietnam may have helped an anticommunist government remain in power in Saigon much longer than would otherwise have been the case. However, in the end, it proved largely irrelevant for affecting the outcome of the political struggle in South Vietnam. Indeed, by Americanizing the war, the United States undercut the credibility of the claims to power of the government it sought to help. In any event, the forms of American military power were not well adapted to guerrilla warfare in the jungles and rice paddies of Vietnam. For this kind of warfare, the activities of the Viet Cong and the North Vietnamese proved more relevant.

If he hoped to assert direct control upon Kuwait, the actions of Saddam Hussein in sending his troops there were most relevant. So were the requests of the United Nations that the Iraqi troops be withdrawn, and the eventual actions of the Allies to defeat the Iraqis. Among the activities of the Persian Gulf War that may have been less obviously relevant (at least to the issue of control of Kuwait) were the imposition of an economic embargo against Iraq, and the bombing campaign against Baghdad. While these clearly attempted to show Allied resolve, they were not directly decisive in the battle for Kuwait, which ultimately required military action by ground forces.

Legitimacy. The fourth important consideration for the effective use of force is legitimacy. There needs to be a judgment that force is justified. Here, of course, comes the question: Justified by whom? *Someone* will always justify the use of force to resolve international conflicts; thus the question really becomes: How broadly is such force accepted as appropriate? There are at least three audiences to consider in making judgments about the legitimate use of force in international conflicts: (1) the decision makers and citizens of one's own nation, (2) those of the nation against whom force is applied, and (3) observers from other nations. For none of these is the judgment a simple yes-or-no response, but a combination of considerations that, when analyzed, frequently suggests when the issue of legitimacy may be a real problem for using force effectively.[3]

Both Argentina and Great Britain felt justified in their respective conquests of the Falklands, since they each considered them as legitimately their territory. Other nations were not so sure about either's claim, but did not consider it an issue of any great importance. This all changed with the Argentine invasion of the islands. Then other nations were required to make judgments: Would they consider the seizure as legitimate? Would they approve of a British attempt to retake the islands by force? The initial response was mostly in favor of the British view, and the United Nations passed a resolution asking for an Argentine withdrawal. When this was refused, the legitimacy of the Argentine position became more in doubt to everyone except themselves. Especially of concern to the rest of the world was their abrupt use of force. European nations united in economic sanctions against Argentina, and the United States (after a fruitless attempt to mediate between Argentina and Great Britain) also declared its general support for the British. With this kind of external support, the final retaking of the islands by British forces was widely seen as legitimate, given the unyielding position that the Argentines had displayed. One of the key factors in the legitimacy of the British position was that most of the people who lived in the Falklands clearly wanted to remain under British control.

In the case of the Bay of Pigs invasion, the Americans didn't want to claim major responsibility, for even they believed that a direct invasion of Cuba would be illegitimate under any standards of international law. This reserve about responsibility was an important factor in dooming the venture to failure. Meanwhile, no one doubted that quashing the invasion was a legitimate use of state power by the Cubans. During the Cuban Missile Crisis the next year, legitimacy judgments were different. By strict standards of international law, Cuba had a right to arm itself—and there were no generally agreed limitations against missiles being included. But there was a kind of unwritten law that a major change would not be introduced that would greatly affect the balance of power. Americans could therefore see any means of removing the missiles as legitimate; even if Russians and Cubans would be expected to have other views. However, even they recognized how the Americans felt; and when the Americans sought to remove the missiles with minimal force (and without a direct threat to intervene to undermine the Cuban government or prevent its general alliance with the Soviet Union) they made a withdrawal more acceptable. President Kennedy even used terms that would appear to minimize the harshness of the U.S. response: calling the military blockade a "quarantine." This made the actions of the United States more acceptable both to its own citizens and to the world of nations generally. This clearly had a role in resolving the conflict with a minimal use of military force.

The legitimacy of American actions in Vietnam were much more doubtful than in the Cuban case. Of course, the argument could be made that the United States was only helping another country (South Vietnam) defend itself. But this argument included the assumption that South Vietnam was properly an independent nation—a view not generally held in either Saigon or Hanoi. It was also based on the assumption that the main problem for South Vietnam was from the North, rather than an internal insurgency. As the war continued, the amount of U.S. involvement became viewed (by most Americans as well as by the rest of the world) as out of proper proportion to either any real American interests in Southeast Asia or to any hope that South Vietnam could emerge as a truly viable nation. Indeed, the legitimacy of the South Vietnamese government was eroded by the overwhelming presence of the Americans, making it appear legitimate to even fewer Vietnamese, either in the North or in the South. In the end, questions of legitimacy and efficacy were central in the American withdrawal and in the ultimate demise of the South Vietnamese government.

Legitimacy worked in another direction in the Persian Gulf case. Here, American involvement was not as a lone outsider, for it had the general support of the world community and the official blessing of the United Nations. The means by which Iraq had taken over Kuwait was generally seen as illegitimate. Almost everyone except the Iraqi government deplored this action. Further, the response of the Allied forces was deliberately planned, with official approval from the U.S. Congress as well as the United Nations. This helped to provide wide participation and support for the military campaign that eventually drove Iraq from Kuwait. The fact that vast resources of oil were at stake also helped the nations involved to justify their involvement— at least to themselves.

In Conclusion. Among the examples viewed, it would appear that the application of force with the strongest combination of capability, credibility, relevance, and legitimacy was that of the Allied response to Iraq's conquest of Kuwait. Conversely, the American involvement in Vietnam was most problematic in all of these areas. Should it be surprising that American force more successfully controlled the outcome in the Persian Gulf War than in the case of Vietnam?[4]

Beyond Brute Force

Coercion Without Force?

So far we have looked primarily at examples of the use or threat of force in international conflicts. Does it also have a role in the internal affairs of societies and states?

Perhaps the role of force is not as dramatic in domestic as in international affairs. Also, coercion may be successfully applied without the direct use of, or threat of, physical force; for if by coercion we mean being controlled against one's own will, it often occurs in response to a higher authority or stronger power, and not only when physical force is at issue. This is true in international as well as domestic conflicts, though it is probably easier to see in matters within a society.

A citizen may not want to pay income taxes but has little choice. That an eventual prison term could result from the nonpayment of taxes may be in the back of the citizen's mind, but this is probably not an immediate consideration. It is just *understood* that one must file the form and pay the taxes.

A student may not wish to take a class required for her major, but she takes it. Of course, she could avoid it and change to another major, but that may not be practical. Thus, although physical force is in no way threatened, the student is successfully coerced to take the class.

A husband may not want to go with his wife to a dinner party. The wife may not be so eager to go herself, but she insists it is a necessary social obligation that they attend. So they go, including the husband (unless he can come up with a good excuse not to).

We can see these examples as instances of the exercise of coercion without physical force. There are also occasions when coercion is supported by a clear and present threat that physical force might be used to subdue the individual's resistance or to reduce his freedom. For some people, payment of taxes might fall in this category, as would avoiding many other violations of the criminal law.

Coercion and the State

The power of the state signifies perhaps the most obvious form of coercion in the modern world. The state is often defined as that organization which claims a monopoly of legitimate physical force within its territorial bounds. Never mind that other organizations may make use of physical force to assert their will; those who lead the state will rarely accept such other powers as legitimate, and will most likely have laws to discourage the use of physical force by those not exercising state power.

This state of affairs is generally accepted by the citizens of modern nations, though one may find here and there a principled anarchist who would like to do away with such state power. In fact, traditional Marxists held to such an elimination of the state as an ultimate goal. But for most of us, this is hardly seen as a viable alternative. We take for granted the coercive power of our states, and only hope that it will be exercised responsibly and responsively, with the welfare of most citizens in mind.

It is easy to forget that the state is a relatively recent invention of humanity. Until about 10,000 years ago there were no states. Only with what we call civilization did states appear and formal governments, exercising power beyond the traditions of family and tribe, begin to function. It is interesting to speculate on the processes that initiated the formation of states, and we have at least some empirical evidence on this subject. Be that as it may, states are now very much with us, and they regularly exercise coercive power over our lives.[5]

Criminal law provides the most obvious form that the coercive power of the state takes. Laws are passed, along with sanctions that may be applied if someone fails to live up to these standards. All violations need not be punished to maintain the coercive power of the laws, so long as the authorities energetically pursue the most dramatic violations and impose severe penalties on those found guilty of the most heinous crimes. There are, in most nations, important safeguards against arbitrary arrest and punishment; it is therefore inevitable that a lot of crimes go unpunished. Nevertheless, those that are punished must give pause to others who may be considering breaking the law.

Coercion in Everyday Life

Physical force and violence are present in the very small as well as the very large units of social organization. Families as well as nations show frequent use of physical force, or the threat of force, to exert influence when a conflict occurs. In both cases we generally deplore the use of force, but still we appear unable to conduct ourselves without its occasional use.

In most families, physical force sometimes occurs in a conflict. This is true not as often among adults (though, as we saw in Chapter 2, such cases occur with greater frequency than we would like to admit) as between adults and children or among children. Spankings are a common form of discipline for young children in even the best of families, and the threat of a spanking may have its intended effect of influencing behavior without such force being often used. Children fighting with each other is also common. Furthermore, fighting is not just the recourse of a schoolyard bully; many children will attempt to resolve even minor squabbles with one another through force.

Wherever people are in relationships that they cannot leave—or can only leave with great difficulty—there is a special vulnerability to the use of force. Nations cannot easily leave the international system (though China attempted this, with fair success, for a number of centuries); they are therefore vulnerable to the military influence of others. Likewise, it is usually difficult for persons to leave their own country, and this strengthens the coercive influence of the state. In families, young children cannot easily leave their parents, and a disruption of family ties is difficult (though not impossible) for adults as well. This durability of relationships gives us many of the things in life that we cherish most, but it also leaves us open to the threat of force being made or exercised.

In spite of the possibility of the resort to force, it is actually quite rare that issues of personal relationships are resolved in that way. Through the process of growing up with other people, we learn alternative ways to deal with others when a conflict occurs. We learn the techniques of avoidance and of verbal aggression for handling especially bothersome individuals, and only rarely (except in the exciting world of televised drama) do we resort to actual force.

But this does not protect us from coercion—from having to do things against our will. Coercion occurs in ways we hardly recognize; we simply accept it as a normal part of life. By being in an organization, we accept the dictates of that organization, even when they are not to our liking. For example, most jobs include tasks we don't really want to perform, but we do them, nevertheless. Is it too strong to say that this is a matter of coercion? We usually do not think of it in such terms, but any relationship of authority includes some potential coercion.

One social psychological experiment of well-deserved fame points very clearly to the potentially coercive effects of authority. In this study, Stanley Milgram introduced subjects to what was supposedly a study of learning, in which one would play the role of "teacher" and another of "learner." Subjects were apparently assigned at random to one of these two roles, though in reality the situation was rigged so that a confederate of the experimenter always became the "learner." Since this was described as a study of the role of punishment in learning, the teacher was induced to punish the learner for incorrect responses with what the "teacher" believed to be electrical shocks (though in reality no shocks were delivered). The teacher (the real subject) was then asked by the experimenter to increase the voltage of the shocks, despite the apparent agony of the victim.

The whole point of the experiment was to see how far people would go in carrying out such orders. That most people do obey up to the point of apparently near-lethal shocks is in itself shocking news to most readers of this study. But when we examine the details, we begin to understand why this is true. The experimenter is completely confident in the directions he gives, and he supposedly knows what it is all about. He has clear authority over the situation and is insistent that the teacher must proceed to higher levels on the shock machine. All of this enhances the experimenter's influence over subjects. The subject may not want to do so, but, despite personal misgivings, usually accedes to the experimenter's request.[6]

When we consider how much of our daily lives is constrained by authority of one kind or another, we begin to see the variety of forms in which we may be constrained against our will. This suggests that the coercive resolution of social conflict, through the dictates of another's or our own authority, remains an ever-present possibility.

Summary and Conclusions

Summary

In this chapter we examined the coercive resolution of social conflicts. This included the successful application of physical force, or of the threat of physical force. We saw, too, that coercion can occur without the use of force.

Anytime one faces influence that cannot be questioned (whether it is backed up by force or not), there is a vulnerability to coercion. As Max Weber taught us, there are different bases upon which social authority can be built, and any of them can offer the possibility of inducing us to do something contrary to our wishes. If we are authoritatively induced to end a conflict or hold back from pursuing it, we can then speak of resolution by coercion.

We opened this chapter with the example of coercive conflict resolution represented by the Falkland Islands Crisis. In this case, the British used physical force to end Argentina's temporary dominance of the islands in dispute. We also examined, more briefly, four international disputes involving the United States: the Vietnamese War, the Bay of Pigs invasion of 1961, the Cuban Missile Crisis of 1962, and the Persian Gulf War of 1990–91. In examining the conditions that determine when the use or threat of force may prove effective in conflict resolution, we mentioned especially four factors:

1. Capability, or whether sufficient force could be made available.
2. Credibility, or whether others believe that the force would in fact be used.
3. Relevance, or whether the force could affect the real interests and decision-making process of the other side.
4. Legitimacy, or whether those involved believe that one has a right to engage in force in this situation.

After examining the possibilities of forcible resolution, we considered how coercion might occur without any direct use of force. A critical institution here is that of the state, generally assumed to have coercive power over its citizens. The state exercises this coercive power with physical force on occasion, but most commonly without it. Criminal law gives us many examples of this coercive power of the state. We also examined the role that coercion can play in our more personal relationships, such as in families. Here, too, we found that force is sometimes used, but that coercion may occur even without the threat of force.

Conclusions

Among the conclusions suggested by our examination of coercion in conflict resolution, we might especially point to the following:

a. Force can sometimes resolve a conflict—or at least serve to dictate a temporary resolution.
b. However, force aimed at coercion does not always coerce. Often the resort to force just makes the conflict less manageable.
c. Authority can be used to dictate conflict resolution without physical force, but this depends on a prior legitimacy of such authority, such as through the accepted power of the state.

8

Negotiation and Bargaining

The General Motors Strike of 1970

Contract Renewal Time

The contracts of the United Auto Workers with America's major automobile manufacturers were up for renewal in 1970, and both the union and the companies had much at stake in these contract negotiations. Union members felt that they had not obtained their proper share from the gains made by the American automobile industry, and the companies felt that the workers—already better paid than in most comparable industries—should be satisfied with little more than a cost-of-living adjustment in their pay checks. Having established a three-year cycle for contract negotiations, with those of all three major manufacturers expiring at approximately the same time, the union felt it was in a position to exercise greater power than in the past. Restlessness among the rank-and-file workers increased the union's determination to push at this time for significant improvements. Furthermore, the companies had been showing generally good profits and could afford, the union believed, a more generous pattern of wage agreements. On their part, the companies felt that their financial positions, though temporarily favorable, had just about the right balance of labor costs and investment for future production. Although the competition from Japan's auto manufacturers was not yet a major concern for American companies, there had been a significant increase in sales by Europeans. The companies could not afford to be complacent about their financial resources.[1]

Thus was the ground prepared for a major showdown in 1970 between the UAW and America's major automobile companies. On only one point did both the union and the companies appear to agree: that they should be able to settle their differences without a strike. The new president of the UAW, Leonard Woodcock (elevated to that position earlier in the year after the untimely death of Walter Reuther), expressed his "sincere hope" to reach an agreement "without a work stoppage." The leaders of General Motors also expressed the desire to avoid a strike, as did those of Ford and Chrysler. Representing the prevailing view was the statement from Lynn Townsend, chairman of the Chrysler

Corporation: "It's my hope that the industry as a whole can negotiate contracts without a strike."[2]

Since General Motors was the largest of the "big three" automakers, they were a special target for the UAW. The union felt that what they could get from GM would set the basis for the contracts with the other two. Therefore, they gave special attention to the opening of contract talks with General Motors on July 15, 1970; and later they extended contracts with the other two companies in order to concentrate their pressures on GM.

The union initially put a lot of issues on the table beyond those of compensation. They wanted time clocks to be eliminated, overtime to be voluntary, a paid dental plan, an unbroken holiday between Christmas and New Year's, a paid day off when a child is born to a worker, and greater freedom to organize white-collar workers in GM plants. Furthermore, they asked that company books be opened to allow inspection of the costs for the environmental and safety improvements the manufacturers had, with considerable publicity, made. Of course, they also expected a substantial wage increase and the restoration of an unlimited cost-of-living clause in the contract. Although they would await a precise offer from the company on a wage increase, the union suggested that increases above 20 percent during the three years of the contract would be reasonable. They were also pushing for an early retirement option, allowing any workers to get full retirement benefits who had been on the job for 30 years or more. There were, in addition, other union requests that would add to company costs, such as funds for a union-controlled educational program and increases in the supplemental unemployment program.

The company did not immediately lay out a proposal. Instead, they sought understanding from the union of some of their problems regarding worker discipline, which they felt were seriously eroding productivity. Unauthorized work stoppages had been a troublesome problem for GM, and they felt that workers were encouraged by the union too freely to pursue petty grievances. The company also pointed to increased medical insurance costs and other special increases that past benefits packages had required. And they emphasized the dangers of inflation, which recent wage increases in a number of key industries appeared likely to exacerbate.

Finally, on September 1, two weeks before the date the union had identified as a deadline for an agreement, the company set forth its detailed proposals. On the all-important issue of wages, the offer was for an initial 7.5 percent increase—but with no changes in the cost-of-living contract clause. On most other issues the GM offer showed little response to the requests that had been made by the union.

Irving Bluestone, chief negotiator with General Motors for the UAW, said of the company's offer: "GM may feel that it has come up with a good offer, but it is essentially a hiccough." President Leonard Woodcock used even earthier language in a meeting with GM workers, calling the offer "crap." The union then presented a list of more focused economic demands, including wage and benefits increases totaling more than $2.50 per hour. The company expressed "shock" at the union's proposals, and Woodcock commented: "The script calls for them to pass from a state of surprise to a state of shock." Both sides began serious preparations for a possible strike.[3]

The Strike

On September 14, the strike began. Immediately, more than 340,000 GM workers went out on strike, and the number of striking workers increased beyond 500,000 before it ended. Both parties seemed to assume that the other must yield in a major way before the strike could be settled. Most people thought that this was likely to happen before very long, for General Motors had nearly all its production closed down while its chief competitors continued to turn out automobiles. The union had specifically avoided striking them, despite contracts expiring at the same time, in order to concentrate its efforts at GM. The union even allowed some General Motors plants that supplied parts to Ford and Chrysler to remain in operation, indirectly increasing the pressure on their main opponent.

The union had accumulated a considerable strike fund (estimated at about $120 million at the start of the strike), so initially the GM workers on strike suffered little economically. However, as the strike continued, this fund became lower and lower, and the likelihood of real hardship loomed for the future. But could the union compromise very far, given the strong promises they had made to the rank-and-file?

About a month after the beginning of the strike, the union moderated its public statements and gave more emphasis to negotiations of local issues. It hoped that getting down to greater detail here would encourage more progress at the national level. But this was not immediately apparent. The company, though willing to talk further about the issues, maintained the basic position it had outlined before the strike.

The UAW called a special convention on October 24, at which time they sought to keep the union behind the strike; now, however, they avoided inflammatory rhetoric. At this convention, Woodcock accused General Motors of foot dragging, and in a pointed comment of warning to members of his own union as well as to the GM leaders, he said:

> I would pray General Motors does not push this strike to the point where our strike fund is drained and we cannot pay any weekly benefits to the families of those on strike. . . . I hope the top management of this corporation is not so shielded from reality as not

to be aware that if they create the bitterness which would flow from such a situation, it will hang over and plague the General Motors Corporation for years and years to come.[4]

Thereafter, both sides began talking more seriously with one another in negotiating sessions and in informal away-from-the-table contacts. The company suggested that they identify a November 10 target for an agreement. While not accepting this formally, the union also expressed a desire for an early conclusion of the negotiations. The size of the primary negotiating groups was reduced in the interests of more efficient bargaining, and supplementary probing was carried on to try to deal with some of the more detailed issues. In expressing GM's desire to move to a speedy conclusion, the head of their negotiating team, Earl Bramblett, said: "General Motors is losing $90 million a day in sales. We want a settlement as quick as we can get it." However, neither side was changing its basic position, and both sides begin to express fears that the strike might last through the rest of the year—a result neither wanted.[5]

The Settlement

Before the strike started, James M. Roche, General Motors chairman, had had occasional contacts with Leonard Woodcock. The relationship between the two men was cordial. Roche had gone out of his way to cultivate positive relationships between them, saying, on one occasion, that Woodcock would be welcome to talk with him personally any time he wished. This was an invitation that Woodcock did not think it appropriate to follow up on during the early weeks of the strike, with all contacts going through the official negotiators. However, when negotiations seemed stalled in early November, his assistants were ready to encourage Woodcock to consider Roche's earlier invitation. When one of them chanced to meet Roche in the lobby of the General Motors building (where the main negotiations were taking place), they engaged in some small talk about the strike; then the union official casually asked if he would be willing to talk with Woodcock personally about the strike. Roche's reply was yes, of course, anytime Woodcock wished. Woodcock seized the opportunity later the same day. He made an appointment to see Roche early in the afternoon.

For this meeting, Roche had his chief negotiator, Earl Bramblett, with him, though Woodcock went alone. Roche and Woodcock talked casually for some minutes, then moved to the matter of the strike. Both expressed concern over the strike's length. Woodcock frankly told Roche that the union's strike fund would be exhausted by the end of the month. He also indicated that he was planning to have a meeting with the General Motors Council, the top union men in their GM division, on November 11, the day after the targeted end of current negotiations. The implication was that either by then there would be an acceptable agreement or else the strike would become much more bitter. As to ideas about a settlement, Woodcock expressed confidence that they should be able to come together on a wage compromise (he had himself been known to indicate that something around an increase of 50 cents per hour might be acceptable to the union). However, he identified further issues where he felt a change in the company's position would be needed to end the strike: movement on an early retirement plan, a return to an unlimited cost-of-living clause, and more money for the supplemental unemployment fund. Roche responded by outlining GM's problems with the strike and pointed to pressures from the federal government to avoid an inflationary settlement. As they ended the discussion, both Roche and Woodcock expressed the hope that the strike would not go on much longer.

This meeting between Roche and Woodcock did not immediately add any new proposals into the negotiations, but its timing and nature helped bring the negotiations to a head. On November 9, the company indicated that it was ready to present some revised proposals. Late that evening—after midnight, in fact—these proposals were laid out in detail. They included an increase of approximately 51 cents per hour in wages for main assembly line workers, plus practically everything else that Woodcock had indicated to Roche would be necessary to induce the workers to end the strike. Active bargaining proceeded on some of the details, but at about 5 a.m., the union representatives indicated they were ready to take the proposal to their General Motors Council. With a recommendation for approval? the GM representatives asked. "Yes," was Woodcock's reply.[6]

The union's full negotiation team had not been involved in the November 9–10 negotiations, so it was now Woodcock's task to seek their approval. When they met, there was clearly some opposition to the agreement; however, when they voted it came out eight to four in favor of the contract. There was then concern that those opposed would take a minority report to the council the following day, but they did not. It was simply reported to the council that the negotiating team recommended ratification. There were some tough questions from members of the council, but Woodcock was able to respond effectively to most of them. He then concluded:

> It is a victory. We took on the world's mightiest, most powerful manufacturing corporation. They said we wouldn't dare. And when we did they said we couldn't win. Well, they were wrong on both counts. We did win. We spent all our money. But we've got a better union. That is what it's all about.

This was greeted by applause and a standing ovation. The critical steps toward ratification had been successfully taken. The vote of the UAW members that followed was 307,533 to 11,540 in favor of the contract. Ratification was formally announced on November 20, and the strike of sixty-seven days was finally officially over.[7]

The UAW-GM strike of 1970 was one of the most important strikes in American history. Other strikes (including one between the same two parties in 1945-46) have been longer and more bitter. But for man-hours off the job and for costs in lost production, no other strike reached the level of the 1970 GM strike. Over 500,000 workers were involved for most of the strike's sixty-seven days, and the costs to General Motors in lost profits have been estimated as in excess of $1 billion. The strike's outcome also had an important impact on the rest of the American economy. The Nixon administration was at that time trying to encourage wage settlements that would not be inflationary, and it did not consider that the UAW-GM accord was in line with these standards. The President's Council of Economic Advisors said:

> It is clear that this settlement, if generalized through the economy, would crowd further upward costs per unit of output and therefore the price level.

But there was little that the federal government could do, and both General Motors and the UAW defended the agreement as responsible in terms of the general public—as well as effective in serving their own interests.[8]

Formal Negotiations and Bargaining

American Collective Bargaining

The United Auto Workers-General Motors contract negotiations of 1970 need to be seen in the context of American collective bargaining. Both American corporations and their unions, where active, wish to preserve their rights to independent action in labor-management affairs. They see this as properly occurring without governmental dictation of how contracts may be arrived at. In the United States, therefore, the government or representatives of the public are not regularly a part of negotiations. When federal mediators are called in, their role is typically only to try to help the parties themselves come to an agreement, not to impose terms. Only rarely does the government intervene to determine the outcome of a labor dispute. All these points applied to the 1970 case study we have just examined. However, in some other countries of the world there would have been less opportunity for the two sides to work out their own solution, regardless of the views of the government or general public.

Part of the independence of unions and companies in the United States stems from their possible recourse to the ultimate weapons they have available:

for management to close down production in a plant and/or lay off large numbers of workers, and for the union to call a strike. Even though these weapons are seldom used, their presence must be considered when representatives of labor and management engage in collective bargaining.

Those who have closely observed American labor-management negotiations have suggested that they tend to have a general pattern. They involve a process that is repeated in most cases of contract negotiations. This process can be characterized as having three main parts: (1) establishing positions, (2) probing for strengths and weaknesses in the positions of each other, and (3) reaching a conclusion.[9]

The opening rounds of collective bargaining are usually occupied with each side stating its case. Each will voice their concerns and outline the kind of agreement they hope to see. While each will listen politely to the other side, usually a big difference between the positions is soon apparent.

Then comes the phase of extended discussions. Each side has stated its case, but these need to be examined in some detail. Especially is each side on the lookout for weaknesses in the positions of the other. This includes searching for clues—sometimes given unintentionally in unguarded moments of the discussion and sometimes intentionally suggested—as to what are the higher and lower priorities in each other's positions.

After a while, there is no more information to be gained from further discussion. Then comes the time for reaching a conclusion. The discussions may be shortened, or drawn out further, to fit the timing of a targeted end of the negotiations. Sometimes this is imposed by the expiration of the contract or by the union's strike deadline. In any event, there is usually a mutual sense of when the bargaining must come to a head. The parties then craft the agreement, or else the parties accept an impasse, often including a strike.

This process has many elements of ritual in the way the parties engage in discussions. Usually both sides include experienced hands who know how the game is played, and so it follows a rough script based on past experience. Those sitting at the table may in fact come to enjoy the conflict they engage in, getting satisfaction from whatever points they make at the expense of each other. Bargaining to them may become a fine art at which they wish to display their talents. For the process to end prematurely would be a big disappointment for such persons. This is well illustrated by the manufacturer who wanted quick action on a contract with his union, so he said to them:

> I know that there's going to be a lot of haggling and I have a good
> idea where it's gonna end up, and I have an offer to make. And here
> it is. I wanta end this thing up. I'm gonna get—wrap it up and get
> outa here tonight. Ten cents an hour.

This was as much as the union had expected to get, but they could not bring themselves to an agreement without what they considered proper bargaining. They indicated that they would consider the executive's proposal as an initial offer. At this he walked out of the room. The result of such premature bargaining was, in this case, a strike.[10]

The underlying reason for lengthy collective bargaining is not so much to exchange information as to demonstrate power to one another. For this it is important to show endurance and a willingness, if no agreement is reached, to call, or take, a strike. Once the sense of relative power is determined through collective bargaining probing, an agreement usually falls into place. As one scholar of collective bargaining has expressed this point:

> "Exorbitant" demands, random actions, cajoling, argumentations, and the like, running through numerous meetings leading to a deadline with its concomitant threat of work stoppage, are all utilized to find out settlement positions. It ought to be obvious, but unfortunately it is not, that collective bargaining is a process of power, not a rational persuasion by the logical presentation of facts.[11]

Most of the general points we have made about collective bargaining may be seen in the UAW-GM negotiations of 1970. Early on was the identification of the basic positions of each side, although serious formal proposals were not made until about two weeks before the contract was to expire. Energetic bargaining ensued, but a conclusion was not soon forthcoming. Both sides then faced the reality of a strike. Only after the strike had continued for about two months, and each side had established the power of its position, was there again serious bargaining. It is likely that the company would have been willing to settle when the contract expired with terms similar to those finally worked out, but sensing that the union would have rejected such an agreement, they did not propose it then. They waited until the union had been weakened and its members were tiring of the continuing strike. Then a compromise settlement was possible that both could define as a victory. They both had to demonstrate their power before they could finally come together.

There are, of course, important variations in collective bargaining from industry to industry and from company to company. In some industries, especially those with a large number of companies facing a highly unionized work force (such as among coal miners and longshoremen), negotiations are apt to be especially bitter and volatile. In industries with a few large companies and a highly organized labor force (such as in the automobile industry) there is apt to be a more orderly approach to collective bargaining. There are also important differences in collective bargaining traditions from company to company. General Motors has come to be known as a hard, but not harsh, bargainer and has, over the years, forged a relatively good working relationship with the United Auto Workers. The historical relationship between General Electric and the International Union of Electrical Workers has been much more stormy, with GE trying hard to circumscribe collective bargaining to a minor role in determining company policies. There are also major corporations, such as IBM (at least as this company existed in the past), with no collective bargaining but with strong traditions of concern for the welfare of workers.

The case of IBM leads to the recognition that not all labor-management relations are negotiated in the form of collective bargaining agreements. In many cases, there is no recognized union to serve as a bargaining agent. This does not mean that no labor negotiations go on. They still occur, but they tend to be less centralized. Consider universities, for example. Most universities do not have labor organizations serving as official bargaining agents for their faculty, but there are other ways that negotiations take place. They occur individually, department by department, and they also occur through bodies of the entire faculty, such as committees of a faculty senate. Whether or not worker demands are as well represented through non-unionized processes is, of course, an open question—answerable ultimately by elections for union representation, organization by organization.

Basic Concepts

As we prepare to move beyond American collective bargaining in our discussion, it may be useful to pause to understand some of the key concepts often applied to negotiations.

Generally, we can use the terms *negotiation* (whether in singular or plural form) and *bargaining* as rough equivalents. Either can be seen as involving a discussion between parties aimed at reaching some mutual accord. The differences between these two concepts are primarily matters of connotation; 'negotiation' most commonly emphasizes the process of interaction that goes on between parties, while 'bargaining' usually emphasizes the underlying positions and the way moves are made to adjust them in the interests of reaching an agreement. Both concepts assume that the parties are voluntarily involved in a search for some kind of agreement that will facilitate the interests of each.

Negotiations typically start with stated positions on each side—whether stated formally or presented by implication. In the UAW-GM negotiations of 1970, neither side presented a detailed plan for an agreement at the start of negotiations, but both freely outlined the nature of what they were seeking. Often these initially stated positions are termed *initial offers,* especially when explicitly made.

Along with the positions the parties present to each other are also the positions they present to themselves. Each typically has in mind a framework of how far they are willing to compromise from the initial offer, if they have to, in order to reach an agreement. For this ultimate fallback position we use the term *reservation price.* Each side therefore has a framework within which they seek to focus negotiations; we speak of this with the term *subjective bargaining range.* This covers the distance between the party's initial offer and its reservation price; it represents where they would be willing to consider proposals without breaking off negotiations. By combining the subjective bargaining ranges of both parties (we assume in most of our discussion the presence of just two parties, though sometimes we may need to identify more participants), we can determine the *actual bargaining range.* The actual bargaining range consists of the common elements in the subjective bargaining ranges of both parties.

An example might be helpful to illustrate these concepts. A property owner wishes to sell a house, and she has a prospective buyer. The owner asks for $120,000 (her initial offer), but would be willing to come down as low as $100,000 (her reservation price) in order to make the sale. Meanwhile the prospective buyer says he would be willing to pay $90,000 (his initial offer), though secretly he would pay up to $15,000 more if he had to (making his reservation price $105,000). Her subjective bargaining range would be between $100,000 and $120,000, or a range of $20,000; while his would be a range of only $15,000—between $90,000 and $105,000. The actual bargaining range would be between $100,000 and $105,000 (given, in this case, by the reservation prices of each), a range of only $5,000. This is, of course, a highly simplified example, for most negotiations do not have such simple dollars-and-cents markers. For example, in the UAW-GM case, there were about four main issues, all involving monetary considerations, but none allowing the precision in quantitative assessment that we have used for our real estate example.

Bargaining tactics are any efforts made to move the other party toward one's own position, thus promoting an agreement on as favorable terms as possible for one's own interests. Negotiators may use a great variety of bargaining tactics in a given set of negotiations, including rational persuasion, misrepresentation of one's own interests, belittling the presentation of the other side, threats, promises, and/or modifying one's own position. Bargaining tactics tend to serve either (or both) of two main objectives: (1) trying to make sure that an agreement is reached, and (2) trying to make sure that the agreement serves one's own interests (rather than those of the other) as much as possible. Bargaining that emphasizes the first of these two purposes usually gets the term *integrative bargaining,* and it is generally cooperative. Bargaining emphasizing the second purpose is *distributive bargaining,* and it is essentially competitive. It is in the nature of most bargaining that both cooperative and competitive forces are involved throughout negotiations, though in different mixtures at different times. In the case of the UAW-GM negotiations, the emphasis was highly competitive as the labor contract was expiring, but it became more cooperative (integrative) during the second month of the strike.

Given the presence of competitive forces, negotiations often involve contests to establish the relative power of the parties. This is generally less effective when carried out by tactics of direct pressure or verbal abuse than by patient exploration of the situations each must face. Real power is given by what alternatives a party has if a speedy agreement is not reached. If one party has good alternatives, or can endure the conflict a long time without an agreement, it has a high degree of bargaining power, whether or not it chooses to use it. In the UAW-GM case, both sides were in good financial condition and had strong bargaining power at the start of the strike, but six weeks later both had become vulnerable. That the union moved more than the company from its initial position in reaching the final agreement should not be taken as too significant a measure of relative power, for this is quite common in American labor-management negotiations. Unions often present inflated initial positions in order to demonstrate to their members how much the union is trying to get for them, while companies usually have less of a need for presenting an initially exaggerated position.[12]

A critical question about bargaining power is that of where the parties would be without an agreement. The applicable concept here is that of the 'BATNA' of each—that is, the best alternative to a negotiated agreement. If an agreement is not reached, what else is available? If the alternatives are bleak for one of the parties, they have low bargaining power. Another term sometimes applied in the bargaining literature is that of the *conflict point:* the point where the parties would find themselves if there is no agreement. In the UAW-GM negotiations, the conflict point for the initial negotiations was a strike—an outcome that was made necessary by the absence of an agreement.

In trying to establish relative power for the distributive bargaining that occurs, it often happens that the parties will misrepresent their actual situations to imply that their alternatives are better than they really are. On the other hand, each party may try to appear to be not much impressed with the arguments of the other. Demonstrating one's patience and not compromising too soon is a means of demonstrating one's relative power. Being able to see the conflict point as something that can be taken in stride is often an important tactic for seeking concessions. In the UAW-GM case, both sides showed this by being willing to experience a strike—until the strike itself became too costly to be continued, and both parties felt forced to settle.

Negotiations, however, never involve purely conflicting interests. There are also common interests, which serve as the foundation for integrative bargaining. This may take the form of discussing issues that both sides have a stake in (such as improving quality or dealing with foreign competition, in the case of the automobile industry). When there is a long-standing relationship between sides, there is usually a recognition that sooner or later an agreement must be made, and that to delay it too much may injure the interests of both. Therefore, the UAW-GM negotiators did a rather interesting dance to signal to one another that it was time to come to an agreement—as the company indicated a target date for an agreement by November 10, and the union called for a meeting of their General Motors Council for November 11. Despite their quarrel, both sides knew they would have to come to an agreement, and they thus provided each other some final help to bring this to pass. As an example of the help that went with integrative bargaining in this case, we may note that when the UAW strike fund ran low, the company agreed to a temporary payment of $23 million per month in insurance costs (so the workers could keep their insurance current without depleting the strike fund), which would then be charged to the workers after the first of the year. Such a deal is not indicative of the relations between mortal enemies, nor is it common for those with only a temporary relationship in a market economy; it is more like married couples who have a spat but still continue to work together in economic and child-rearing matters. Earl Bramblett, the chief negotiator for GM, expressed this point in commenting after the agreement that both sides really won. As he put it, "A continuing relationship requires no loser."[13]

Negotiation and Coercion

We often think of negotiation and coercion as the two main ways of solving a dispute. Of the two, we prefer negotiation, for, as Winston Churchill once put it, "Jaw, jaw is better than war, war." Sometimes, however, we feel that force or coercion becomes necessary—usually, as we put it, as a 'last resort.' This framing of the choices available for conflict resolution leaves out some of the most promising ways to deal with conflicts, as subsequent chapters on adjudication, mediation, and arbitration will show. But the framing of negotiation and coercion as simple opposites also fails to recognize how much one may sometimes depend on the other. Negotiations may be an important part of a process of coercion, and the potential for coercion may be a factor assisting negotiation, as was most abundantly clear in the arms control agreements the United States and the Soviet Union formed in the closing years of the Cold War.

The primary cases we have used to represent coercion and negotiation have each had elements of both processes. The Falkland Islands controversy can also be seen as a case study of international negotiations, and the UAW-GM negotiations of 1970 clearly included coercive aspects.

By 1971, negotiations between Argentina and Great Britain over the Falklands/Malvinas question had been going on for several years. Although in some respects the issues were difficult to resolve through negotiations, both sides made a serious effort to do so. This resulted in the 1971 Communications Agreement between the two countries. David Scott represented the British and Juan Carlos Beltramino the Argentines. Without much publicity, they reached a limited agreement offering mutual cooperation among the British, the Argentines, and the Falkland Islanders. The British would build certain facilities on the islands (most notably an airstrip and shipping facilities), which would allow closer contact with the mainland. Meanwhile, the Argentines agreed to run an air service to the islands. The Falkland Islanders would achieve greater contact with the outside world through such measures and, it was assumed, become closer to Argentina in the process. Scott himself assumed that the Falklands would be flying the Argentine flag within a few decades, but the issue of sovereignty was not faced directly in these negotiations. Instead, there was a special 'white card' to be used when the islanders traveled to the mainland; this would allow the Argentines to consider the visit as internal and the British to consider it as international. Meanwhile, the islands would continue to be administered as a colony of the British Crown.

At first, all major parties seemed satisfied with the agreement reached. Even the islanders felt that it would serve their interests, since no loss of their British citizenship would be involved. Within a few years, however, this mutual understanding became unglued from all sides. The British delayed or abandoned some of the promised projects, claiming a lack of funds. The islanders began to feel more and more that they had been forgotten by the government in London. Meanwhile, a new government came to power in Argentina which was intent—for reasons of popular nationalism—on opening again the issue of sovereignty over the Falklands. Within a few years, the Falklands/Malvinas conflict was as bitter as ever.[14]

Despite our use of the UAW-GM conflict in 1970 as an example of negotiation, both sides used what can only be considered as coercive tactics. The union's deliberate attempt to focus its energies on General Motors, working without contracts for its main competitors to put maximum pressure on GM, was a major coercive tactic. For its part, GM delayed the detailed presentation of its proposals until there was little chance for extensive negotiations before the contract deadline, placing the union in a position of either yielding on most points or calling a strike. The strike itself was a weapon used by both sides to force each other to give up much of what they sought at the beginning, and this coercive strategy had some success for both sides.

We think of negotiation as involving parties freely meeting with one another in search of a mutually satisfactory agreement. That is often true enough; but the line between negotiation and coercion is sometimes blurred.

Negotiation Everywhere

Varieties of Negotiation

Negotiation occurs not only in formal bargaining sessions, but also in innumerable everyday situations we all face. Where will a couple be going for vacation next summer? By what hour must a teenage daughter be back home? How much of his vegetables must Junior eat before being allowed dessert? To what channel will the TV be tuned? So on and on are the questions of every-day life that involve bargaining and negotiation.

So far in this chapter we have discussed labor-management bargaining and international negotiations. There was also a brief illustration from real es-tate sales. These are all situations in which negotiation is readily seen to take place. Less obvious is the negotiation within an organization or on an inter-personal level. However, we should recognize that any time that persons must deal with each other despite differences in interests (perceived or real), there is the basis for negotiation. And that is just about everywhere.

In fact, the very basis of our social life together can be seen as bound up in a form of negotiation. What we consider to be reality is in large part the con-sensus reached after some sparring and debate with others—a consensus in which different interests may be expressed in various ways. To see our basic social arrangements as a 'negotiated order' is only extending slightly the ne-gotiation metaphor from the more formal settings in which we most easily rec-ognize negotiation phenomena. Of course, as we extend the idea of negotiation into all kinds of social exchanges, we must recognize that we usually do not have explicit bargaining or extended discussions about the substance of an agreement. The bargaining frequently happens so quickly and in such small pieces (as when we decide what purchases we wish to make in a supermarket) that the way the entire structure is a product of negotiation is often difficult to see.

Negotiation in the Laboratory

If we see negotiation as a general social process, we can try to abstract out its essential elements and study these under carefully controlled conditions. This is what laboratory studies of negotiation do.[15]

Some laboratory studies have looked especially at market conditions, and how bargaining may differ under different market conditions. For example, how does bargaining differ when parties have essentially similar market power, as compared with situations of unequal power? Or what are the effects upon negotiation of highly competitive markets, as compared with less competitive markets? Often using points earned as a substitute for money (though some-times using real money), behavioral scientists pursue such questions through experiments. Their results are not usually surprising, for they tend to confirm what economic theory would generally predict; for example, more bargaining activity is found under conditions of equal power than unequal power, and more negotiation occurs under the less competitive market conditions. Nevertheless, it is useful to establish with greater precision the economic principles gener-ally understood as applying to bargaining behavior.

But economic theory is sometimes silent on important points about bargaining. Consider our earlier real estate example. A seller asks $120,000 for a house, and a buyer offers $90,000. Since the seller is willing to come down to $100,000 and the buyer go up to $105,000, economic theory suggests that there should be a deal within this actual bargaining range of $5,000. Of course, we cannot be sure there will be a deal. Since each is pushing for their own interests, they may never realize that there is this overlap in their subjective bargaining ranges. In this case, there will be no deal, despite the fact that each would have their interests served by an agreement. Such misperception is not unusual in situations where each side is intent upon hard bargaining, that is, where distributive considerations overshadow the integrative interests that the parties have. But let us go beyond this issue and assume that the parties will come together on a sale. At what point will the sale take place? Somewhere in the range of $100,000 to $105,000—that is all that can be predicted by conventional economic analysis. Beyond this, the solution is, as they say, "indeterminant." All possible outcomes within that range can be justified as economic solutions. It is often said that where the parties actually end up will be determined by their 'relative bargaining power.' But what does this mean? How do we identify the factors that go into such relative power? Cannot we make some better prediction than that the result will be "somewhere" in the bargaining range?

We have just identified what is sometimes called "the bargaining problem." Of course, there are many other problems concerning bargaining, but this question is a persistent one: Where within the actual bargaining range is an agreement to be struck? Are there not patterns of bargaining that allow us to make a better prediction than that the outcome is indeterminant? Although traditional economic theory cannot give us an answer, some of the models that game theorists have devised can give us solutions. These answers are very hypothetical, for they assume certain logical conditions that may not always apply. Nevertheless, a formal solution for the bargaining problem identified by John Nash has received rather wide acceptance because of its logical elegance. We do not need here to go into detail as to just how the Nash solution overcomes the indeterminacy problem; we only point out that there have been formal, mathematical analyses of bargaining solutions that allow us to go beyond standard economic theory.

More generally, many experiments have been performed on factors that may or may not promote agreement in mixed-motive situations. Literally hundreds of experiments have explored one or another variable relevant to negotiated agreements under controlled laboratory conditions. It is very difficult to sum up this research in a few generalizations; nevertheless, there are some points that repeatedly show up in the research:

1. The more complete the communication between negotiating parties, the more likely are they to reach mutually satisfying agreements.
2. The more parties anticipate future interaction in similar negotiating situations, the more likely will they be to reach mutually satisfying agreements.
3. Negotiators often have levels of aspiration that define what they expect; these expectations are often more important in identifying where agreements will occur than is formal analysis of actual bargaining ranges.
4. Agreements are especially likely to be reached at points where there is a sense of equity, in that there is a reasonable balance in what both sides gain.
5. Agreements are often identified at points that naturally stand out within a bargaining range. For example, easily identified round numbers are more likely to be the focus of an agreement than are less common markers.

How to Negotiate

Practical as well as theoretical research has focused on the process of negotiation. One of the leading universities for this kind of work has been Harvard, and the Harvard Negotiation Project has become a leading source of inspiration for all kinds of negotiation. One rather ambitious example of how theory and practice can be combined may be seen in Howard Raiffa's *The Art and Science of Negotiation*. Here, formal models of negotiation are combined with rich case studies and numerous practical applications. A less theoretical, and much more popular, work coming out of Harvard has been a little book by Roger Fisher and William Ury entitled *Getting to Yes*. Here the authors give numerous practical hints on how to conduct successful negotiations.[16]

Fisher and Ury have several main points around which they organize their advice. These include the following (stated in slightly adapted form):

1. Separate the people you are dealing with from the problem that you have with them. Concentrate on the problem without denigrating the other party, and make your relationship with them as positive as circumstances will allow. Remember that they have important needs and values, just as you do.
2. Focus primarily on interests, not positions. When the other party presents a bargaining position, seek to uncover what interests are behind it. Then try to focus the discussion on how these interests of the other party, as well as yours, can be best met.
3. Before coming to an agreement, make sure all main options have been considered—both for you and for the other party. Invent options that may not be obvious but which add to the understanding of the range of possibili-

ties. Discuss the special values of those options that might allow gains for both parties.

4. Strive for a sense of fairness by seeking general principles and objective criteria that can serve as a framework for your agreement. With principles recognized as fair to both sides, no one needs to lose. Both sides can feel that a fair agreement has been the result.

Thus, instead of "positional bargaining," Fisher and Ury advocate what they call "principled negotiation." Instead of trying to wear down an opponent's position, we should try to focus the issues on their merits, then search for the principles that will allow both sides to come away with a sense of mutual gain.

Getting to Yes has had widespread, and well-deserved, circulation among conflict resolution professionals. It is clearly written and is filled with helpful pointers for would-be negotiators for all sorts of occasions. However, there are some possible reservations and criticisms about this approach to negotiation. Fisher and Ury's strong argument against positional bargaining, for one thing, is apt to be impractical in formal negotiations, which traditionally use the comparison of positions as a way of defining the central issues. True, even here much may be gained by trying to go behind the positions to the underlying interests the parties have; but it is unlikely that positional bargaining can be eliminated easily. This is especially the case in labor-management negotiations, where certain rituals of negotiation are well established by past practices; each side has come to depend on them and wants to appear engaged in hard bargaining to satisfy its supporters. Not to allow such negotiators to present and defend their positions would rob the negotiations of much of their dramatic style and psychologically invigorating opportunities for verbal combat.

Another problem with Fisher and Ury's advice is that it may not always be as easy as they suggest to find central principles and objective criteria to use as the framework for an agreement. It is likely that two sides in negotiations will view the proposed principles differently, leading to an argument over whose principles are to be favored as "most fair." Also, the search for what they call "objective criteria" may be sometimes out of reach. True, it is always worth trying to see if there cannot be some basis besides power for determining (and above all, for justifying) a solution to the problem under consideration. But it is not often easy to agree on just *which* "objective" criteria are the most compelling.

Multilateral Negotiations

Most of our discussion in this chapter has assumed that negotiation is between two parties. This is, of course, a simplification. Most negotiations involve more than two persons, and negotiations between organizations typically involve further negotiations within each organization. For example, in the UAW-GM contract negotiations of 1970, rather critical negotiations were involved on the union side before the proposed contract was submitted to a vote of the rank and file. A strong minority within the bargaining committee dissented; though they agreed to keep their dissent private, once the vote had been taken. This was a major factor in the ease of final ratification. While we do not know what dissension there may have been on the company side, it is fair to assume there was some division within General Motors management over what kind of deal should be considered acceptable.

As the number of parties involved in negotiations increases beyond two, some kind of coalition formation is almost inevitable. As Georg Simmel pointed out long ago, even a three-person group tends to break down into a coalition of two against one. In larger groups, the tendency to form into coalitions is usually even more apparent. Negotiations then proceed both between leading coalitions and within each coalition. The political processes of a modern democracy are mainly expressed through various coalitions among the electorate, with leading politicians serving as power brokers to negotiate between the main coalitions.

Democracy and Negotiation

Our reference to democratic systems of government leads to the mention of one rather important feature of the modern world. Political systems based on negotiation are increasing at the expense of those based on coercion. The difference is not a night-and-day contrast, for even the most authoritarian political regimes have involved negotiations among leading groups, and democratic systems still operate with an ultimate claim to coercive power. Nevertheless, there has been an important shift in emphasis as market systems (based mainly on implicit negotiation) have replaced more traditional and authoritarian economic systems, and as the idea of consent of the governed has replaced traditional authority in giving legitimacy to political systems. Once we allow mechanisms for widespread citizen participation in selecting and influencing governments, we open the door widely to negotiation between all kinds of groups and their representatives. These form into pressure groups and political parties, and their leaders (including those officially elected and others who work more behind the scenes) negotiate with one another over major issues of public policy. As a result, we have the phenomena of modern democratic politics—directly expressed in the complex forms of multilateral negotiation that have accompanied the growth of the idea of 'consent of the governed.'

Summary and Conclusions

Summary

In this chapter we examined how processes of negotiation operate to resolve social conflicts. Negotiation can occur whenever there is a combination of conflict of interest and interests in common between parties. The purpose of negotiation is to control the interest conflicts in order to form a more effective working relationship between parties. This working relationship is sometimes embodied in formal agreements, though often the informal products of negotiation are as important as an explicit written agreement.

We used the 1970 contract negotiations between General Motors and the United Auto Workers as an initial example. Before a contract agreement was reached in this case, there was a strike lasting more than two months and involving more than 500,000 workers, certainly one of the largest strikes in American labor history. But more important for us than the economic impact of these negotiations was their embodiment of a common theme in negotiation: Two parties having significantly opposed interests still, sooner or later, must work out their differences in the interests of the more important needs they have in common.

In our more general discussion of negotiation in American collective bargaining, we saw that a common pattern is a series of three subprocesses: (1) establishing the positions of each party, (2) probing for strengths and weaknesses in these positions, and (3) reaching a conclusion. Critical questions often involve those of relative power, which must be recognized in some way through the negotiation process.

A number of key concepts help us understand basic negotiation processes. These include initial offers, reservations prices, subjective bargaining ranges, actual bargaining ranges, distributive and integrative bargaining tactics, the importance of each party's BATNA (the best alternative to a negotiated agreement), and the conflict point.

When we talk about negotiation we have primarily in mind voluntary discussions between parties aimed at producing a mutually satisfactory agreement. Although this is basically in contrast to conflict resolution by coercion, there are ways negotiation and coercion are sometimes combined.

Negotiation occurs in innumerable varieties. Those forms discussed in the early part of the chapter (emphasizing labor-management relations) are only a small part of the total range of negotiation phenomena. We noted that negotiation occurs at all levels, from the interpersonal to the international, and in ways that develop both explicit and implicit agreements.

In studying common features of negotiation, we briefly reviewed findings from some of the experimental literature. We also noted some general lines of advice that may be suggested to make almost all kinds of negotiation more effective. Finally, we recognized that negotiation frequently involves more than two parties, and we noted the close relationship between the rise of democratic institutions and the increased importance of complex forms of negotiation for political problem solving.

Conclusions

A number of conclusions were suggested throughout our discussion. Among them, the following apply quite broadly to the process of negotiation.

a. Negotiation is the most common method applied for the resolution of conflicts. The most formal kinds of negotiation may require specialists and special settings; however, everybody negotiates something every day.

b. Negotiation has become increasingly important in the modern world. Trends toward increased individualism, reliance on markets for economic decisions, and democratic political institutions all tend to expand the voluntary discretions available for most people, and therefore the opportunities for negotiation.

c. Negotiations most likely to be effective are those in which the parties focus on mutual problem solving, rather than who may be winning or losing.

9

Adjudication

Costs of Negligence

The Suit

At 6:13 P.M. on November 22, 1950, a commuter passenger train left the New York City station. It had only begun its journey when suddenly it was hit with full force from behind by another passenger train of the same line. In one of the greatest railroad disasters of American history, seventy-five persons were killed, mostly in the last car of the train rammed by the engine of the other train. The cause of the failure of the second train to stop was never fully identified, partly because its engineer was among those persons instantly killed.[1]

One of the persons killed in this accident of the Long Island Railroad was John Donelon, age thirty. He was on his way home to Merrick, where his wife, Muriel, and their four-year-old son were planning to meet him. He was employed by the William H. Weintraub Agency, an advertising firm, where he had been working for less than two months. His current salary there was $100 per week, a figure that seemed, for that time, neither remarkably large nor small for a person in his position. However, his earning power became a more critical issue after his death than while he lived, for his wife brought suit against the Long Island Railroad Company to seek compensation for their negligence. About two years later the case of Mrs. Donelon against the railroad came to a court trial. We will follow the events of this trial as a special example of the process of adjudication.

Mrs. Donelon was represented by Louis Nizer, a well-known trial lawyer. The Long Island Railroad Company was represented by Walter Doyle, an attorney with experience in railroad cases. The Judge was Francis G. Hooley. There was also a jury which would be expected to weigh the claims in determining an appropriate figure for compensation. Negligence was not at issue; given the circumstances, the railroad company conceded responsibility for the accident. The question then became simplified to how much Mrs. Donelon should be paid for this disruption in the life of her family.

Testimony Begins

The first to take the stand during the trial was Mrs. Donelon herself. Her attorney asked many detailed questions about her husband, designed to give the jury a favorable image of him and a positive view of what his future should have been. It thus clearly emerged that he was a man who was strongly devoted to both his work and his family; also, he was a public-spirited and well-informed citizen. Such items as the way he loved to sing with his son, how he planted azalea bushes around their house, and his daily reading of *Time, Newsweek* and *U.S. News and World Report,* as well as the *New York Times*—all helped to make concrete the positive nature of this man whose life had been suddenly ended. The defense attorney objected to any questions that seemed to reflect on John Donelon's financial prospects, but he did not protest against other personal details becoming part of the record. In his chance at cross examination, Doyle, the attorney for the railroad, tried to confirm the basic facts of Donelon's employment and that he had been unemployed in the past. It was thus established that his 1950 gross earnings were $3,825.84 up to the time of the accident, and that his earnings for 1949 were $4,219.07. It was also made clear that he had been in his new job only five weeks, and that there were apparently no written records of a positive evaluation from his previous employer.

Nizer, as Mrs. Donelon's attorney, then called a series of witnesses to testify to the quality of Donelon's work. The president of the National Export Agency (a previous employer) and two officials of the Weintraub Agency (his last employer) all presented concrete details about the outstanding work Donelon had done for them. The defense attorney sought to make clear that these currently stated evaluations were not backed by written records made when Donelon was actually working. Over Mr. Doyle's objection, however, Nizer convinced the judge to allow a brief informal note written by a vice president of the Weintraub Agency to get into the record:

> This is just to let you know that your boy, Jack Donelon, is doing
> a real fine job. Thanks for bringing him in. He is just the remedy
> we needed for this export headache and, unless I miss my guess,
> he is going to be a pretty important guy around here before too long.

Judge Hooley allowed this to become part of the evidence only when it became clear that its writer would later appear on the stand and could be cross-examined about the statement.[2]

Two clergymen, including the pastor at the church where the Donelons worshipped, were next called to the stand by Mr. Nizer. They testified to the religious devotion and good works shown by Mr. Donelon. The defense found little here to object to or to refute during cross examination.

Further Evidence

Next Mr. Nizer called an insurance actuary named Richard Fondiller to the stand. Although Fondiller had outstanding qualifications and was able to get some of this knowledge about life expectancies into the record, Nizer was unsuccessful in his main objective. This was to show that the life tables then under general use by the courts were badly out of date and would therefore underestimate the number of years that might reasonably be assigned to the life expectancies of either John or Muriel Donelon. When the defense objected to this line of questioning, the judge sustained the objection. In defense of the tables currently in use, Judge Hooley said, in part,

> The American Experience Tables of Mortality came about by Act of the legislature. I have never in my years of practice and seventeen years here on the bench used any tables other than the tables that I find at the end of the Civil Practice Manual.

When Nizer persisted briefly on this point, the judge replied, "I may be wrong, but I am going to follow what I regard as a safe course. I am not going to pioneer this."[3]

Then was developed by Nizer another rather unusual line of evidence aimed at giving scientific documentation of the deceased's aptitude for future advancement in his line of work. Rules of evidence prevented a simple presentation of information available about his aptitudes, for all evidence had to be properly qualified. Nizer had laid the foundations for his new evidence by getting Mrs. Donelon to acknowledge that several cardboard boxes of miscellaneous papers had been discovered among her husband's things, and the contents of one of these was presented as a part of the material for the case. Later, Donelon's neighbor, Myron Berrick, who was a psychology student, identified the contents of one of those boxes as test results from psychological testing he had given Mr. Donelon as part of his own training in psychology at New York University. But here came a challenge from the defense. Since Mr. Berrick was only a student at the time he had administered the tests and still had not completed his doctoral training, he was not qualified to interpret the meaning of the test results. Besides, the original tests were no longer available—all they had was Berrick's assertions that those papers represented results that could only have been those of the testing he had administered. There was no handwriting of Donelon's on the papers, and the testing service from which the tests had been obtained no longer had the originals. At any rate, Mr. Berrick was not professionally qualified to make any interpretation of these results. What was left were only some pieces of paper that one witness had claimed to be results of psychological testing.

To interpret the meaning of these test results, Nizer called on William D. Glenn, a leading psychologist in the area of psychological measurement. Glenn had been Berrick's professor at the time that the tests had been allegedly administered to Donelon. Although the defense objected to Glenn's analysis of materials he had never seen before, the judge allowed this questioning to continue until its relevance could be shown. Dr. Glenn was therefore allowed to give his interpretation of the test scores recorded in the cardboard box found among Mr. Donelon's things. They turned out to be highly unusual test results. Among other things, they showed the following percentile scores of Mr. Donelon:

- 99 on a test of general intelligence
- 96 on a retail selling aptitude test
- 94 in accuracy of arithmetic calculations
- 99 in interest in personal and social affairs
- 97 in ability to form close personal relationships
- 95 in ability to take part in social groups
- 90 in a test for mental health

It is understood that for a score of 99, less than 1 percent of the comparable population would score higher, and for 90 it would be less than 10 percent. Therefore, these scores were all extremely high, though there were some others in which Mr. Donelon's results were not above the average range (such as in mechanical interest, finger dexterity, and personal self-confidence). From this evidence, Professor Glenn inferred a most favorable estimate of Donelon's business potential. He said, in part:

> In the area of intelligence he is an extraordinarily capable individual, capable of considerable growth, tremendous growth in the area of practical judgment and aptitudes, all of those areas are high, extremely high. His interests were integrated at a mature level and related to his abilities. . . . My evaluation of his capacity for growth, for success, based on these findings, is that it is extremely high.

Dr. Glenn was about to indicate that if Donelon were being considered for a job, he would give him a very favorable recommendation; but that testimony was not allowed since Dr. Glenn had no personal knowledge of Donelon's actual work activities.[4]

Before the exploration of evidence regarding Donelon's unusual test scores could be completed, the defense suffered another unexpected turn in the case. Judge Hooley suddenly announced a reversal of his previous ruling on the admissibility of testimony challenging the life expectancy tables generally used by courts. He had done legal research since that earlier ruling that convinced him these life tables had not in fact been kept up to date. He was therefore ready to consider evidence in favor of an alternative set of calculations. Clearly, this had the prospect of extending the period of time to which the railroad company's liability might apply.

The reader should recall that Donelon's death was only one among seventy-five in that horrible accident of the Long Island Railroad. The company had many other suits still pending, and this judge's new ruling threatened to increase significantly the railroad's liability in all these cases. True, they could appeal such a ruling about life tables, but suppose they lost in the appeal? Then liability for all the other cases would have to be reconsidered, as would cases already settled according to the old life expectancy tables. In short, the company faced a chaotic situation in which they would have great difficulty in limiting their liability in the manner they had counted on.

Settlement

This prospective change in life tables, in addition to the surprising evidence about Donelon's unusual test scores, led the railroad suddenly to pursue an out-of-court settlement with great energy. Before the trial started, they had offered Mrs. Donelon a settlement of $25,000; acting with Mr. Nizer's advice, she had refused this offer and chose a court trial when the company failed to increase the offer. Now with the trial well along, the railroad was ready to increase their offer substantially. They proposed a figure of $80,000, then increased it to $90,000. Nizer advised Mrs. Donelon not to accept this. The next day Mr. Doyle sought to get the parties together in special conferences with the judge. After Judge Hooley determined that the railroad might be prepared to offer $112,500, he encouraged agreement from Nizer and his client. Nizer still believed that a jury would give Mrs. Donelon more than this offer; but she could not count on getting the money soon, given the opportunity for an appeal. The judge spoke frankly to her in acknowledging that some of his rulings might not be supported by a higher court. In the light of this, Mrs. Donelon was advised by Nizer to accept the proposed settlement, which she did. When the court resumed a short time later, Judge Hooley told the jury:

> Members of the jury, the Court is pleased to say to you that the parties have amicably settled their differences. The Court encourages these settlements. No high pressure is used on either side. Parties make their own bargain. You must not feel that your time is wasted because you did not have a chance to pass upon it. . . . You have done your share in bringing it about. The case goes out of the Court forever; there are no appeals, no re-trials. Thank you very much.[5]

The American Judicial Process

Criminal Law and Civil Law

In this section we will try to summarize the judicial process as it operates in the United States.

In the United States, as in most countries of the world, there is a clear distinction made between criminal law and civil law. Criminal law defines crimes and provides for their punishment by agents of the government. Civil law deals with disputes between private parties and identifies the way such disputes may be adjudicated. 'The state' is always the party initiating the action in a court case under criminal law, and the purpose of the hearing is to determine guilt or innocence and to apply an appropriate punishment, if guilt is established. In a civil case, the court simply weighs the merits of the claims of both sides and makes a judgment as to a proper conclusion.

There are a number of detailed differences in procedures between these two kinds of court cases, and these vary from state to state. However, it is generally more common that a jury will help form a judgment in severe criminal cases (especially by making a judgment as to the facts of guilt or innocence) than in civil cases. Also, the standards of evidence tend to be different for the two kinds of cases. For criminal cases, guilt must be established 'beyond a reasonable doubt'; while civil cases are typically guided by a weaker standard of 'the preponderance of the evidence.'

Although the power of the state is used in declaring the outcome of both criminal and civil cases, this power is more direct in the case of criminal law. Separate arms of government provide prosecution and judgment, but both are agents in carrying out the will of the state as set forth in the law. Because this is intended to control quite directly the behavior of citizens, there is a strongly coercive element here. In the case of civil law, the state is involved only when properly petitioned by one of the parties. It therefore serves primarily as a neutral agent in upholding the law as it applies to the settlement of private disputes. Because we have already dealt with the coercive powers of the state in a previous chapter, we limit our discussion in this chapter mainly to the judicial process within the civil law framework.[6]

General Procedures in Civil Suits

A civil case starts when one party files a petition against another party. The party initiating the action is the plaintiff, and the other party, from which the court will demand a response, is called the defendant. If the judge in whose court the case is initiated believes the claims of the plaintiff are without merit, he or she may simply dismiss the case without any hearing. If a hearing is to be held, each side usually engages in pretrial 'discovery' to help establish the basic facts. This may include 'interrogatories' which the opposing party is required to answer. Both sides must also usually provide sworn testimony before the trial; such 'depositions' are given in the presence of attorneys for both parties.

It is necessary (except in some relatively minor cases) for each party to have an attorney, and the attorney guides the case through the judicial process. The attorney acts to serve the interests of his or her party. If the case comes to a court trial, the attorneys are responsible for getting the relevant evidence before the court. The judge presides in order to see that only relevant evidence is presented, and that it is presented in a proper manner.

In a court case, the attorney for the plaintiff presents evidence first. This includes the calling and questioning of witnesses (each of whom may also undergo a cross-examination by the attorney for the defendant), and the introduction into the trial of relevant documents or other exhibits. After the plaintiff's attorney has completed presenting evidence, it is then the turn for the defendant's attorney to call witnesses and submit other evidence (with the plaintiff's attorney given a chance to cross-examine any witnesses presented). All witnesses must give their testimony under oath. The judge serves to keep the case moving according to correct procedures, but he or she normally does little to establish the evidence beyond ruling on the objections made by one of the attorneys about the evidence presented by the other. After both sides have presented their respective cases, each gives a 'summation' of its position. Then the court, with or without the assistance of a jury, makes its decision.

Where a jury is involved, it helps weigh the evidence, as guided and directed by the judge. In some cases this may take the form of recommending the extent of payments to recompense a plaintiff. However, the jury does not interpret the law; that is always the responsibility of the judge.

Once a decision is announced, the losing party may decide to appeal to a higher court. This can normally be done only if there is a claim made that the judge allowed inappropriate procedures to be used or made an incorrect ruling about the law. If the case is heard by an appeals court, the full case is not tried again; the evidence initially given, if properly presented, still stands. But the decision may be reversed if the appeals court determines that the judge made serious errors in the procedures allowed or in the interpretation of the law. Appeals courts are usually reticent to change the decision of a lower court, so this happens rarely. However, a court judgment may be effectively delayed while an appeal takes place.

Many of these procedures are illustrated by the case study with which we started this chapter. The plaintiff in this case was Muriel Donelon, and the Long Island Railroad Company was the defendant. Most of the action in the case was controlled by the respective attorneys, Mr. Nizer for the plaintiff and Mr. Doyle for the defendant. The judge made important rulings, and a jury was present to help weigh the evidence for damages. That the case was settled before the trial had run its full course is also a fairly typical pattern for civil cases; in fact, most are settled out of court before a trial begins. That this was not the case here was largely due to the confidence of Mr. Nizer that he could get a much better settlement from a jury in court than would be possible in a pretrial agreement.

The Long Island Railroad case shows how carefully a judge must rule on what evidence is admissible. Judge Hooley repeatedly was asked to rule on objections by the defense against certain evidence being presented. He realized that the evidence of psychological tests was unusual, and he was very careful to see that it was properly qualified. (For example, Mr. Berrick, who administered the tests, was not allowed to give any interpretation of them; and Professor Glenn was permitted to interpret them only over the objections of the defense.) Continually, there was great sensitivity as to what evidence could be considered relevant.

Relevant evidence according to court procedures may be very different from what most lay persons would consider relevant. In most states, for example, attorneys must avoid any mention of the presence or form of insurance in cases such as the Donelon case. Presumably, a jury should not take that into account when they are weighing a case on its merits. Also, any outside-of-court negotiations between the parties are not to be mentioned in court. Such information might influence a jury, so it is kept secret. A practical consideration here is that courts would like to see more outside settlements, thus reducing the court loads; this would not be facilitated unless both parties were forced to avoid any mention of their negotiations in court. So it was that very suddenly in the Donelon case the jury was informed that the parties had reached an agreement, and that the case was therefore no longer before the court.

Key Points

To understand how adjudication is carried out in the United States, there are some general features it is helpful to note. These include at least seven key points:

1.   The law is made by judges.
2.   The law seeks perfectly consistent rationality.
3.   The framework for considering cases is adversarial.
4.   Court procedures are highly formal.
5.   Lawyers are essential.
6.   Courts have a highly selective view of truth.
7.   Few cases ever go to a court trial.

Let us consider each of these points in turn.

1. The Law Is Made By Judges. There is often the misleading impression created (encouraged by elementary and high school texts in American government) that legislatures make laws and judges only help interpret and enforce them. To believe this, however, misses one of the most important facts about justice in the United States, namely, that the law is created by judges.

The United States follows Great Britain in adhering to a common law tradition. This means that law is not only what is contained in statutes, but what grows out of common sense and reasonable judgment. This idea has its roots in the Western traditions of natural law, based in part on ancient philosophies and more directly on medieval notions of how God's will (or, in postmedieval times, Nature's basic principles) should exert a controlling influence in the way courts exercise their powers of judgment. In effect, this leaves up to judges to determine what the law really is, case by case. They may be guided by laws passed by legislatures, but such laws only have meaning as they are interpreted by judges.

A special feature of the powers of judges in the United States is provided by the institution of judicial review. Even when a legislature passes a law that has clear dictates, it is up to the courts to decide if it is a valid law. Judges use the Constitution as a test. The question then becomes: Is the new law consistent with the Constitution—including the way the Constitution has come to be interpreted by the United States Supreme Court? If it is not, the courts may simply declare a law to be null and void. This power of judicial review is not itself explicitly given in the U.S. Constitution. However, it has been an established part of the American system of government ever since 1803, when the Supreme Court first claimed this power in the case of *Marbury* v. *Madison.* The newly appointed Chief Justice, John Marshall, then carefully asserted this power in a case that there was practically no way to challenge (partly because his ruling supported the power of his political opponents and partly because the Act of Congress which he overruled was itself controversial). This power, once assumed by the Supreme Court, gave to judges throughout the court system the opportunity to make judgments about the constitutionality of a wide variety of legislative enactments. It helped to confirm the central role of judges in the making of law.

2. The Law Seeks Perfectly Consistent Rationality. Few institutions are as fully rationalistic in their approach as are the courts. Judges are allowed to make and interpret law largely because it is expected that they will do so in a thoroughly rational manner and that they will follow clearly consistent patterns of interpretation.

In any court case, precedent clearly controls the way the judge applies the law. He or she rules not only in the way considered most fair, but also—and even more so—on the basis of consistent principles of law. These principles have been established in previous cases, and the judge now must apply them to the current case.

If a losing party believes a judge did not follow the correct procedures or principles of law in a court case, the judgment may be appealed. The appeal is almost never on the basis of evidence presented in the first trial (unless there is a claim that the judge inappropriately ruled on what evidence may be allowed); rather, the appeal must be on the basis of an inappropriate interpretation of law. In other words, the appeal is only successful when the first judge made a serious mistake. Because judges hate to be reversed on appeal (and appeals courts hate to have to reverse a decision), judges are exceedingly diligent in trying to interpret the law the same way that courts of appeals would do. This means that a good judge must be a scholar of the law, studying what rulings have been made elsewhere—in other places as well as in the present jurisdiction—in order to apply the law in a proper manner. All this leads to the assumption that there is a single framework of law, which is to be applied with perfectly consistent rationality to any case that comes before a court.

3. The Framework for Considering Cases Is Adversarial. Court cases are always presented in terms of one party versus another. The plaintiff makes a complaint, and the defendant must seek to counter the claims of the plaintiff (sometimes by initiating a counter suit). In any event, both parties are in a contest against one another in the way the court (as a supposedly neutral umpire) considers the case.

Historically, modern court systems emerged as substitutes for trial by combat. In medieval times, disputes were often settled privately, with the decision going to the party with the greatest influence or physical strength. As a romantic refinement during the age of chivalry, a noble knight might take the case of another person (sometimes an ordinary person, more commonly a lady of unusual beauty, and still more commonly a more powerful noble to whom he had sworn allegiance), settling the dispute with another party in a joust between champions. In modern courts, it is typically the attorney who assumes the role of champion, going forth to do battle in court.

In order for the judge to be able to assume a role of impartiality, it is considered important for each side to be able to present its case in competition with one another. Out of this conflict, with the law as interpreted by the judge providing the final arbiter, justice is expected to emerge.

4. Court Procedures Are Highly Formal. In order to uphold both their neutrality and claims for rational consistency, courts must adopt highly formal procedures. Each side must understand certain formal ground rules for the way a case is tried. The procedures follow a clearly set pattern, and evidence must be presented according to this pattern. The judge must frequently rule on matters of proper evidence and procedure, preserving the integrity (and, in a sense, sanctity) of the court. It is these formal procedures, along with the Latin jargon surrounding them, that helps to make the court a place of mystery—and with a logic all its own.

5. Lawyers Are Essential. The formal nature of courts necessitates having a lawyer if a party is to proceed according to all the proper rules. Only an attorney can normally know the special rules and procedures of a court well enough to get a case heard. Indeed, only an attorney can effectively advise a party as to the most appropriate court for a case, to say nothing of the proper form to follow in submitting the case, or in pleading a defense to the case brought by another party. Attorneys must 'represent' the client if his or her case is to receive careful consideration in a trial. They serve somewhat as the knights in the days of old, going forth to do battle on behalf of a client. So important are they in the American system of justice that more attorneys are currently practicing their profession in the United States than in all the other countries of the world combined.

6. Courts Have a Highly Selective View of the Truth. Although we may like to believe that the truth is something that will naturally emerge through a full and fair investigation, this is not always what people find when they go to court. Rather, the way evidence must be presented is so limited by formal rules that much of what most people consider relevant can never be considered by a court. Furthermore, the standards of justice applied in a decision by a judge frequently represent technicalities that few outside the legal profession can understand. When juries are involved, what is accepted as true (by the 'preponderance of the evidence' in a civil case—as contrasted with the higher standard of 'beyond a reasonable doubt' for a criminal conviction) is even less predictable than when a judge alone tries the case. This is one of the reasons that most litigants in civil cases do not seek a jury trial even when they have a right to demand one.

7. Few Cases Ever Go to a Court Trial. The proportion of the civil cases filed with a court that go through a full trial is usually reported as being less than 10 percent. Some general estimates run at less than 5 percent, and the proportion is no doubt even lower in some jurisdictions.[7]

Why is a full hearing of a case so rare? Part of the answer lies in the cost of pursuing a case through a full trial. Fees for attorneys gradually mount as the pretrial discovery process goes on, making many litigants impatient to get the case settled. Moreover, court dockets are often crowded, requiring a long time, sometimes several years, before parties can get a trial scheduled. Judges generally encourage out-of-court settlements (sometimes even taking a leading role in trying to bring the parties together); their own work (and that of others involved with the court) is greatly reduced if a settlement occurs before a trial.

Even though most cases never go to a court trial, those that do serve to set the framework for the cases settled out of court. It is through the judgments made in court cases that attorneys gather information about how other cases might be decided if taken to trial. This information then helps their clients to identify what they might reasonably anticipate in a settlement.

Also, note that some cases are intended more to establish a principle than to get settled. These cases force courts to take positions in matters that may previously have been ambiguous. If a suit is of this nature, there is no good reason for an out-of-court settlement; indeed, the motivation is strong to pursue an appeal if the initial decision is not satisfactory. Court trials are the only way to resolve such matters of legal principle.

Our Opening Case

Many of the preceding key points about the American judicial process may be illustrated in our opening case dealing with a tragic accident on the Long Island Railroad. Although it is not clear in this case that Judge Hooley sought to make law, his willingness to hear new evidence about life tables could well be a precedent for later cases. He was sensitive to this possibility and torn between the desire to follow established procedures and the need to hear new evidence that he personally considered appropriate. That he was aware of breaking new ground led him to encourage Muriel Donelon to accept a settlement— in part because of the uncertainty of how an appeals court might rule on some of his procedural decisions. The adversarial nature of the court process is well illustrated by the way Mr. Nizer's efforts for Mrs. Donelon were strenuously opposed by Mr. Doyle. That this was done through a highly formal process was also evident. The role of the lawyers, Nizer and Doyle, was clearly central in the way the case was presented, and ultimately settled. Nizer had to go to great pains to get the evidence on John Donelon's psychological test results before the court, because the ability of the court to accept relevant material was highly limited. Only some of what most would see as 'the truth' could be part of this trial. Finally, the case did not ultimately receive a court decision. It was settled out of court before the trial was completed; it is different here from most cases in that it even went to trial in the first place. In many respects, therefore, our opening case illustrates the key points we have made about how the American judicial process works.

Legal Cultures Elsewhere

Our discussion has focused upon the judicial process as it is found in the United States. It should be understood that slightly—or greatly—different procedures would apply in other societies.

In simpler societies, such as those in which the great span of human prehistory was spent, there was often nothing at all similar to what we know as judicial procedures. What justice was dispensed was often carried out by individuals or families rather than by governmental structures. An instructive Native American example is given by the anthropologist Robert Lowie, showing both the presence of formal procedures along with a private framework for settling disputes. Reports Lowie:

> When two Crow warriors claimed the same honor, one might challenge the other to an ordeal. Each impaled some meat on an arrow, touched it with his lips, then raised it aloft, and called upon the Sun as a witness, saying that if he lied he was to die. Then, if shortly afterward the oath-taker died or lost a close relative, the tribe regarded him as the perjurer, the honor in litigation going to his rival.

Formal trials were not common in preliterate societies, though they could be found in many areas of Africa. Lowie gives an example from the Lobi tribe, where trials "give an opportunity for forensic eloquence and serve as general entertainment." He continues:

> At one open air Lobi trial for larceny the defendant was asked by the presiding elder to express his side of the case. He admitted the theft of several chickens belonging to relatives in order to get money for gambling. The plaintiffs were then heard, whereupon the judges discussed the matter among themselves and decided on severely reprimanding the offender. During the proceedings villagers of both sexes attended and several times questioned the magistrates and the defendant.[8]

In more complex societies, trials are often conducted by formal agencies of the state. However, religious courts often handle many cases as well. For a long time in Western European history, courts of the church existed side by side with those of the state, and many important cases were tried by the church. Although that is no longer common in European nations, the more traditional Islamic nations (such as Saudi Arabia) still see the legal system of their government as an extension of basic Islamic law.

An adversarial system of justice applies in most Western nations. However, most of Europe takes much more literally the enacted laws of legislatures than is the case with Great Britain and the United States. The common law tradition in which judges are the primary formulators of law is mainly an Anglo-American phenomenon. Also, the adversarial system may be less emphasized in other parts of the world. In China, for example, there is a long tradition of the good of the whole society taking precedence over the interests of disputants within civil disputes. This leads to a different emphasis throughout the judicial system.

The Law in Action

Social Factors in Adjudication

Throughout the operation of courts, in both criminal and civil cases, there is a general assumption that adjudication primarily involves the bringing together of (1) the law, and (2) the facts. The law is seen as something already established, that simply needs to be applied to the present case. Each case involves some important facts, and these need to be seen in relation to whatever established law is most relevant. It is the primary role of the judge to see that the facts and the law are properly brought together.

But litigation often does not involve a simple and impartial weighing of the facts in relation to the law. The law in action embodies many aspects of social institutions that are not codified in the law. These include such factors as the nature of litigants (whether individuals or organizations, for example), the particular styles of judges and their time pressures, the nature of the local community, and the economics of the legal profession.

Consider the matter of personal injury claims from automobile accidents. In theory, there is a body of law relating to liability for injuries; that, in relation to the facts of a particular case, should provide the basis for adjudication. However, first of all, these cases almost never go to court. They are settled between an insurance adjuster (usually representing a major insurance company) and the claimant (either as a particular individual claiming injury, usually the case with minor claims, or through an attorney). The settlement that occurs is not necessarily dictated by either the most relevant law or the detailed facts about an accident. More critical than such factors are the nature of insurance companies as bureaucratic organizations and the particular responsibilities assigned to insurance adjusters. The adjuster is under pressure to settle cases quickly and without undue costs to the company. A primary concern is his or her relationship to the company, rather than either liability law or the particular facts of a case. Therefore, the persistence with which an individual presses a claim often has more to do with the final settlement than does a thorough study of the facts of the case. Also, facts tend to be interpreted according to general damage categories and liability rules of thumb, rather than in terms of actual negligence. As one who has thoroughly studied the process of claims adjustment concluded, "legal relationships cannot be understood as a product of the formal law alone, but must be understood in terms of the interplay between the formal law and aspects of the situation in which the law is applied."[9]

Ordinary Litigation

When we think of litigation and adjudication, we especially remember what we have heard about cases with millions of dollars at stake or some case with special courtroom drama. Most litigation, however, is a far cry from the picture given by popular television shows. The issues are generally rather mundane and, except to the parties directly involved, not very interesting. Furthermore, as previously noted, they almost never go to court. What can we say about this great majority of litigated cases? What kinds of cases are they, and how are they settled?

One very ambitious research study which sought to answer such questions as we have just posed was carried out in 1978 through 1980, with the most thorough reporting of the results made in the early 1990s. This was the Civil Litigation Research Project, briefly described in Chapter 2. Without again reviewing the detailed procedures, we may say that this research investigated various samples of cases of civil litigation in both federal and state courts. We are here concerned with some of the main findings of this study.

What kinds of cases were most common, according to the Civil Litigation Research Project? In both state and federal courts, the most common kinds of cases involved torts (claims for damages from wrongful acts of another party) and commercial or contract claims. In state courts, domestic relations and property disputes provided other major categories of cases. Federal cases were more likely than those of state courts to focus on matters of civil rights and discrimination claims, and actions or benefits of governmental agencies. Most cases were initiated by, or on behalf of, individuals. They were often directed to organizations, though other individuals were the defendants in almost half of the federal cases and a somewhat lower proportion of the state cases. Economic values at stake were mostly under $5,000 for state cases (with a median of about $4,500) and under $20,000 for federal cases (with a median of about $15,000). About 92 percent of the cases never went to trial; and of those going to trial, an unstated number were settled before the trial had run its full course (as in our opening example of a suit against the Long Island Railroad).[10]

Noting that most cases are settled without a trial, we need to understand more fully how they get settled. This is typically done through contacts between attorneys representing the primary parties. These are usually rather simple negotiations, for the economic values at stake are typically quite modest. Thirty hours is about the average amount of time spent by an attorney on a case. Of this, only about 10 percent of the time (or about three hours) is devoted to settlement negotiations, and such negotiations are usually focused on monetary values. An emphasis on money is especially strong when a case is handled by the attorney on a contingent fee basis. In his review of patterns of settlement negotiations, as found in the Civil Litigation Research Project, Herbert Kritzer makes the following points:

- Most cases are settled with one or two exchanges of offers and/or demands.
- Most lawyers devote relatively small amounts of time to actual negotiations.

- A large portion of initial offers and demands are very close to the acceptable settlement.
- Relatively few cases involve substantial shifts in offers and demands in the course of the bargaining.
- Plaintiffs are less likely to engage in tactical bargaining (i.e., making demands that are substantially different from the acceptable outcome) than are defendants.
- Contingent-fee lawyers do not obtain higher effective hourly rates by engaging in tactical bargaining.[11]

All of this suggests that the attorney's primary role in most civil cases is neither as a strong advocate to get the most for the client nor as one who simply gives legal advice—two popular images of what the practice of law is mainly about. Nor is the attorney ordinarily pushing for a court trial to demonstrate forensic skills. Rather, the lawyer is largely an agent for getting the case settled as efficiently as possible but without neglecting the client's interests. Kritzer calls this role that of the "justice broker."

The economics of litigation have an important influence on the patterns just discussed. The attorney's fee is not large in cases where not a great deal of economic value is at stake, and spending a lot of time on such cases would not benefit the attorney as much as would having a relatively large number of cases. Also, from the client's point of view, an early settlement is less costly than lengthy litigation. Both of these interests are served by a lawyer who assists in getting a settlement without a great deal of fuss. Efficient settlement, however, is not always speedy; and often lawyers use court dates as a spur to their bringing a long-delayed case to a conclusion. In the Civil Litigation Research Project, the average time from the initiation of a case to its termination was about 420 days.

Although most litigation does not result in an actual trial, lawyers get their framework for negotiated settlements from the judgments reached for similar cases in court. As Kritzer expresses this point, "The settlement of many (if not most) cases relies upon the adjudication of others." The lawyer's knowledge of such other cases is a critical part of successfully filling the role of the justice broker.[12]

Small Claims Courts

The research just discussed does not include the very small cases which are usually handled by special courts, often called "small claims courts." Parties in such cases are often not represented by lawyers. Nevertheless, they are expected to present their case within the framework of established legal procedures. This is sometimes quite difficult, for most people are not used to thinking in legal terms. Research into small claims litigation suggests that there are especially two problem areas: First, many litigants do not comprehend the burden that the adversarial system imposes on them; and second, many litigants do not understand the remedial power of civil courts, often believing that the government has direct power to make things right. As a result of such misunderstandings, litigants are often greatly frustrated when they become involved in a court case. This is especially true for people from low educational and socio-economic levels, who have a much less positive view of the judicial process than do others.[13]

Adjudication, Coercion, and Negotiation

Adjudication, the use of courts to decide disputes, has been set by our sequence of chapters to provide a contrast for both coercion and ordinary negotiation. However, as we examine the reality of what happens to cases filed in courts, we must recognize how much they depend on a combination of adjudication, coercion, and negotiation. Litigation is apparently aimed at adjudication; why else would a court case be filed? When a case is tried in court, the power of the state is applied to the outcome, and this power has strongly coercive characteristics. The state and its agencies of coercive power will stand behind the judgment rendered. But actual adjudication, in the sense of a trial in court, rarely takes place at all. As we have seen, negotiation is the primary means of resolving most cases filed with civil courts, although the cases that do get full adjudication in court are used as an important framework for such negotiated settlements.

Summary and Conclusions

Summary

In this chapter we considered what happens when a dispute is taken to court. Adjudication refers to a settlement by a court. We focused on what happens in civil cases, rather than those involving criminal charges. In civil cases one party (the plaintiff) goes to court to demand something from another (the defendant). The court then makes a decision on the issues in dispute, unless a negotiated settlement occurs first (as it usually does).

Our opening case study involved the accidental death of a railroad passenger. We used this case to examine some of the operations of the American judicial system. In this case, a widow won a substantial sum in the settlement of a negligence case, largely as a result of the clever work of her attorney.

We considered the following key points regarding how the American judicial system functions: (1) the law is made by judges; (2) the law seeks perfectly consistent rationality; (3) the framework for considering cases is adversarial; (4) court procedures are highly formal; (5) lawyers are essential; (6) courts have a highly selective view of truth; and (7) few cases ever go to a court trial. We also noted how the American judicial system may differ from the systems of courts in other societies.

In discussing 'the law in action,' we sought to discover how most civil cases in America are handled. Of particular importance is the role of attorneys in helping their clients to obtain settlements without actual court proceedings. Even though few cases go to trial, judgments for those that do provide a primary framework for the way negotiated settlements are made in the others. Attorneys play an especially important role because of the formal nature of litigation and the lack of understanding of judicial procedures on the part of most of their clients.

Conclusions

Among the main conclusions that grow out of our consideration of adjudication are the following:

a. The formal and adversarial nature of adjudication through the American court system makes this both a difficult and expensive way to resolve disputes.

b. Anyone who seeks to make use of this as a means of resolving a conflict should be encouraged to seek the advice of a skilled attorney. However, the efforts of an attorney are often applied more to negotiate an out-of-court settlement than to win a case in court.

c. Although most cases are settled without a trial, those cases that do go to court provide a framework for negotiations that resolve the other cases.

d. Adjudication depends for its effectiveness on both the coercive power of the state to enforce judgments in selected cases, and the ability of parties and their clients to negotiate voluntary settlements for most cases. Adjudication therefore does not work independently of coercion or negotiation as an approach to resolving conflicts.

10

Mediation

Agreement at Camp David

The Road to Camp David

When Jimmy Carter became President of the United States in 1977, the Middle East was one of the priority areas for his foreign policy. There were important strategic reasons why this should be so. The 1973 war of Israel with Egypt and Syria had briefly brought America closer to a nuclear confrontation with the Soviet Union than at any time since the Cuban Missile Crisis of 1962. Moreover, the oil embargo that the Arab states imposed upon Western nations in 1973 and 1974 had emphasized the vulnerability of Europe and the United States to the effects of conflict in the Middle East. Finally, Carter had a deep personal interest in what his Christian heritage identified as the 'Holy Land.'[1]

The United Nations had suggested a general framework for achieving peace in the area, including a plan for negotiations at a multinational conference in Geneva, Switzerland, to be convened jointly by the United States and the Soviet Union. With this in mind, Carter began to concentrate extra attention on questions regarding Israel and its Arab neighbors. He arranged to meet personally with the leaders of Israel and the major Arab states in the first few months of his presidency. He was particularly impressed with the willingness to pursue peace of Anwar el-Sadat, the Egyptian leader. A sudden change in Israeli leadership resulted in a new prime minister, Menachem Begin, whose authority and intentions remained to be tested.

Contacts continued during the summer and early fall of 1977, with American diplomats trying to plant the seeds for successful negotiations between Israel and its neighbors. There were few concrete signs of progress until President Sadat, on November 9, announced his willingness to go to Jerusalem to try to get negotiations going. His visit there followed on November 19-21 and included a dramatic speech to the Israeli parliament (the Knesset). This visit provided an enormous symbolic change in the relationship of these two nations that still remained officially at war. It also caused considerable alarm in the capitals of other Arab nations.

However, the official discussions that followed between Israel and Egypt, including a December meeting between Begin and Sadat, appeared to be unproductive. President Carter was concerned that the movement toward peace was stalled, and he began to consider the idea of inviting these two leaders, at the same time, to his special presidential retreat at Camp David, Maryland. When the months of 1978 continued with little action toward effective negotiations, Carter made his invitation official. Both Israel and Egypt recognized the importance of the United States in supporting (with material aid as well as through diplomatic efforts) any move toward peace in the Middle East; and both Sadat and Begin accepted Carter's invitation to Camp David.

The First Day

On the afternoon of September 5, 1978, both Prime Minister Begin and President Sadat (together with their special foreign policy advisors) arrived at Camp David. They had come for an indefinite stay, though expecting to be there only several days. Sadat was seeking to develop a comprehensive framework for peace, as was Carter. Most of Carter's national security staff, however, thought that only an agreement on a set of principles for future negotiations was practical at this time, and Begin tended toward the same assessment. Few of those arriving that day would have believed that the negotiations could continue for thirteen days.

Despite the opposition of his own press secretary, Carter asked that all meetings be closed to the press. Only the barest of information about the nature of the meetings was to be released. The facilities at Camp David were simple but ample. Sadat, Begin, and Carter occupied lodges near each other, and suitable facilities were nearby to meet the communication needs of all three governments.

Of the two most important guests, President Sadat arrived first, and Carter had a frank but brief discussion with him regarding the forthcoming meetings. Both understood that the objective was a comprehensive settlement of major issues dividing Israel, Egypt, and the Palestinians. Soon Begin also arrived, and that evening Carter attempted to set the stage with him for comprehensive negotiations (detailed discussions with Sadat being scheduled for the next day). Begin expressed doubts about what might be possible, though he agreed to proceed with a discussion of all issues. It became apparent in this opening conversation that security needs would be of paramount importance for Israel.

In these opening contacts, President Carter made clear that the Americans would be playing a very active role in the negotiations, feeling free to set forth their own proposals on the main issues at any time.

Day Two

On Wednesday morning, September 6, President Carter met with Sadat. The Egyptian leader had with him a draft for a written agreement that would deal with all major issues. However, he confided to Carter that he would be flexible in the negotiations on most of the points. On only two points would he be inflexible: land and sovereignty. The entire Sinai area must be returned to Egypt, and Egyptian sovereignty there must be accorded full recognition in future dealings with Israel.

That afternoon, the first joint meeting of Begin and Sadat with Carter was held. Carter tried to keep himself in the background, encouraging Begin and Sadat to talk directly with one another. Begin early made clear his skepticism regarding how much they might be able to achieve at Camp David. He also expressed great concern about protocol and the procedures to be followed. This led directly to the first agreement reached by the three leaders: that no formal meetings were to be held on the Jewish Sabbath, Saturday.

Sadat followed Begin with an argument for a comprehensive peace settlement. Begin listened intently. Carter later recalled this as "the last time I remember the Prime Minister waiting patiently for someone else to finish speaking."[2]

The leaders then moved to a discussion of more specific issues. Sadat used this occasion to read the proposals he had written in advance. Carter felt the tension rise as Sadat neared the end of his document, which had so many points to which the Israelis would take strong objection. Carter recalls:

> When it was over, no one spoke for a while, and I tried to break
> the tension by telling Begin that if he would sign the document as
> written, it would save us all a lot of time.

This apparently helped end the session with a note of humor, and the leaders agreed to meet again the next day.

That evening Carter asked each of the other two leaders to join him in a stroll around the camp. Sadat declined, but Begin accepted. As they walked and talked, Begin expressed his strong criticisms of Sadat's plan.

Day Three

Early on Thursday morning, Carter, with his two top foreign policy advisors, had a meeting with Begin, with his foreign and defense ministers (Moshe Dayan and Ezer Weizman, respectively) to explore further the Israeli positions. Soon it became apparent that the Jewish settlements in the Sinai area were a major roadblock in the way of an agreement with Egypt. Also, the Israelis placed central emphasis on their security needs regarding any West Bank changes, but they were not precise about just what those needs were. This made Carter impatient, and he showed some anger. He told the Israelis:

> You are as evasive with me as with the Arabs. The time has come to throw away reticence. Tell me what you really need. My belief is that Sadat is strong enough to make an agreement here—and impose it on other nations. I believe I can get Sadat to agree to your home-rule proposal if you convince him and me that you are not planning to keep large parts of the West Bank under your permanent control.

The Israelis tried to specify their concerns a bit more, and then Begin insisted that no more progress could be made until Sadat withdrew his statement of proposals. The Israelis first made this a condition for further negotiations, but then softened their position. Said Begin, under some pressure: "All right. We will not ask for withdrawal. We will simply say it is unacceptable."[3]

Later in the morning, Carter met with both Sadat and Begin. Carter describes the role he tried to assume as follows:

> At the very beginning, I decided to withdraw from the discussion between Begin and Sadat. While they talked, I took notes without looking up, and they soon refrained from talking to me or attempting to seek my opinion.

However, this approach did not produce much progress. Soon Begin and Sadat were engaged in a heated discussion which implied mutual bad faith. Begin resisted the proposals set forth by Sadat, and Sadat reacted with anger, finally stating that "minimum confidence does not exist any more since Premier Begin has acted in bad faith."

Carter then moved into a more active role to keep the talks from breaking up completely. He pursued some specific points to seek a clarification of their respective views, which turned out to be a bit less completely opposed than either had assumed. Carter then sought to list the issues that had to be faced in their negotiations. It turned out to be a long list, including demilitarization of the Sinai, Israeli settlements in occupied territories, the question of a Palestinian state, maintenance of Israeli defense forces in the West Bank and Gaza areas, the devolution of power to Arabs in these areas, the meaning of 'full autonomy' for Palestinians, diverse sovereignty claims over the people of the West Bank (including Jordan as well as the Palestinians), the special status of Jerusalem, the future relations of Israel and Egypt, the problem of Palestinian refugees, the special problem of Israeli airfields on the Sinai, the role of Jordan and other Arab states in further peace negotiations, and the future role of the United States in supporting any agreement. Begin and Sadat agreed that this was a formidable list, but both also expressed a willingness to continue the discussions. As Carter describes the ending of this meeting:

> We adjourned under considerable strain. Begin expressed his complete confidence in Sadat, and it was quite conspicuous that Sadat did not make a similar statement in response.[4]

The three leaders resumed their negotiations in the afternoon. There was some progress toward clarifying positions, but still a wide gulf between them. Carter was now playing a very active role in encouraging efforts toward compromise, but the issues seemed obdurate. Israeli settlements in the Sinai seemed a particularly sensitive issue for both sides as the talks appeared ready to break down completely. Carter describes the ending of this meeting as follows:

> They were moving toward the door, but I got in front of them to partially block the way. I urged them not to break off the talks, to give me another chance to use my influence and analysis, to have confidence in me. Begin agreed readily. I looked straight at Sadat; finally, he nodded his head. They left without speaking to each other.

Although they did not realize it at the time, this was to be the last meeting at Camp David in which Begin and Sadat negotiated directly with each other. They did meet again as the talks concluded, but nearly all future movement toward an agreement involved the Americans talking separately with the Israelis and the Egyptians. Although staying for another ten days in lodges near each other at Camp David, Begin and Sadat would both avoid direct contact with one another.

Days Four and Five

Carter met with his advisors concerning how to handle the discussions, which obviously depended on the Americans playing a strong role if they were to be continued. They decided on a plan to develop a series of drafts for a possible agreement, seeking input from both sides as to how they would need to be revised.

On Friday Carter had separate talks with Begin and Sadat. Begin emphasized the special relationship Israel had with the United States, and pleaded that Israeli settlements in occupied territories be left out of any American proposals. Carter resisted having his hands tied on either count. When he met with Sadat, Carter could talk much more frankly, and he described to the Egyptian leader how he planned to proceed:

I would spend the Jewish Sabbath concluding my work on the draft, preparing a summary of the agreements and differences, and having the texts typed for distribution. After study, each group should present its views to me, and I would relay them to the other. The time for the three of us to meet together was over. I would continue to meet individually with the two leaders, back and forth, until the best possible compromise had been evolved, at which point the three of us, along with our key advisors, would all meet.

This actually describes quite well the way the rest of the Camp David negotiations were to be conducted.[5]

Carter spent nearly all day Saturday working, with the help of his aides, on a comprehensive proposal to be given to both Israeli and Egyptian delegations. Shortly after midnight the document was finished. The draft covered nearly all issues involving Israel, Egypt, and the Palestinians. Only two issues did Carter deliberately leave out, because he sensed they would be too difficult to resolve before other issues had been agreed to. As he later commented:

We had decided to call for the removal of all Israeli settlements from the Sinai, and a freeze on settlements in other occupied territory until all negotiations were complete; but we would not include this request in the first draft.

This draft agreement was to undergo significant change over the next few days, but it did present the parties with a concrete proposal which could be used as a base for negotiations.

Days Six through Ten

On Sunday the leaders took a break from negotiations for a tour of the Gettysburg battlefield. Both Begin and Sadat joined Carter in his limousine—with the understanding that there were to be no negotiations during this outing, as well as no interviews with the press (which, excluded from Camp David, eagerly sought any scrap of information available). Late that afternoon Carter presented his draft to the Israelis. The intention was to hold meetings with both Israelis and Egyptians that day, but the talks with Sadat had to be postponed. Two long talks with the Israeli group were not over until 3:00 A.M.

The Israelis had many objections to Carter's proposals, and at times the discussion became quite heated. Early in the discussion Begin requested that the document not be given to the Egyptians before the Israelis had reacted in detail to all its provisions. This was in line with a pledge President Ford had made to coordinate with Israel any peace proposals the United States might give to the Arabs. Carter would not agree to this limitation, but by lengthening their talks that day he was able to get considerable information about Israeli views. These views showed much resistance on numerous issues; but Begin's associates proved helpful in maintaining some flexibility. To take advantage of this, Carter began to explore some of the issues with members of the delegation apart from the formal meetings that included their prime minister. Begin apparently was willing to accept this, and Carter was to take considerable advantage of this opening. In dealing with the Egyptians, however, all of Carter's contacts were directly with President Sadat.

Monday, September 11, 1978, was the day President Sadat almost broke off the talks. The Israelis had shown no willingness to withdraw their settlements from Sinai or to accept full Egyptian sovereignty over this area. These were the two issues on which Sadat was not willing to compromise. However, he continued to discuss with Carter some possible further changes in the proposed agreement, and he reluctantly accepted a three-year period of phased Israeli withdrawal from the Sinai. He promised to study the proposals further, postponing till late that evening his final decision on leaving the talks. During the rest of the day Carter was kept busy with several discussions with Israelis, and these showed some signs of promise on a number of issues. The next morning Carter talked with Sadat, who still kept guarded what would be his decision about leaving—and Carter didn't press the question. Later in the day, after some serious discussions about possible effects of an agreement upon other Arab nations, Sadat indicated that he was willing to continue further. Then it was Begin's turn to have a frank discussion about his fears regarding the use of Carter's proposals as the basis of an agreement. It was not clear whether they could be sufficiently modified to meet his objections, let alone those of Sadat. Begin made suggestions about the announcements that might be released if the talks were ended at this point.

On Wednesday it was back to the drawing board for Carter. Relieved that neither Begin nor Sadat had broken off the talks, he began an extensive revision of his proposals for a settlement. He tried to include elements to meet the concerns of both sides, based on his recent conversations with them. As the Americans revised their proposals, they worked closely with aides from both sides. This allowed each party to know the thinking of the Americans—as well as the views of the other side—as the draft agreement was reshaped. The biggest issue on which the Israelis were unwilling to accept Carter's proposals was that of their settlements in Sinai. On most other issues there seemed room for further compromises. However, the Sinai differences seemed insurmountable.

When on Thursday there still appeared to be no way for the two sides to come together on Sinai issues, Carter reluctantly began preparations to end the talks. He describes how he had felt at that time:

That evening I began to list the differences between the two nations, and was heartbroken to see how relatively insignificant they really were, compared to the great advantages of peace. I sat on the back terrace late into the night, but could think of no way to make further progress. My only decision was that all of us should work together to leave Camp David in as positive a mood as possible, taking credit for what we had done and resolved to continue our common search for an elusive accord.[6]

Days Eleven through Thirteen

As Carter was beginning preparations on Friday morning to try to end the talks as smoothly as possible, he was surprised to receive the news that Sadat had ordered a helicopter to take him from Camp David. As Carter later recalled: "It was a terrible moment. Now, even my hopes for a harmonious departure were gone." Nevertheless, he sought out Sadat and argued strongly against his leaving at that point. Finally, says Carter,

> I told Sadat that he simply had to stick with me for another day or two—after which, if circumstances did not improve, all of us simultaneously would take the action he was now planning.

Sadat relented after hearing Carter promise that he would not try to push for anything less than a full agreement, all terms of which must be implemented to consider the other parts valid. Sadat then told Carter, "I will stick with you to the end."[7]

Saturday had previously been identified as a nonworking day, but on Saturday, September 16, there were numerous discussions, mostly between Americans and Israelis. It was again the Sinai settlements that appeared to be the stumbling block. Finally, Begin agreed to submit to his Knesset the question, "If agreement is reached on all other Sinai issues, will the settlers be withdrawn?" This appeared to break the logjam, and serious attention could then be given to other details in the draft agreement.[8]

Sunday morning Carter approached Sadat with the planned changes. Except for a few points (most of which Carter was sure could be changed to meet the needs of both sides), Sadat was willing to accept the revised agreement. On one point, Carter admits to a bit of manipulation in order to help confirm an early agreement:

> The only serious problem was his desire to delete the entire paragraph on Jerusalem. I knew that the Israelis wanted the same thing, but I confess that I did not tell Sadat. I reserved this concession just in case I needed some bargaining points later on.

After a few more changes, both the Israelis and the Egyptians were ready to accept the third major American formulation of an agreement. Actually, there were to be two agreements: a Framework for Peace in the Middle East, and a separate Framework for the Conclusion of a Peace Treaty Between Egypt and Israel. At the last minute, however, there was a dispute over the language in which the Sinai issue was to be referred to the Knesset. After hurriedly meeting with both sides on this, Carter formulated a final revision on this issue. He then sent it to both parties with the instructions: "This is the exact language to be used. Do not use any other language on or off the record." This was accepted by both sides, and Carter at last realized that the Camp David discussions had been a success. He could then have preparations made for the public announcements to follow, for the friendly handshakes between Sadat and Begin in front of television cameras, and for the final signing at the White House in Washington of what came to be known as the "Camp David Accords."

Aftermath

Israel and Egypt both moved to fulfill their promises regarding the Sinai. The Israeli Knesset, in an emotionally charged session, did give the go-ahead to a phased withdrawal of their settlements in the region, and steps were initiated to assure the demilitarization of the Sinai peninsula. Based on such progress, Egypt and Israel signed a formal peace treaty on March 26, 1979.

However, progress on the more general plans for peace in the Middle East did not come so easily. The language regarding moves toward self-determination for the Palestinians in the West Bank and Gaza areas had been left vague in many ways, and it soon became evident that Egyptian and Israeli views remained quite different. Furthermore, Israel established new Jewish settlements in the West Bank, which Sadat, and Carter, felt were contrary to the Camp David understandings. Sadat then (in 1980) broke off further peace discussions with the Israelis. Nevertheless, the Sinai agreements were still followed by both Egypt and Israel, and the two nations continued to have diplomatic relations.

It was fifteen more years before the issues regarding the status of Palestinian self rule in the West Bank and Gaza areas would again be seriously negotiated. This was to involve the state of Israel in direct negotiations with the Palestine Liberation Organization, a political group with whom the Israelis had previously avoided any contact. As these new negotiations have recently developed, the pattern of agreements being formed seems to rather closely resemble the framework Carter had urged for Israel and Egypt in 1978 at Camp David.

Sadat had almost no backing (at least in public) from other Arab nations for the agreements he made with the Israelis. Indeed, most Arabs vehemently opposed his moves toward peace with their bitter enemies. That this opposition included some segments within Egypt was made clear on October 6, 1981, when Sadat was assassinated while on military parade in Cairo. Still, his top assistant, Hosni Mubarak, then assumed power and generally continued the policies that Sadat had initiated.

In his memoirs, President Carter recalls the thirteen days he had spent at Camp David, most of this time in his Aspen Lodge near the respective quarters of Prime Minister Begin and President Sadat. Other affairs of his presidency took a back seat during those two weeks, while Carter gave his main attention to mediating the conflict between Egypt and Israel. Reflecting on those very busy days, Carter has said:

> It seems extraordinary how many intense hours I spent cooped up in the small study at the end of the back hall at Aspen. Some of the most unpleasant experiences of my life occurred during these days— and, of course, one of the most gratifying achievements came at the end of it.

Similar feelings can be expressed by many other mediators who have involved themselves fully in the problems presented to them by parties in conflict.[9]

The Nature of Mediation

Key Features

Mediation is a process by which a third party seeks to help persons involved in a dispute come to a mutually satisfactory resolution of their conflict.

As mediation has come to be practiced in the United States during the final decades of the twentieth century, it has certain key characteristics:

1. *Mediation is assisted negotiation.* The mediator's role is to facilitate negotiation between parties who have difficulty in resolving a conflict on their own.
2. *The mediator is a neutral third party.* The mediator avoids taking sides in attempting to move the parties toward agreement.
3. *Mediation is voluntary.* Although mediation is sometimes initiated by a court order (and thus not fully voluntary in this respect), continuing in mediation is voluntary for the parties, and no agreement is reached that is not mutually accepted.
4. *Disputants retain responsibility.* The mediator may guide the negotiations, but responsibility for any decisions of substance always remains in the hands of the disputants.
5. *Mediation is private and confidential.* What goes on in mediation sessions is not expected to be shared with others. Sessions are conducted in a private place, and there is no official record of what is discussed.

In addition to these central features are a number of characteristics that usually (though not always) are seen as important features of mediation. Let us add some of these additional points to our list of what constitutes mediation.

6. *There are no sanctions for failure to reach an agreement.* If agreements are voluntary, it must also be acceptable not to agree. When agreement is not reached, no blame for this is cast upon either party.

7. *The process of negotiation is informal.* Disputants use everyday language and informal procedures. There are no formal rules of evidence or procedure.

8. *A written agreement is usually the objective.* To confirm agreement, the mediator tries to get the result in writing. When both parties agree to the same statement of a resolution, their dispute can be considered as concluded.

9. *Litigation is viewed as an alternative to mediation.* If an agreement cannot be reached through mediation, the parties are free to pursue their case in court. Usually, though, during the period of mediation the parties must suspend any litigation that may be involved.

10. *Clients generally pay for the services of the mediator.* The mediator charges for his or her services, and this charge is usually borne by the parties themselves.

11. *The mediator is a trained professional.* The mediator has taken special training to develop the skills suitable for the conduct of mediation.

12. *The mediator facilitates clear communication, and emphasizes mutual problem solving as the objective.* The mediator helps the parties talk to one another clearly about their differences, then guides them to structure the discussion in terms of the problem(s) they must solve together— rather than on who might win what at the other's expense.

Variations

Mediation, as we have just characterized it, is applicable to many kinds of situations. Some of the most commonly recognized applications of mediation are:

- Labor-management contract disputes
- International conflicts and diplomacy
- Domestic relations cases, including divorces
- Ordinary civil cases (court cases pursued through mediation)
- A variety of relatively minor disputes often categorized as "community mediation"

Among Western nations, mediation has a longer history in labor-management disputes and international conflicts than in the other categories listed above. In the United States, only within the past two decades or so have family mediation, community mediation, and mediation of ordinary civil cases become generally accepted as ways of resolving such disputes.

At the present time there seems to be no end for what might be included under community mediation—including involvements in ethnic conflicts, neighborhood disputes, small business deals gone sour, tenant-landlord disputes, and conflict within schools.

So far our discussion of mediation has reflected primarily the practices used in the United States and other Western nations. We should also recognize that other societies practice mediation, often with significant differences from what we have described.

In the Middle East, for example, mediation is often part of the process of conflict resolution in local communities. However, in contrast to practices in the West (where neutrality typically suggests the mediator should have no past relations with the disputants), a mediator for Middle East disputes is often a community leader who may be well acquainted with the parties. Furthermore, such a mediator is often more active in suggesting solutions—even exerting strong pressures toward recommended outcomes—than is the mediator of the West.[10]

In the Far East, likewise, mediation is also well established. In fact, there has probably been, and continues to be, more mediation practiced in China than in all the rest of the world combined. There is a long history of community mediation in China. Centuries ago a tradition was developed in the villages of disputes being resolved by informal local leaders rather than official magistrates. This has continued into the modern period, and even in major cities today, there is an attempt to identify those who will mediate disputes within local areas. Mediators in cities are thus identified by 'street committees,' which are somewhat parallel to traditional practices in rural villages; and these mediators can handle all kinds of local cases—from disputes within families to those between local organizations. Within work organizations there is also a wide range of forms, including mediation by the labor organization, mediation by management, and mediation under the sponsorship of the Communist Party (which is included as a recognized part of nearly all work organizations).[11]

In China, Korea, and some other nations of the Far East, the mediator is not so much a neutral third person who simply tries to serve the individual interests of the parties (and help them resolve their differences) as she is an agent of society who insists that harmony must be maintained for the good of the social order. With this in mind, the mediator is often well known by the disputants, and she (usually the mediator is a female) does not draw back from telling what she thinks they should do to solve their dispute. She often sees her role as more that of an educator—helping people see what they should do, and why—than that of a neutral facilitator of discussion. All these are important differences in emphasis from the key characteristics of mediation that we listed. Still, in the Far East, most of the characteristics do apply, though with less emphasis on privacy, a written agreement, or the alternative of litigation. Also, one of the twelve characteristics we listed almost never applies, at least in China. This is the way the mediator is paid. In the West, he or she is usually paid by the clients. In China, mediation is almost always provided as a free public service (like drinking water or garbage collection) supported by some local unit of government.

Jimmy Carter as a Mediator

The role played by President Carter during the Camp David Middle East negotiations of 1978 was clearly that of a mediator. He well exemplified most of the characteristics we have identified. He tried to get the parties focused on the issues and provided himself as a third party to encourage agreement. He did his utmost to provide privacy for the discussions and to cultivate the trust of both sides.

In some respects, however, the Camp David Accords do not illustrate the usual image of mediation. Some of these are minor differences from the typical patterns we identified. For example, the alternative to agreement for Egypt and Israel was not litigation, but a continued state of war. Also, Carter collected no fees for providing his services, and he had no formal training for the practice of mediation. More importantly, Carter did not act in the ways we expect of a neutral third party. His approach to the two sides did not appear, at least on the surface, to be an evenly balanced one. Clearly, he had better personal relations with Sadat than Begin, and he used very different approaches in dealing with the Israelis and the Egyptians. He would have long and heated arguments with the Israelis to try to convince them to yield on certain points, while his contacts with the Egyptians were much more in a matter-of-fact style (and conducted more personally and confidentially with their leader). Did that make him less of a neutral? Probably not in a basic sense, for his purpose was still to work out a solution that would be of clear benefit to both sides. He just felt (and with justification) that, given all the past ties of Israel to the United States as well as the special opportunity provided by Sadat's peace initiative, different approaches were necessary for dealing with the two sides.

Several features of Carter's Camp David mediation were especially notable in helping to produce the outcome. One was his audacity in organizing the talks in the first place. He placed the prestige of the United States and his presidency on the line with little assurance that there would be a productive outcome. Of course, the absence of an agreement might not have been a disaster for the United States, but it clearly would have been an embarrassment, given the high profile of preparations for the talks. Following upon his audacity in planning the talks was Carter's persistence in pursuing them. If it had not been for Carter's insistence that the talks continue, they would have ended after two or three days with no substantial progress made. Only his personal pleas to Sadat kept the Egyptian leader from leaving early, and only his impassioned arguments with the Israelis about the possible benefits to them of an agreement induced them to continue with talks that so often seemed hopelessly doomed to failure.

Carter showed special mediation skills by his flexibility in adjusting to the needs of the particular situation. The very active role he ended up playing as a go-between was not the laid-back approach he started with. At the beginning, his intention was primarily to create the conditions under which Sadat and Begin could conduct negotiations with each other. But Sadat and Begin were unable to deal with each other in a productive fashion. Carter then assumed a much stronger role with each side as he provided the link through which essentially all negotiations took place. Such a series of separate meetings with each side is not the pattern most mediations take; mediators often use separate meetings as a tool, but seldom are they given the predominant role they held in the Camp David talks.

Another technique used by Carter with great skill was the single-text approach. As mediator, Carter knew that his first draft for an agreement would not be fully acceptable to either side. Nevertheless, it gave a focus for negotiations. As the negotiations proceeded, the text for a proposed agreement was revised, twice in major ways and many more times in minor ways. But the single text always remained as a framework for the discussions. Not always do mediators find the single-text approach practical. It requires great skill in laying out initial proposals both sides will at least find worthy of discussion, and this in turn must be based on a rather thorough understanding of both parties. At times, however, this single-text approach is a very useful tool for mediators, and it certainly proved valuable in the Camp David case.

Despite the relative success of the Camp David talks, we must also recognize that Carter did not succeed in all he set out to achieve. The agreement that emerged at the end of thirteen days still had important points that were subject to different interpretations by the two sides. This led both Egypt and Israel to abandon the comprehensive plans for the West Bank and Gaza that they had both apparently agreed to at Camp David; and little progress was to be made for well over a decade on questions that directly involved the Palestinians. However, the basis for peace between the nations of Israel and Egypt was achieved— which was no small achievement, given the previous hostilities.

Carter was to continue to display his skills as a mediator both during and after his presidency, though never with quite the dramatic results obtained in the Camp David negotiations of 1978. Later examples included three different international mediation attempts in 1994, all at least partly successful, which caught the attention of the world. These involved the dispute between the United

States and North Korea over nuclear inspection issues, allowing for a transfer of power in Haiti on the eve of American military intervention, and bringing about at least a temporary truce between the warring sides in Bosnia. In these efforts, Carter was acting as a private citizen and not with the power of the American presidency behind him. In some respects that limited his influence, but there were also advantages. With his mediation efforts not being directly sponsored by the U.S. government, he had more of a free hand in the way he could discuss the issues involved.

Some Other Attempts

Some of the case studies of previous chapters provide illustrations of attempted mediation, even though this was not the primary form of conflict resolution used.

In April of 1981, Alexander Haig, the American secretary of state, spent approximately three weeks trying to mediate between the British and the Argentines on the issue of the Falkland Islands. This followed directly after the Argentine invasion of April 2. The United States seemed a natural party to provide mediation, given their favorable relations with both Argentina and Great Britain. However, Argentina proved to be unwilling to consider any proposal that would involve withdrawing their forces, and Britain would consider only solutions that included such a withdrawal. Haig finally announced the failure of his mediation efforts, and the United States moved rapidly to give their moral support to the British.

Mediation for major labor-management disputes in the United States is provided by the Federal Mediation and Conciliation Service, and this service was available for helping to settle the UAW-GM strike of 1970. However, neither side took an initiative in inviting such mediation. Finally, J. Curtis Counts, the director of this federal agency, made a point of talking to each side to see if mediation might be feasible. This was on October 30, when the strike had been going on for about six weeks and was still not close to settlement. Counts emphasized the interest of the federal government in seeing the strike settled and asked if mediation would be helpful. Both sides, however, declined the invitation at this point. Later, Woodcock, the head of the UAW, had second thoughts, and he telephoned Counts on November 9, suggesting that he might be useful as a mediator after all. The next day Counts arrived in Detroit, only to find General Motors ready to make their final proposals. Later that same evening GM did present the UAW with these proposals, and they served as the basis of the final agreement. Therefore, mediation was not part of the settlement process, but it probably would have been if the strike had continued even a short time longer.

There was no official mediation provided in the court case of *Donelon* v. *Long Island Railroad*. However, near the end of the trial, Judge Hooley played something like the role of a mediator when the parties came together for an informal settlement conference. He urged them to reach an agreement and helped defend what he considered a reasonable figure for a settlement. No one was obligated to reach agreement at this point; either party could have pushed the case onward to the final judgment. But the two sides did come to an agreement, and the judge promptly announced the dismissal of the case.

These three examples serve to illustrate that mediation—though still not often used, and, when used, not always successful—remains a viable approach for resolving a wide variety of conflicts.

The Success of Mediation

The Conflict Resolution Movement

There has been a rapid growth in the use of mediation in the United States during recent decades. This has been part of a general trend utilizing several different, but correlated, forms of conflict resolution.

First may be mentioned the peace movement, focused especially on international issues, but also suggesting a broadly based effort at understanding and promoting nonviolent means of resolving conflicts. Associated with this is an academic field of conflict and peace scholarship, usually called "peace studies." There are a number of schools with thriving academic programs in this area, and several journals (such as the *Journal of Conflict Resolution* and the *International Journal of Conflict Management)* provide for the publication of important research.

On the local community level, many groups function to encourage the empowerment of those with little money or normal access to power. This grass-roots conflict resolution movement has been directed to such areas as domestic abuse, the control of crime, and the problem of violence in the schools. Accompanying these concerns has been a desire to promote nonadversarial forms of dispute resolution, embodied in such ventures as local dispute resolution centers. Where these centers exist, they usually provide mediation as their central service.

There is also what may be called the "ADR movement." This is a movement within legal circles to encourage the use of alternatives to standard litigation through the courts. ADR stands for "alternative dispute resolution," and such procedures as mediation and arbitration are proposed as often more effective than traditional litigation. These approaches have become ever more popular as court case loads build up at accelerating rates. As this is written in the mid-1990s, about half of the states in the United States have some kind of statewide rules or legislation to encourage the use of mediation for court cases. Most of these states have developed these frameworks since the beginning of the 1990s.

Family Mediation Results

Family mediation offers both an illustration of the rapid growth of mediation in a relatively new area and some results of research showing its relative effectiveness.

In 1981 California became the first state in the United States to require mediation for all domestic cases involving contested child custody and visitation rights. Under this legislation, each superior court of the state was required to provide divorcing couples with appropriately qualified mediators. Subsequently, family mediation has become more widely applied elsewhere in the United States, sometimes on a voluntary basis and sometimes by court order.

Research has now accumulated to help us assess the effectiveness of family mediation. We shall take note especially of studies comparing the effects of divorce mediation with what may occur through more normal divorce procedures. A recent review of such research has indicated the following patterns.

1. *Outcomes.* Out-of-court settlements appear to be reached in slightly over half of mediated cases, compared to slightly under half of other divorce cases.
2. *Client satisfaction.* Nearly all studies show higher client satisfaction with mediated divorces than with the more common adversarial procedures.
3. *Client costs.* Nearly all studies show lower costs with mediation than with the more common forms of litigation.
4. *Compliance.* Some studies show more short-term compliance with mediated agreements than with other procedures; however, over the long term, the differences are not usually significant.
5. *Psychological effects.* Few studies show long-term effects that give a clear advantage to either mediated cases or ordinary litigation. There may be some more favorable reactions with mediation in the short term—for both clients and their children—but long-term psychological adjustment appears mostly determined by factors other than the procedures used in obtaining the divorce.[12]

Most of the research on the effectiveness of family mediation has a major problem in the self-selection of subjects. Even though respondents are similar in the mediated and nonmediated cases, the voluntary nature of mediation means that there is almost never complete random selection between the two groups. That persons who choose mediation have more favorable results with it than those who do not is hardly a remarkable result. However, several studies have closely approached a random assignment of subjects to treatment groups through an unusual degree of cooperation on the part of authorities. Perhaps the best known instance of this is a study done in Denver, Colorado, and reported by

Jessica Pearson and Nancy Thoennes. They obtained, through a case assignment process, a random assignment of divorcing couples to either mediated or nonmediated treatments. Although a few of those assigned to mediation dropped from the treatment (leaving a less than perfect random assignment), nearly all of the 470 cases involved fit into well-matched groups. The results of this study clearly indicated higher user satisfaction in the mediated group. Results with mediation are generally rated as more fair, more effectively focused on the real needs of children, and allowing more clear communication of points of view than those obtained otherwise.[13]

More recent research by Robert Emery and Melissa Wyer also followed procedures that made it close to a true experimental design, and this research also shows that "mediation greatly reduced the frequency of custody hearings, allowed settlements to be reached in half the time, and substantially increased the satisfaction reported by fathers." For mothers the results of this research regarding satisfaction were not as clear-cut as with fathers, leading these authors to suggest a significant gender difference in satisfaction with divorce mediation.[14]

Views from the Bench and the Bar

Earlier we mentioned the rapidly growing popularity of mediation and other ADR techniques in legal circles. The legal community has ordinarily taken the lead as state after state has moved to establish statewide ADR legislation or court rules. But this has been with a significant level of conflict, as many attorneys see ADR procedures as undermining the basic practices of the American court system. On the other hand, some attorneys and judges see the nonadversarial nature of mediation as a great advantage, for they see some of the exacerbations of conflict produced by conventional litigation procedures. In addition, there is the practical consideration of overloaded court dockets, often a special concern of judges.

Some interesting patterns are indicated by research on attitudes and recent experiences with mediation in one state within two years after it adopted statewide ADR rules emphasizing the use of mediation. Indiana implemented statewide ADR rules on January 1, 1992. Data for a series of Indiana studies were gathered by the author and his colleague, Morris Medley, from the fall of 1992 through the spring of 1994. This research showed a rapidly growing use of mediation in regular civil cases, though with little change in family mediation. Although there were wide variations in attitudes toward (and experience with) mediation in legal circles, the following are among the general patterns to emerge from these studies:

1. Judges are more favorably inclined toward mediation than are attorneys. Attorneys are only moderately in favor of the increased use of civil medi-

ation, and they are almost evenly split on the desirability of mediation for divorce cases.
2. Among attorneys, younger attorneys feel more favorable toward mediation than do those who are older. However, most legal-practice variables appear not to be strongly related to attitudes toward mediation.
3. Among the factors that most judges and attorneys found favorable about mediation were the greater responsibility mediation put on the parties directly involved, the greater opportunity given them to express their concerns, and the expectation that mediated agreements were more likely to be kept than decrees in other cases. Most also saw mediation as taking less time in bringing a case to a conclusion than other procedures.
4. In their experiences with mediation, attorneys saw as especially critical to success the ability of the mediator, the helpful effects of the mediation process itself, the willingness of the parties to compromise, and the desire of parties to avoid greater financial costs. When mediation does not succeed, the unwillingness of the parties to compromise and the role played by some attorneys to hinder mediation were seen as among the most common factors.[15]

Results with International Mediation

Mediation is less likely to show success with complex issues than it is with simpler issues. Also, when hostilities have developed to a high degree, mediation is not so likely to prove successful. These points are well illustrated by considering the role of mediation in international relations.

We saw in Jimmy Carter's activities at Camp David in 1978 that some very intense conflicts can be mediated. But in this same case study, we saw just how difficult the task of mediation can be. Generally, the success rate in international mediation has not been high. One study found the following results regarding the success of 364 attempts at international mediation since 1945:

•   In only 17 cases (about 5 percent) was mediation fully successful.
•   In 64 cases (about 18 percent) mediation was partly successful, involving a cease fire or partial settlement.
•   In 283 cases (about 77 percent) mediation was either not accepted to begin with or unsuccessful in its application.

In attempting to identify the differences between successful and unsuccessful attempts, this study indicates that conflict intensity and complexity were key factors. The more intense and more complex disputes were unlikely to allow successful mediation. Dispute duration was also apparently a factor, especially if related to intensity and complexity.[16]

These findings make all the more impressive what Jimmy Carter was able to achieve as a mediator at Camp David.

Summary and Conclusions

Summary

We used the role of Jimmy Carter during the Camp David Middle East negotiations of 1978 as our opening case study of mediation. Despite enormous differences, Israel and Egypt were able to work out an agreement on some of the main issues dividing them—largely due to the persistence and skill of President Carter.

In identifying the key features of mediation, we gave special emphasis to five points: (1) Mediation is assisted negotiation. (2) The mediator is a neutral third party. (3) Mediation is voluntary. (4) Disputants retain responsibility. (5) Mediation is private and confidential. Beyond these main points, there is great variation in the nature of mediation for different kinds of conflicts. Also, different societies and cultures emphasize different approaches in mediation.

Mediation has shown rapid growth in the United States in recent years, both as part of a broad-based conflict resolution movement and as a special tool for court-related alternative dispute resolution (ADR). Evidence has been reviewed which broadly supports the effectiveness of mediation for divorcing couples and for other kinds of civil cases. Despite President Carter's success at Camp David, international disputes are usually not very likely to be resolved through mediation.

Conclusions

Two conclusions seem to follow from the materials presented in this chapter:

a. There is no simple recipe for successful mediation. Beyond some generally applicable principles, what is effective varies greatly from one kind of mediation to another, from one case to another, and from one society or culture to another.

b. As a means of dispute resolution, mediation is rapidly growing in popularity in the United States at the present time. Among the reasons for this are the heavy load handled by the courts in conventional litigation, the desire of many people for less confrontational ways of handling disputes, and evidence for mediation's success in producing effective agreements.

11

Arbitration

Three Cases

Costs of Freedom

Instead of focusing on a single case study to introduce the subject of arbitration, we will briefly examine three different cases. These cases all involved American public school teachers who, in the early 1980s, found themselves in trouble because their ideas of academic freedom were not shared by their school administrators.[1]

A foreign language teacher in Ohio, whom we will call Ms. Arnold, was highly critical of the way foreign languages were treated in her school system. She made her views publicly known through the local media. After being warned to be careful about the way she presented her views on such matters of school policy, she was careful not to use the classroom as a general forum for airing her ideas. Nevertheless, when asked by students for her views on the treatment of foreign languages, she responded briefly. For this she received an official reprimand and was reminded of her duty to avoid any discussion with her students of that subject. The next day she asked one of her students if he had complained to the principal. The student said no; but that afternoon Arnold received another written reprimand. The principal viewed Arnold's actions as a case of insubordination, given the prior order not to discuss the issue with students.

A case in the state of New York involved a social studies teacher, whom we will call Mr. Bellugi. He had been teaching in his system for almost twenty years, and his general ability as a teacher was not in dispute. What was questioned was the appropriateness of some of his comments directed at the president of the local board of education. The setting was a party for the social studies department at a local country club. He used the occasion for loudly and personally criticizing the board president, saying such things as "I had two of your kids in school and I can't believe they were your issue. I can't understand how such nice kids could have a father who is such a no-good son of a bitch." A particular issue seemed to be the board president's past circulation of materials attacking protesters of the Vietnam War. Bellugi said to him, "For years you have been cranking out hate literature on your printing press, but you never had the nerve to sign it." For this outburst, the school board brought disciplinary proceedings against Bellugi.[2]

A somewhat different issue of academic freedom surfaced in an Illinois school, where English classes were taught by a teacher we will call Mr. Charters. Several years earlier Charters had been among a group of teachers who sought approval for a course on the Bible as literature. Unsuccessful in this, Charters nevertheless introduced Biblical materials in some of his own classes, especially in two remedial English classes. Rather routinely the principal approved his course plans, but later had second thoughts. Further examination showed extensive use of the Bible and closely related materials, and the principal's approval was then withdrawn. Nevertheless, Charters proceeded with his plans, including listing the Bible as a course text. Immediately after the start of the new classes, the principal and the English department chair met with Charters and told him that "in no course in our curriculum is the Bible in any version one of our texts; therefore, it is not to be used." Charters felt that this was an improper order, and he persisted with his teaching plans. About a week later, however, he abandoned the project after receiving a written warning from the superintendent of schools. Charters continued to advocate his curriculum ideas and eventually filed a formal grievance over what he considered to be the infringement of his academic freedom.[3]

In all three of these cases, the local teachers' association gave encouragement to the teacher under fire. In both the Ohio and Illinois cases, the teacher's cause was supported as a formal grievance within the prevailing employment policies of the school district. While New York state law provided a somewhat different framework for hearing disciplinary cases involving public school teachers, the teacher there also had considerable support from his teaching colleagues.

Some Issues

Some issue of free speech or academic freedom is present in each of the above three cases. These freedoms do not provide absolute rights, but need to be interpreted in the light of particular contexts that may on occasion limit them.

One of the factors that may limit speech in an academic setting is the content of what is said. Does the challenged expression deal with something related to the person's role as a teacher? All three of our cases could be so construed. However, the relevance to one's teaching duties varied. It was most clearly relevant in the case of Ms. Arnold, it was not so clear in Mr. Bellugi's case, and the relevance was definitely in dispute in the case of Charters.

We may consider discipline for a teacher's utterances more likely to be proper when a teacher is acting within the school itself. For Arnold there was apparently no official objection to her voicing her views in the community, but she was challenged for expressing them to students. Bellugi was clearly not in the school at the time of his objectionable remarks, and no students were then present; but the setting was still a school-related social function. The case of Charters was directly an issue regarding the school curriculum.

Another factor that might limit academic expression is the manner in which speech is uttered. Intemperate or abusive speech is more likely to be objectionable—especially if expressed to those higher up in the academic hierarchy. Clearly this was part of the issue for Bellugi. We have no evidence that speech was intemperate in the other two cases, though in both of these there was some challenge of a principal's authority.

How Can These Cases Be Resolved?

In each of our three cases, an outside arbitrator was obtained to seek a resolution. This was part of the grievance process established by teacher contracts in the local school systems in the Ohio and Illinois cases; in the New York case it was provided by state law for appealing a teacher disciplinary issue. In each case, the arbitrator was asked to decide on the issue in question. Each party had a chance to present its side of the dispute, after which it was understood that the arbitrator would make a decision. Both parties were then expected to accept this decision.

We will later describe what the arbitrator actually decided in each case. Meanwhile, the reader is encouraged to consider what his or her ruling would be if called upon to arbitrate these disputes.

The Nature of Arbitration

What Is Arbitration?

In arbitration, the parties take their conflict to an impartial third party, who provides them with a decision that allows them to end their conflict.

Although the above definition describes arbitration in general, we must immediately recognize that arbitration can take on many different forms. Among the main distinctions made between forms of arbitration are those concerning (1) whether or not arbitration is freely chosen by the parties, (2) whether or not parties have agreed to be bound by the arbitrator's decision, and (3) whether or not basic policy or economic issues are at stake.

Voluntary Versus Compulsory Arbitration. Sometimes parties in conflict will decide to seek arbitration on their own initiative for a particular dispute. Such voluntary arbitration is rare. Much more common are cases for which the parties have previously committed themselves to arbitrate certain categories of issues. Arbitration then is not optional for individual cases. It fits into a previously established framework, and the parties may not choose whether or not to be included. They automatically find their case in arbitration.

Nonbinding Versus Binding Arbitration. Sometimes parties are not bound in advance to accept the arbitrator's decision. It may be advisory only. In such cases, the arbitrator's role has much in common with that of a mediator, the main difference being that the arbitrator must, after hearing both sides, formally put forward a proposed resolution for the conflict. More common is binding arbitration, where the parties have agreed in advance that they will accept whatever the arbitrator's ruling may be. Their previous agreement providing for arbitration also binds them to accept the decision. In such binding arbitration, it is as though the parties had agreed to an enforceable contract with a few blanks remaining to be filled—and the arbitrator's job is to fill in those blanks.

Interest Versus Rights Arbitration. At times arbitration deals with basic policy or contract issues. Arbitration is then usually termed "interest arbitration," in the sense that basic economic interests are involved. For example, a labor-management contract may, especially if mediation has failed to achieve agreement, be submitted to an arbitrator's ruling. Much more common is arbitration for particular grievances interpreted within the framework of a previously established contract. This is often called "rights" arbitration, in that the dispute involves a determination of what is appropriate within agreements already determined. The arbitrator must interpret the merits of the case presented by the parties in view of the established contract. The vast majority of labor-management contracts in the United States have provisions for the arbitration of grievances that cannot be settled more informally. In contrast, very few labor-management contracts themselves are decided through arbitration.

Other Distinctions

The possibilities for forms of arbitration are extremely rich. The way an arbitrator's decision is limited can be an important consideration for some types of arbitration. Especially for contract arbitration, parties sometimes agree to accept final-offer arbitration. This means that each side presents its final negotiating position to the arbitrator, who then must choose between them. This provides a special incentive for the parties to move toward a negotiating position that appears reasonable, and frequently this encourages an earlier agreement—without, in the end, requiring an arbitration hearing after all.

Several states have developed a variation of final-offer arbitration for public sector labor disputes that allows each party to give two final offers. This gives the arbitrator the option of choosing any one of four positions. It is suggested that this tends to add a greater incentive for negotiating flexibility to be shown by the conflicting parties, as well as giving more options for the arbitrator to choose from.

Another distinction sometimes made is between public and private arbitration. Is arbitration provided by a public body, as is often the case in Europe, or is the arbitrator in private practice? In the United States, most arbitrators practice privately, using such groups as the American Arbitration Association to help them identify disputes suitable for their involvement.

One can also make a public-private distinction in regard to whether a work unit is in the public sector or the private sector. Contract arbitration is more likely to be found in public-sector work settings than in private enterprise. This is because public employment is more directly under governmental control, and private companies and their unions both tend to resist outsider settlement of their basic contract disputes. In some other countries this is less often the case than in the United States. Australia and New Zealand are examples of nations in which arbitration is much more widely practiced for labor-management contracts. One of the American states, Kansas, tried to impose binding arbitration on labor-management contract disputes back in the 1920s, but that experiment was soon declared unconstitutional. In contrast, grievance arbitration in America is widely practiced in the private sector, where it is a part of most contracts (probably more than 90 percent) negotiated through private collective bargaining agreements.[4]

We can also distinguish arbitration cases on the basis of the degree of formality in their procedures. Arbitration hearings can be very informal. When this is the case, they seem to be very similar to mediation sessions. On the other hand, some arbitration sessions involve procedures that are almost as formal as those of court cases. The degree of formality depends largely on the nature and seriousness of the dispute, though also a person serving as arbitrator may choose one or another style.

Up to this point we have been thinking mostly of an arbitrator as an individual, but this is not always the case. An arbitrator may be a panel of any number that is mutually agreed upon. Important cases often use a panel of three arbitrators. A common practice is to have each of the parties choose one arbitrator (not formally tied to the party but known to be sympathetic), and these two arbitrators together then choose the third member of the panel. The third (and most clearly impartial) arbitrator is most influential for the final decision, though the other two arbitrators ensure that all relevant points receive full consideration.

The Arbitration Process

Ordinary Arbitration

As implied earlier, the most common situation for arbitration involves an employee grievance under a contract that calls for mandatory arbitration when such disputes occur. It is what is usually termed as "rights," rather than "interest," arbitration, and the decision of the arbitrator is to be binding. This was true with each of the three cases we examined at the start of the chapter.

In such a typical case, the process starts with a grievance of an employee or a group of employees. Before it becomes considered as an arbitration case, it must pass through several steps. The process here varies from one work organization to another, but we will consider what might be involved in a typical case.

Initial Processing

Suppose an employee of a unionized company feels she is given improper assignments by her supervisor. She may seek out the union shop steward about her complaint, and he may talk with the supervisor. Assuming that the problem is not resolved in this way, the employee may file a formal grievance. The personnel department takes note of this, and checks with the supervisor about the case. The local union also receives notification of the grievance, and they indicate their backing of the employee. If she lacks the union's backing, the employee may decide not to proceed further; however, If she has the support of the union, the company must give her case careful attention. Company managers will seek to inform themselves about the grievance which is now being pursued by both the individual and her union. They will review their policies to assure themselves that the employee's supervisor had acted appropriately. If not, they will try, as diplomatically as possible, to rectify the situation. On the other hand, if they believe that the supervisor's actions were justified, the case is ready for arbitration.

Getting an Arbitrator

In our hypothetical case, the labor-management contract calls for compulsory arbitration of grievances that cannot be otherwise resolved. The contract also includes a standard arbitration clause, suggested by the American Arbitration Association, by which both parties agree to binding arbitration for any dispute regarding the application of the contract. Either the union or management may initiate a request for arbitration of a specific case. Unless they agree together on an appropriate arbitrator, they seek the assistance of the American Arbitration Association for identifying someone. This Association will give each side the same listing of arbitrators they would recommend for the case. Each party can then cross out any names on the list that it considers unacceptable and give a rank order preference for the arbitrators remaining. A representative of the Association would then, keeping in mind the preferences of both sides, seek to get the agreement of a particular arbitrator to take on the case.

The Hearing

After accepting a case, the arbitrator informs himself about its basic facts. He then fixes a time and place for a hearing, notifying both parties at least five days in advance. The arbitrator has general authority to control the hearing, though if any party seeks legal representation, any attorneys so chosen are included. If either party requests a stenographic record of the proceedings, this is granted.

Whichever party formally initiated the arbitration request usually presents its position first, including any documents or other supporting exhibits. Then it is the other side's turn. The arbitrator then ask questions of both parties and/or their witnesses, seeking whatever further information he believes would be helpful. At the conclusion of the hearing, the arbitrator returns home with whatever documents he has collected and personal notes he has made.

The Conclusion

Within thirty days after a hearing has concluded, the arbitrator announces his decision in written form. Although only a brief statement would suffice, the arbitrator usually provides several pages of his own analysis, showing why he decided in the way he did. This is then expected to close the case. Of course, a party that is dissatisfied with the decision may appeal to the courts. However, the courts are hesitant to hear any cases that have already received decisions from an arbitrator. They consider the arbitration award as part of the labor-management contract which must stand unless there are very unusual circumstances. Cases that have been appealed to the U.S. Supreme Court make it clear that arbitrators have a wide range of discretion in the way they may rule.

Some Variations

As just indicated, the courts are hesitant to decide cases that have already been arbitrated. However, some cases do go to court. Usually this is when an important principle has been part of the arbitrator's decision, and the courts are willing to consider the case in terms of the legal precedent of that principle.

The Torrington Case

One such case that led to a court review involved a dispute over paid time off for voting on election days. This practice had been followed for many years at the Torrington Company. However, during collective bargaining negotiations with the union, the company indicated that it intended to discontinue the practice. This was not a major issue, however, in the breakdown of collective bargaining and an ensuing seventeen-week strike. When, finally, an agreement was announced, the new contract was silent on the relatively minor matter of time off for elections. But the strike had created a mood in which the union was prepared to challenge the company on even minor matters. When the company denied paid time off at the next election day, the union challenged this decision. Since the parties involved could not agree on how to handle this issue, it became a formal grievance to be decided by an outside arbitrator. The decision of the arbitrator was that the company had an obligation to continue a practice that had long been understood as a part of employees' rights, so long as the contract did not explicitly change this understanding. Employees were to continue to receive paid time off for voting, even though the company had previously announced, before the current contract was signed, that the practice was to be discontinued. The fact that the contract was silent, the arbitrator ruled, left the practice the same as it had been understood before the latest agreement.[5]

The company appealed this arbitration ruling to the courts. They felt that a principle of some importance for both the company's authority and for labor law was involved. In accepting the case, the U.S. District Court agreed. What was even more unusual, they gave a decision that reversed the judgment made by the arbitrator. The court ruled, in part, that

> Labor contracts generally affirmatively state the terms which the contracting parties agree to; not what practices they agree to discontinue. This agreement made no provision for "paid voting time" and the arbitrator exceeded and abused his authority when he attempted to read into the agreement this implied contractual relationship.[6]

Now it was the union's turn to appeal. The general importance of implied rights for workers made this also a matter of principle for them, and they took the case to the United States Court of Appeals. After careful consideration, this court also held that the arbitrator had exceeded his authority. Written contracts, they held, need to be seen as more precisely binding than his decision had allowed.

What then becomes the importance of unwritten past practices? Are they not effective bases for a grievance? Here the courts have appeared to support the general tendency of arbitrators to take past practices, even if not formalized by written contracts, into account in their rulings. When contracts contain ambiguous language about a practice, past usage may take precedence over any attempt at a new interpretation. However, when a contract has clear provisions, past practices are not relevant. What the Torrington case involved was apparently something between these two possibilities—past practices had been explicitly denied by management during contract negotiations, but the ensuing contract was silent on the issue. Here the courts have accepted the silence in the new contract as decisive, provided that the company indicated its intention to change their policies in advance of the contract. That is the fine line that the Torrington case seems to draw, in exemplifying how arbitration rulings may, when special matters of principle are involved, become appealed to the courts.

Arbitration in Major League Baseball

Earlier, we mentioned briefly the possible option of final-offer arbitration, where each side makes a final offer and the arbitrator is limited to deciding between them. One of the most interesting examples of this procedure may be found in American major league baseball.[7]

For more than two decades, final-offer arbitration has been used to decide the salaries of major league baseball players when the player and the owner are unable to come to an agreement on their own. Similar to much grievance arbitration, individuals provide the cases for arbitration; however, the actual subject for arbitration concerns the players' basic monetary interests rather than their rights under a contract. It is their individual contracts that are to be decided.

Beginning in 1974, the owners and players agreed to accept final-offer arbitration for setting players' salaries, and this has been continued in subsequent general agreements between owners and players. It should be pointed out, however, that players in their initial seasons are not eligible for arbitration, and more experienced players, as free agents, are also not normally covered by arbitration procedures. Nevertheless, well over a hundred players per year in recent years have requested arbitration, and of these about one-fifth actually complete the arbitration process (with the others settling before the arbitration process is completed).

An example will help show how arbitration can work. In 1986, Don Mattingly of the New York Yankees had a very good year. His batting average was .352, and he hit thirty-one home runs. Although his gross salary was $1,375,000 that year, he had high hopes for a sizable increase for 1987. He asked for a raise to $1,975,000—a $600,000 increase—in his final demand. The club only offered $1,700,000—a $325,000 increase. An arbitrator was therefore given the case and was forced to choose between $1,975,000 and $1,700,000. The arbitrator selected the player's figure as more reasonable, thus making Mattingly's award higher than any previous arbitrated salary in major league baseball.[8]

Players affected by arbitration do not have freedom to move from club to club; the special exemption of baseball from antitrust legislation leaves them under monopoly conditions, with the owners holding the upper hand. The establishment of final-offer arbitration was seen by players as a means of increasing their power in relation to the owners, making salaries more what they would be under free market conditions. Most scholars who have studied the economics of major league baseball agree that this has indeed been the general result: that arbitrators, though quite arbitrary in their decisions from case to case, have the long-term result of bringing salaries closer to what would approximate free market conditions.[9]

The American Airlines Case

Contract arbitration is sometimes mandated in the public sector, usually along with a ban on a union's right to strike. For the private sector, contract arbitration is rare. However, it sometimes does occur as a way of settling a

bitter strike when negotiations seem to be at a genuine impasse. An example
of this may be seen in the dispute between American Airlines and its flight attendants' union late in 1993.[10]

American Airlines had been losing money for some time, so they sought
to lower their operating costs by changing their work rules. Related to this was
a request for a reduction in the attendants' coverage of flights and for an increase in the proportion of retirement benefits to be paid by employees. Although collective bargaining during 1993 brought progress in many areas, the
union and management were unable to agree on these particular issues and on
the final level of pay. The flight attendants, approximately 22,000 strong, began
their strike on November 18, after intense negotiations (assisted by a federal
mediator) had failed to bring about a settlement. Although management sought
to keep their flights operating normally, the strike soon gave promise of caus-
ing major disruptions in Thanksgiving travel plans.

However, the strike was over before Thanksgiving. Just three days after
it started, it ended. Both sides wanted an early settlement, but neither was prepared for a quick change in positions. Under these conditions, the solution appeared from an unlikely source: President Clinton's White House. Sources close
to the president understood that both sides wanted to end the strike as soon as
possible. After only a few hours of White House intervention, a conclusion was
reached and the flight attendants announced their readiness to go back to work.
What President Clinton suggested was that each side accept binding arbitration
of the main issues remaining. Both quickly agreed.

The union saw this conclusion as a victory; they had proposed such arbitration earlier. Management was more reluctant to accept this limit on their
powers, but the pressure of the White House proved decisive for them. Said the
chairman of American Airlines, Robert L. Crandall, in a news conference: "For
any citizen or any company or any union to say 'No, I won't do that' to the
president requires an awfully good reason." On its part, the White House min-
imized its use of pressure tactics. "This was not our agreement, this was their
agreement," said a White House spokesman.[11]

Although different parties may give different versions of the final negotiations, it is clear that White House intervention hastened an end for the strike;
it is also clear that binding arbitration was the formula that both sides could
agree to for accomplishing this.

The dispute between American Airlines and their flight attendants is unusual in several respects. Seldom will either party in collective bargaining seek
out contract arbitration as a solution—they are too jealous of their own freedom of action for that. Even more rare is White House intervention, for both
sides are wary of governmental involvement, and the White House ordinarily
likes to avoid taking part in major controversies. Nevertheless, in this particular instance, President Clinton did become involved, talking personally on the

telephone with the leaders of both sides. And this time, the agreed solution took the form of contract arbitration.

Decisions in Three Cases

Arbitration in Schools

School systems are among the organizations that may, as a last resort, call in an arbitrator to settle a grievance raised by an employee. This occurred in each of the three cases with which we opened this chapter. We now reveal what the arbitrator decided in each case. The reader should bear in mind that another arbitrator might have made another decision for any of them.

Arnold's Case

In the case of Ms. Arnold, who was highly critical of her school's foreign language program, the arbitrator recognized her right to express views publicly regarding the program. This was her right as a citizen. As a member of the school staff, however, she was expected to be very careful in the way she expressed views to students. On the basis of the evidence available to the arbitrator, he concluded that she had indeed been circumspect in her comments to students. Her initial reprimand from the principal was therefore out of order. However, she should not have raised with a student a question about the basis of this reprimand. She was therefore out of line in her follow-up. The second letter of reprimand was appropriately kept in her personnel file, though the first letter was removed.

Bellugi's Case

For Mr. Bellugi's case, there was an arbitration panel of three persons: one named by the school board, one named by the teachers' group, and a neutral one approved by both groups. The decision turned out to be a split one. The teachers' arbitrator felt that Mr. Bellugi's comments to the school board president had been within the bounds of permissible speech. It was not made within the school setting, and there was no clear harm done to the instructional program of the school. The other two arbitrators, however, saw Mr. Bellugi's comments in a different light. They made clear first of all that the right of free speech was not an absolute, as U.S. Supreme Court opinions had confirmed. They quoted the court as saying that "There are certain well-defined and narrowly limited classes of speech, the prevention and punishment of which have never been thought to raise any Constitutional problems." They saw Mr. Bellugi's intemperate remarks to the president of the school board as within the bounds of speech that could properly be regulated. As the chief arbitrator expressed their conclusion, Bellugi's remarks were "offensive and especially disrespectful to the president of the board of education in the District where the respondent taught." According to this ruling, the teacher was appropriately disciplined for his comments.[12]

Charters' Case

Mr. Charters found little sympathy from the arbitrator for his attempts to include the Bible as assigned reading in the courses he taught. He had indeed been guilty of insubordination in the way he pursued his curriculum ideas. "He could not, under any circumstances, continue to teach the unit merely because he believed that his supervisor exceeded his authority," said the arbitrator. Neither academic freedom nor constitutional free speech were involved, in the arbitrator's view; rather this was simply a case of "a recalcitrant teacher who, upon finding his students' knowledge of Scripture to be less than to his satisfaction, set out to remedy this perceived shortcoming under the guise of a literature course." But in so doing he did not fulfill the curriculum requirements of his school. Instead, he apparently sought to instill in students a particular religious viewpoint, and he was not completely honest about these intentions. "In fact," said the arbitrator, "from the source materials he eventually produced, it is clear that the content of the course was a fundamental Christian view of Biblical material. Not one of the cited references was an academic literary work." Mr. Charters' grievance was therefore dismissed by the arbitrator.[13]

Summary and Conclusions

Summary

In arbitration, the parties take their dispute to an impartial third party, who provides them with a decision which allows them to end their conflict.

We opened the chapter with three cases of grievance arbitration involving public school teachers. Each case raised an issue of academic freedom or free speech. We then described some of the main general forms that arbitration may take. These include voluntary versus compulsory arbitration (based on whether or not the parties are bound in advance to seek arbitration), nonbinding versus binding arbitration (based on whether or not parties are required to accept the arbitrator's decision), and interest versus rights arbitration (based on whether basic understandings are at stake or only the interpretation of previously determined agreements).

We used binding grievance arbitration, the most common form of arbitration in the United States, for describing a typical arbitration process. The steps in this process include: (1) the initial processing of the grievance, (2) getting an arbitrator, (3) holding an arbitration hearing, and (4) obtaining a conclusion. In order to point out some of the various forms that arbitration may take (in addition to simple grievance arbitration), we considered three additional cases: *(a)* a case involving court appeals over the interpretation of past practices, *(b)* the special form of final-offer arbitration used for determining the salaries of American major league baseball players, and *(c)* an airline strike in which governmental intervention was applied to obtain an arbitrated solution.

Conclusions

Two main conclusions are suggested by the materials reviewed in this chapter:

a. Arbitration is extremely varied in the forms that it may take, and it can be applied to many different kinds of circumstances.

b. The popularity of arbitration continues to grow. This is in part because it has many of the same advantages as mediation (such as privacy and flexibility) while at the same time sharing with adjudication the prospect of an authoritative decision.

12

Many Roads to Resolution

The Spink County War*

In the late nineteenth century, many local areas of the United States experienced what has been called a "county seat war." This term refers to a bitter struggle between rival towns over which one is to be named as the county seat. We will here describe one such case, as it occurred in Spink County, South Dakota.[1]

When Spink County was organized in 1879, county records were temporarily located in Ashton. This town soon became Old Ashton, as it was bypassed by the railroad and another Ashton was located along the tracks. Meanwhile, other towns had rapidly sprung up, including Redfield. In the county seat election of 1880, Redfield probably had ninety-four votes, exactly one-half of the votes cast, but not the needed majority. We say "probably" because someone apparently reworked the poll books later, making a final determination of the count uncertain.

Four years later the issue again came up for a vote, and, in an election with obvious irregularities on all sides, Redfield again had a plurality but not the necessary majority. At least, that is the way the count was announced. Redfield proponents doubted the accuracy of the count and, besides, they felt that a proper reporting of the earlier election would have given them the county seat in 1880.

As a group of men, including leading citizens of Redfield, were discussing the situation one night in December, 1884, someone suggested that direct action was called for. Others agreed, and before the night was over a systematic plan for forcibly seizing the records from Old Ashton was both formulated and successfully carried out. The next morning the county records were in protective custody at the Redfield city hall, rather than at the courthouse at Old Ashton.

News of the midnight seizure of the county seat soon spread throughout Spink County. Citizens of Ashton and the northern part of the county were

---

outraged and proceeded to form their own action group. Early in the morning of December 7, about three hundred men gathered at Old Ashton and prepared to march southward toward Redfield. By the time they approached Redfield their ranks had been increased to about a thousand men. At the eastern edge of Redfield the forces from Old Ashton paused to send a series of ultimatums to the Redfield leaders.

Meanwhile, Redfield had prepared its defenses. Every available gun in the city was prepared for action, and men were positioned to stop any invading force. As the day wore on, Redfield received three delegations from those encamped east of town. But all demands for removing the county records away from Redfield were rejected. Finally, about mid-afternoon, the decision was made by the visiting forces to move upon Redfield. There were to be three divisions of the attacking forces. All would move in a body toward town. Then groups at the end would separate, moving to the right and left. The orders of these groups were to set fire to the first buildings reached and to shoot to kill any resisting forces. Meanwhile, the central force was to advance directly to the city hall to seize the county records.

The advance was ready to start when the whistle of an approaching train provided a temporary diversion. The train was not a regularly scheduled one. In fact, it had been specially and hastily arranged to bring back a court order from a judge in Milbank, 128 miles away. Three Redfield citizens had left early that morning to seek a temporary injunction against removal of the records from Redfield. Now these men returned on the train, injunction in hand.

With this new turn of events, the invasion was stalled. Then the two sides started serious negotiations. Finally, an agreement was reached. The records were to remain in Redfield until or unless a court ruled otherwise; the county commissioners (mostly non-Redfield men) were to take charge of the records at Redfield; and if a court ordered their removal, there was to be no resistance by Redfield forces.

This ended the most active phase of the Spink county seat war. A force of militia was sent to Redfield by the territorial governor, but it arrived too late to find any chance for decisive action. There continued to be legal skirmishing, resulting in the county records being moved back temporarily to Old Ashton. In 1886 there was another election on the issue, and this time Redfield clearly won. Ever since, Redfield has proudly held its position as the county seat of Spink County, South Dakota.

Forms of Resolution

How did the citizens of Spink County, South Dakota, resolve their conflict over county seat location? As our account describes, there were at least four different modes of resolution attempted, all of which had some effect upon the way the issue was settled. These included elections, physical force, direct negotiations between the conflicting parties, and adjudication.[2]

In most states, county seats were supposed to be decided by a special election on the issue. In Dakota Territory, when Spink County was first organized, the petition for organization was followed by a temporary location of the seat of government. However, a permanent seat could only be established by an election, with a majority of those voting needed to establish a permanent location (or later to remove the county seat from one town to another). When this election was held in 1880, there was considerable controversy about the way the votes were counted. The election of 1884 was also in dispute. That there were disputed elections on such an issue should not be surprising, for there were often election irregularities in the early histories of American (especially midwestern) counties. Although ultimately the issue was decided in the election of 1886, that was only after six years of uncertainty regarding where the legitimate seat of government for Spink County should be.

During the period of electoral uncertainty, the citizens of Spink County sought to resolve the issue of county seat location by force. Both sides used this approach, and each had some degree of success. Physical force first moved the county records from Old Ashton to Redfield, and another application of force was about to take them back when this counterattack was stalled. Given the willingness of both sides to use force to resolve the issue, it is a wonder that no one was physically injured in the conflict. Participants in county seat wars elsewhere have not always been so fortunate, for several such conflicts have been known to result in fatalities.

With the impasse that developed over the use of force, direct negotiations between leaders of both sides of the Spink dispute were attempted. These did not seek to settle the issue of county seat location once and for all, but they did bring the parties away from the brink of physical confrontation with a temporary agreement that all could live with. These negotiations were successfully concluded, and the armed citizens of Spink County could then return to their homes. They had reached a compromise which would leave the permanent location of the county seat to be decided later, but would specify how county business was to be conducted in the meantime.

Ultimately, the courts had responsibility for settling the issue of county seat location. When an election was disputed, the issue could be taken to court, allowing a judge to make a determination. Not always, however, was the losing side of a county seat war willing to live with the judgment of a court of law. At least, not without further action or appeals. Eventually, of course, a court had to approve a final determination of the issue, but sometimes that could involve several years. In the case of Spink County, court appeals had not been concluded when the citizens decided to take the issue into their own hands. But their actions were restrained by a temporary injunction, for they did recognize the ultimate legitimacy of the courts to act in such cases.

What, then, was the primary means of conflict resolution for the Spink county seat war? We cannot give a simple answer, for elections, force, direct negotiations, and adjudication all had a significant role in determining the outcome.

Going beyond Spink County, we discover that most local disputes over county seat location in American history have been decided by some combination of elections and adjudication. These have been the primary means for resolving this kind of issue. Often an election has been decisive by itself, but on numerous other occasions a court has been required to interpret the election. At times litigation has gone on for years over such an issue.

Elections and adjudication, however, have not been the only ways that county seat conflicts have been resolved. We saw in the Spink County case that force and direct negotiations between parties to the conflict both played a role in producing the outcome. Elsewhere, each of these approaches has on occasion been the primary means by which a county seat conflict has been resolved. There have been several cases where a forceful resolution has been decisive, and several others where direct negotiations provided the primary solution for the conflict. But we need not stop with just these four approaches to resolution. In his study of county seat wars, the author has also found a number of other ways of trying to resolve these conflicts. Let us illustrate a few of them.

1. Resolution by Redefinition. In some county seat wars, the county in question has been redefined to remove the bitterness of a dispute. Sometimes this has taken the form of dividing the county into two, allowing each of the contending towns to be the county seat for their respective counties. This occurred, for example, in the history of Edwards and Wabash counties, Illinois, on the basis of a negotiated agreement that prevented a direct physical attack of a body of partisans determined to change the county seat of the original county. In other cases, the county boundaries might be changed, leaving one of the contending towns less able to obtain the prize. State legislatures have sometimes cooperated in such a resolution. For example, in Allen County, Kansas, the contest was a close one between Iola and Humboldt, until the state legislator from the area—who happened to be from Iola—arranged for the county boundaries to be changed. By combining part of Allen County with its neighbor to the south, Iola was left much more clearly in the center of the county and there were fewer voters to support the cause of its rival.

2. Resolution by Purchase. County seat elections have sometimes been bought by those with enough money to spend on the issue. In the county seat war in Gray County, Kansas, a wealthy supporter of Ingalls wrote checks of over $100 each to secure votes; meanwhile, proponents of the other town, Cimarron, promised $10,000 for the solid backing of a critical precinct. Needless to say, this conflict required court action before it could be decided, and ultimately the Kansas supreme court made the decision. One of the judges later described the decision in favor of Ingalls as based on the judgment that "there was a little more fraud committed by the Cimarron side than by the Ingalls side." An even more impressive example of an attempted (and successful) resolution by purchase occurred in the case of Potter County, Texas. The owners of the Frying Pan Ranch didn't like where the courthouse had been located, so they purchased the entire town of Amarillo and moved it to a new location on land that they owned. The county seat naturally followed.

3. Resolution by Arbitrary Outside Influences. Legislatures sometimes intervened in a county seat conflict in ways that contradicted the standards they had themselves set up. For instance, they approved Wilmot as the new county seat of Roberts County, South Dakota, even though Wilmot had obtained the county records by force after losing an election to Travare. On one occasion, no less a body than the Congress of the United States intervened in a county seat contest, when in 1888 they passed a special act to create Latah County in Idaho Territory, to define its boundaries, and to establish Moscow as its county seat—thus ending the dispute between Moscow and Lewiston over the county seat honors for the previously existing Nez Perce County. Other examples of arbitrary outside influences could include events popularly referred to as "acts of God." For example, in the case of Tom Green County, Texas, San Angelo seemed defeated by a rival named Ben Ficklin until that latter town was wiped out by a flood in 1882.

4. Other Imaginative Forms of Resolution. In two cases of county seat conflicts, the author has found stories about the issue being decided by a tournament between champions of the rival towns. In one of these two cases, the information is not well documented; however, in the other case, the story is repeated as fact in more than one book. Unfortunately for a good story, further investigation has shown that the wrestling match (which did occur between champions of rival towns in Webster County, Iowa) was actually not decisive in establishing the location of the county seat. Another imaginative way of resolving a county seat struggle was used by some early residents of Douglas County, South Dakota. When it was shown that their county organization, including the initial location of the county seat, was fraudulent, they seized the county records and caused all of them to be permanently "lost"—thus requiring a completely new organization of the county.

Many Roads

What could be more simple than a county seat contest? There is only one issue: which town is to become the county seat. There were usually only two contenders. Also, legal guidelines were readily available regarding how the issue was to be properly decided. Still, as we have seen, this did not always allow the settlement of the issue to proceed in a simple manner. Indeed, there were a great variety of methods used in resolving even such a simple kind of conflict.

How much more do we need to be alert to the variety of forms of conflict resolution available for our more complex conflicts! There is not just one way to resolve a conflict. There may be a preferred way, one that is most commonly applied for that kind of conflict. But there are always other ways that can be tried as well. The variety of methods for resolving conflicts is surely as great as the variety of ways that conflicts may be pursued—which is a great many ways indeed.

Intractable Conflicts

Despite the many ways one might try to resolve a conflict, we should still recognize that some cases just do not seem capable of resolution by any method. For many years, the Cold War between the Soviet Union and the United States appeared to be such a conflict. There might be resolution of specific issues, such as in arms control agreements, but it seemed inevitable that the basic conflict would just go on and on. On a smaller scale, this has seemed true of the conflict in Northern Ireland between Irish Catholics and Protestant Unionists. The political and ideological currents run so deep that a general settlement seems impossible. The Middle East is another area where long-term hostilities and political complexities seem to produce unending conflict.

These examples, however, all also suggest that no conflict is completely without resolution. The Cold War appears to have ended with the disintegration of the Soviet Union, and Russia and the United States are (at this writing) on generally friendly terms. Recently there have been new signs of a relaxation of hostilities in Northern Ireland. In the Middle East, movement toward workable agreements now involves Palestinian Arabs and Israelis—despite tremendously complex difficulties. Even those conflicts that appear most intractable can sometimes yield at least partial resolutions. And, eventually, even the most bitter disputes may finally get resolved.

A conflict over the county seat that seemed to many of its participants as incapable of resolution occurred in Cass County, Illinois. For no less that thirty-nine years the struggle continued between Beardstown and Virginia. Elections, forced removal, appeals to the courts, and special state legislation were all applied to try to resolve this issue—but it never seemed to stay resolved. Finally, in 1876, the Illinois supreme court made a ruling in favor of Virginia, which appears to have ended the most bitter period of conflict. At any rate, this town has served as the county seat ever since then.

So even a conflict that rages on and on for decades eventually can yield to a resolution—in one way or another!

Summary and Conclusions

Summary

We have used county seat wars—bitter struggles between towns over which is to be the seat of county government—as a means of considering a wide variety of forms of conflict resolution. There is not just one proper way to bring a conflict to an end. Among county seat conflicts, we saw all of the following applied in obtaining conflict resolution: elections, adjudication, force, direct negotiations, redefinition of the unit of government, purchase by one party, arbitrary outside forces (including 'acts of God'), and still other highly imaginative approaches that fit none of these categories.

Conclusions

One main conclusion seems to follow from what we have examined in this chapter. It is that there are many different ways to resolve a conflict, and that any given conflict may be dealt with by more than one method of resolution.

Not all conflicts respond to even the best considered attempts at resolution. Some conflicts appear impossible to resolve. Although they might be managed to control clearly undesirable consequences, the basic conflict seems to go on and on. Even such apparently intractable conflicts, however, sooner or later may yield to concerted attempts at resolution.

Epilogue: A Debate

Idealist: I find that encouraging, don't you?

Realist: Find what encouraging?

Idealist: That even though a conflict seems intractable, sooner or later it will get at least partially resolved. Also, that there are many different ways to go about trying to resolve a conflict. Even the same kind of conflict is capable of being resolved in a variety of ways. This means that there's always hope—as long as we can keep trying.

Realist: But it may sometimes take more than a generation for a conflict to wear itself out so that people can go on to other things. Don't forget, taking care of one conflict only allows us to get all worked up about something else. We never really reduce the amount of conflict in the world. We just attend to different issues at different times.

Idealist: But we can reduce the amount of conflict by resolving particular disputes. I just don't buy the idea that there has to be a certain amount of conflict. Where in the world do you get that idea?

Realist: I'm not saying that we are always involved in conflicts to the same degree. But, fundamentally, conflict is a part of life. It's always there. Sometimes we can manage our conflicts to avoid violence or other especially costly results. But we never eliminate conflict. That's why I object just a bit to the title of this book, *Conflict Resolution*. It implies that we really do end or resolve conflicts. But seldom is a conflict completely over, no matter what is done to 'resolve' it. We should therefore be talking more about 'conflict management' than 'conflict resolution.'

Idealist: I think that's overly pessimistic. People can, by concerted action, do something about their conflicts. Take what is going on in Northern Ireland right now as an example. This conflict, which has seemed so intractable for generations, now appears headed for a political settlement. It took a lot of hard work by many people—in Great Britain and the Republic of Ireland, as well as in Northern Ireland—but now it appears to be paying off.

Realist: Yes, take Northern Ireland, but don't hold your breath! As I recall, this conflict was 'resolved' by a political solution back in 1973, and before that in 1920. No matter what kind of political deal may be cooked up now, you can bet your bottom dollar that Northern Ireland will continue to see a high level of conflict between Protestant Unionists and Catholic Nationalists—in one arena or another.

Idealist: Maybe *all* conflict won't be eliminated, but at least things will be a lot better than they've been. That ought to count for something.

Realist: Yes, it does—or at least it will, if that is the way things turn out. But such conflicts have a kind of momentum of their own that is not easily resolved by a political deal. What you call resolution by "concerted action"—I think that is your term—is only a small part of conflict management.

Idealist: But cannot we say that sometimes a conflict is resolved by the way parties can come together to reach mutual agreement?

Realist: Sometimes, but not often. In fact, as much conflict is managed by indirect processes as by what you call resolution by 'concerted action.' Take economic conflicts, for example. Most of these are managed by market forces, without anyone really trying to deal directly with them.

Idealist: But that's just part of the background for dealing with conflicts. What's really important is the way we use our freedom to work together with others in making the world a better place. This requires intentional action. Adam Smith's 'unseen hand' cannot take us very far here.

Realist: And sometimes trying to deal with a conflict through, as you call it, "intentional action" only makes matters worse. That's been the case with almost all our most bloody wars. Get people to be more moderate and rational about their conflicts without trying to completely 'resolve' them and you'll have a much safer world.

Idealist: You have a point there—people can make conflicts worse, trying to resolve them in unproductive ways. We must learn from such mistakes. But always we need to have the idea in mind of the kind of peaceful and just world we are trying to create.

Realist: But whose concept of peace and justice will you be following? Whatever we identify by such terms will represent the values of our culture, but not necessarily those held in other societies. The basic realities consist of people with their interests, asserting them in conflict with one another. We may rationalize what we are trying to attain in terms of concepts such as peace and justice. But, really, we're all just pursuing the interests of ourselves and our groups.

Idealist: I cannot accept that! Our ideals have a reality of their own, motivating us as we seek to resolve our conflicts. To ignore this is to ignore what is most distinctively human.

Realist: Well, I don't know about that. I think that the most distinctive thing about humans is their intelligence. And this intelligence is wasted when we try to resolve conflicts too quickly according to the dictates of one or another of our ideals.

Idealist: So you would just let conflicts go on, without trying to do anything about them?

Realist: Well, no. But I'd be careful about what I'd do—making sure that I thought through what the long-run consequences are likely to be.

Idealist: Okay. I can't argue with that. But we still need some sense of direction to give coherence to whatever we do. And we get this direction from our ideals and values.

Realist: Very broadly this is true—but we always ought to recognize that other people might have different ideals and values.

Idealist: Of course, and we can talk with them about these values, coming thus to understand one another better—just as you and I have been doing here.

Realist: But that doesn't resolve the conflict. You and I will continue to hold different views.

Idealist: Maybe, but I still hope that I can help you see the light! For example, read carefully the previous parts of this book, and I'm sure you will see that my basic views on conflict resolution are supported.

Realist: That's funny! I thought this book has supported my position!

[So the debate continues, though with the *Reader* allowed to have the last word in this exchange.]

NOTES

Prologue

Please note: These notes do not give complete bibliographical information. Brief citations are generally made to works by names of authors and publication dates. Fuller information about each of the sources so indicated is given in the bibliography.

1. The story of the Garden of Eden is found in the second and third chapters of the Book of Genesis.

2. The political philosophy of Thomas Hobbes (1588–1679) provides the classical statement of this second myth. Our quotation describing conditions in his "state of nature" is from Hobbes (1651/1909), p. 97.

3. Our third myth has its classical statement in the political philosophy of John Locke (1632–1704). See especially Locke (1690/1956). Our quotation used to represent this general viewpoint is from the American *Declaration of Independence.*

4. Books here cited are those of Plato (1968) and Machiavelli (1512/1950).

Chapter 1

1. Works cited here are Thucydides (1943), Aristotle (1962), and Sun Tzu (1988). All of these were written several centuries before the Christian era.

2. The issue of the *Journal of Conflict Resolution* here cited is that of vol. 37, no. 4 (December 1993).

3. Our definition of social conflict is broader than what would be preferred by many other scholars. The author believes that such a broad definition allows for a more comprehensive treatment of subject matter than would a more limited definition. In Chapter 4 we will note some other conceptualizations that may be used.

4. The classic modern sociological statement of the importance of social conflict and its positive functions for society is that of Coser (1956).

Chapter 2

1. This research is discussed more fully in Savin-Williams (1987).

2. Interesting comparisons can be made between the findings of Savin-Williams and those reported by Waal (1982) on chimpanzees.

3. Savin-Williams (1987), p. 170.

4. Gelles (1987), p. 4.

5. Ibid., p. 152.

6. This experimental research is reported in Walker et al. (1974).

7. Walker et al. (1974), p. 309.

8. See Haydu (1989) for this case of historical analysis.

9. The source for this quote is Haydu (1989), p. 101.

10. Our source here is Ember and Ember (1994).

11. The quotations in this paragraph are from Ember and Ember (1994), pp. 642–43 and 643, respectively.

12. This research is presented in Garcia (1991).

13. Garcia (1991), p. 833.

14. Our source here is Harrington (1985).

15. Our understanding of this research project is largely based on Kritzer (1990).

16. See Druckman (1994).

17. The main source for our discussion of Axelrod's work is Axelrod (1984).

18. The scholar cited is believed to be Percy W. Bridgman, though a specific citation cannot be made. The author remembers this being mentioned during his long-ago graduate school days, in a lecture by Fritz Heider.

Chapter 3

1. Our primary source for the 1932 Einstein-Freud exchange of letters is Freud (1964). Einstein's letter is found on pp. 199–202. Our quotations come from pp. 199 and 201. Freud's letter is on pp. 203–15. We use brief quotations from pp. 208, 210, 212 (three quotations), 213, 214, 215.

2. Our closing quotation is from Einstein (1933/1949), p. 81.

3. The present section draws extensively from the author's previous works, especially Schellenberg (1982), pp. 19–38, and Schellenberg (1993), pp. 141–47.

4. The primary sources for Darwin's ideas are Darwin (1859/1927 and 1871/1893).

5. A more extended discussion of social Darwinism may be found in Schellenberg (1982), pp. 22–28, 38.

6. A highly readable statement on the uncertain nature of evolution, in the light of recent evidence for "punctuated equilibrium," may be found in Gould (1989).

7. Key sources for the main ideas of sociobiology include Wilson (1975 and 1978).

8. Key sources for the ideas of ethology include Lorenz (1963/ 1966) and Eibl-Eibesfeldt (1975/1979). Waal (1989) describes important recent research on aggression and conflict resolution behaviors among several main kinds of primates.

9. For a general overview of recent developments in the study of genes and behavior, see Mann (1994). The particular case of manic depression is reviewed in Marshall (1994).

10. For further background on this research, see Mann (1994).

11. See especially Plomin and associates (1994).

12. A summary of the evidence cited in this and the following paragraph is given in Bouchard (1994).

13. For further information regarding the physiology of aggression, see Moyer (1987a, 1987b), Svare (1983), and Berkowitz (1993).

14. The quotation is from Moyer (1987b), p. 24.

15. This quotation is from Scott (1975), p. 62.

16. Many sources may be consulted for further details regarding Freud's theories. The author has previously provided his own summary (Schellenberg, 1978, pp. 11–37).

17. This quotation is from Freud (1930), p. 80.

18. For further information on this research, see Adorno et al. (1950).

19. Rokeach (1960) represents an early move from the focus on the authoritarian personality to that on a more general openness to new experience and ideas.

20. Twin studies suggest that about 45 to 50 percent of the variability in the openness dimension of personality may be accounted for by heredity, with only about 10 percent accounted for by a shared family environment (Bouchard, 1994). However, it should be noted that measures of "heritability" (on which these figures are based) vary a great deal with studies of different groups and should therefore be interpreted with great caution.

21. The original statement of the frustration-aggression hypothesis is found in Dollard et al. (1939). A revised statement is found in Miller (1941). Berkowitz (1969) represents a modified version of the theory, and his most recent summary may be found in Berkowitz (1993).

22. For some early evidence on the relation of pain to aggression, see Buss (1961) or Azrin et al. (1964). For a recent summary, see Berkowitz (1993).

23. Berkowitz (1969, 1993) suggests important cognitive qualifications for the frustration-aggression hypothesis. On evidence regarding catharsis of aggression, see Berkowitz (1962), pp. 196–228; Berkowitz (1993), pp. 337–44; or Bandura (1973), pp. 139–54.

24. Discussions of classical and operant conditioning may be found in any book on the psychology of learning. See, for example, Bower and Hilgard (1981), King (1979), Schwartz (1978), or Tighe (1982).

25. See especially Berkowitz (1993), pp. 69–79.

26. An interesting set of studies of the application of operant principles to control unruly adolescent behavior is given in Hamblin (1971).

27. For a general discussion of social learning theory, see Bandura (1977). In Bandura (1973) this perspective is applied especially to aggressive behavior.

Chapter 4

1. Quoted in Campbell and Skinner (1982), p. 145. Campbell and Skinner probably give the best biography of Smith available. For a more informal overview of Smith's life and thought, see Heilbroner (1967), pp. 38–67.

2. Smith (1759/1976), p. 319.

3. Both quotations in the paragraph are from Smith (1759/1976), p. 110.

4. Smith (1776/1910).

5. Smith (1759/1976), p. 82.

6. Smith (1776/1910), vol. 1, p. 13.

7. Smith (1776/1910), vol. 2, p. 155. The quotation in the following paragraph is from vol. 1, p. 400.

8. The quotations in this paragraph are, respectively, from Smith (1759/1976), p. 87, and Smith (1776/1910), vol. 2, p. 180.

9. Park and Burgess (1921). Our quotations are from pp. 507, 510.

10. Simmel (1908/1955). Our quotations are from pp. 17–18, 25.

11. Coser (1956). The propositions we have listed are either quotations or close paraphrases from, respectively, p. 38, 47, 64, 71, 95, 103, 137.

12. Simmel (1908/1955), p. 110. The quotations in the following paragraph are both from p. 111.

13. Ibid., p. 112. The quotation in the following paragraph is from p. 114.

14. Our quotation is from Simmel (1908/1955), p. 116.

15. Simmel (1908/1955), p. 120. Our quotations in the following paragraph are from pp. 121, 122.

16. Blumer first used the term in his article for Schmitt (1937). See also Blumer (1969), from which we have quoted basic premises from pp. 1–5. Another good survey of symbolic interactionism is in Stryker (1980).

17. Strauss (1978). The identification of factors in the following paragraph is from pp. 99–100, mostly in his words but without his punctuation or italics.

18. Lewin (1948 and 1951). For more on Lewin's life and theories, see Schellenberg (1978).

19. Deutsch (1949) gives the original statement of Deutsch's theory. A later statement is contained in Deutsch (1973), on which the following three paragraphs are based.

20. The quotation here is from Bertalanffy (1955), p. 76. See also Bertalanffy (1968).

21. For a general discussion of functionalism in sociology, see Turner and Maryanski (1979).

22. Homans (1958). For a fuller version of Homans' theory, see Homans (1961).

23. Blau (1964) and Thibaut and Kelley (1959) are among the early examples of social exchange theory.

24. See especially Walster et al. (1978).

25. For examples of this later work in exchange theory, see Cook (1987).

26. The quoted material is from Boulding's essay in McNeil (1963), p. 180.

27. See especially Boulding (1962).

28. This Boulding does especially in a small book entitled *The Economy of Love and Fear* (Boulding, 1973).

29. Pruitt and Rubin (1986).

30. Kriesberg et al. (1989).

31. Northrup (1989).

Chapter 5

1. Our chief sources of information about Marx's life are McLellan (1973) and Suchting (1983).

2. The quotation in this paragraph is from McLellan (1973), p. 283.

3. Marx and Engels (1848/1955), p. 9.

4. Tucker (1978), p. 297. Our earlier longer quotation is as used by Ellwood (1938), p. 330.

5. "Audacity, audacity, and still more audacity!" This passage is as quoted by Barnes and Becker (1938), vol. 1, p. 646. The earlier quotation in this paragraph is from Marx and Engels (1848/1955), p. 46.

6. A good summary discussion of Weber's theories is found in Duke (1976), pp. 37–72.

7. See Weber (1904–05/1958).

8. The brief quotation here is from Dahrendorf (1979), p. 54.

9. Dahrendorf (1957/59).

10. A good summary of critical theory is that of Honneth (1987).

11. See Plato (1968).

12. The quotation here is from Book One, 342-D of *The Republic,* as translated in Plato (1968), p. 20.

13. Our main source here is Hamilton, Madison and Jay (1787/1949).

14. Hamilton, Madison and Jay (1787/1949), pp. 9, 10.

15. The quotations in this paragraph are, respectively, from p. 9, 11, 11.

16. The extended quotation is from Hunt and Walker (1974), p. 3.

17. Gordon (1964), p. 30.

18. Here and elsewhere in this section we draw heavily upon Hunt and Walker (1974).

19. Bernard (1981), with our quotations from pp. 23 and 91.

20. Morganthau (1948/1973), pp. 3–4.

21, See especially Galtung (1980).

22. See especially Wallerstein (1974). Also Wallerstein (1987).

23. Gumplowicz is here cited as quoted by Ellwood (1938), p. 488.

Chapter 6

1. Richardson, as quoted by Cuzzort (1969), p. 115.

2. The quotation here is from Cuzzort (1969), p. 130.

3. See Richardson (1960a) and Richardson (1960b). For a good summary of Richardson's work, see Rapoport (1960), pp. 15–46. See also Cuzzort (1969), pp. 110–30.

4. Richardson (1960a). We have also depended on Rapoport (1960) as a general background to help us interpret Richardson's discussion of arms races throughout this section.

5. Quoted in Cuzzort (1969), pp. 129–30.

6. Bernoulli (1738/1954).

7. Von Neumann and Morgenstern (1944).

8. For our discussion of utility theory, we draw extensively on Luce and Raiffa (1957) and Rapoport (1960), as well as von Neumann and Morgenstern (1944).

9. Although the absence of interpersonal comparisons of utility has its attractions, it also has its problems. It does not allow for the extent to which our own judgments of utility are based on what we observe in others—something that monetary values have an advantage in allowing.

10. Savage (1964).

11. See especially Boulding (1962) and Isard and Smith (1982).

12. Von Neumann and Morgenstern (1944).

13. For fuller discussions of game theory by the present author, see Schellenberg (1982), pp. 167–200, and Schellenberg (1990).

14. See especially the discussion of "the bargaining problem" in Schellenberg (1990), pp. 97–105. The original source for Nash's solution is Nash (1950).

Chapter 7

1. Main sources used for historical information on the Falkland Islands, as well as the war there, have been Hasting and Jenkins (1983) and *Sunday Times* Insight Team (1982).

2. Hoffmann and Hoffmann (1984), p. 178.

3. It should be acknowledged that in our discussion here we are using 'legitimacy' in the broad sense of referring to whatever will be generally considered justified within or among societies, rather than in the more limited sense of what is legal.

4. A further discussion of the role of force in resolving conflicts may be found in Schellenberg (1982), especially pp. 225–34.

5. Evidence for factors behind the emergence of states is discussed by the author in a section entitled "How States Began" in Schellenberg (1993). For a discussion of the general evolution of states into modern times, see especially Tilly (1992).

6. The experiment here described is reported in Milgram (1963) and, with fuller discussion, in Milgram (1974).

Chapter 8

1. In our study of the General Motors strike of 1970, we draw especially upon Serrin (1973).

2. Quoted by Serrin, p. 3.

3. Bluestone's quotation is from Serrin, p. 47; those of Woodcock are from pp. 48, 55.

4. Quoted by Serrin, p. 206.

5. Bramblett is quoted in Serrin, p. 213.

6. This concluding exchange is described by Serrin, on p. 265.

7. The quotation from Woodcock is in Serrin, pp. 284–85.

8. The quotation here is from Serrin, p. 278.

9. Our discussion in subsequent paragraphs draws heavily upon Douglas (1962). See also Schellenberg (1982), pp. 204–11.

10. Cited by Douglas (1962), pp. 280–81 (including the quotation).

11. Jensen (1974), p. 16.

12. For evidence that unions usually bend more than management in collective bargaining, see Hammermesh (1973).

13. Bramblett is quoted in Serrin (1973), p. 305.

14. Hastings and Jenkins (1983, pp. 22–27) discuss this agreement and its demise.

15. A somewhat more detailed discussion of laboratory studies of bargaining and negotiation is found in Schellenberg (1982), pp. 211–15.

16. Books here indicated are those of Raiffa (1982) and Fisher and Ury (1981).

Chapter 9

1. Our information about this tragic train accident and of the trial that followed is based on the account of Nizer (1961), pp. 319–65.

2. The quotation here is from Nizer, p. 330.

3. Judge Hooley is here quoted by Nizer, p. 360 and p. 361.

4. Dr. Glenn's testimony is described by Nizer, pp. 343–55, with the quotation from p. 348.

5. Judge Hooley's final comments to the jury are found on pp. 364–65 of Nizer (1961).

6. In the paragraphs that follow we draw generally upon a variety of sources, including Jacob (1984).

7. The evidence on the frequency of settlements is discussed briefly by Kritzer (1990), p. 73.

8. Our descriptions of the Crow and Lobi court procedures are from Lowie (1940), pp. 289–90 and p. 290, respectively.

9. In this paragraph we have drawn especially upon Roos (1970), with the final quotation from p. 232.

10. Evidence in this paragraph is from Kritzer (1990), p. 84 (on categories of kinds of cases), p. 37 (on individuals or organizations as involved in suits), and p. 31 (on monetary values—though, remember, these are in dollar values of the late 1970s).

11. These six points are quoted from Kritzer (1991), pp. 132–33.

12. The quotation here is from Kritzer (1991), p. 137 (emphasized by italics in the original).

13. Evidence on small claims court problems is provided by O'Barr and Conley (1988). Evidence on class-related attitudes to the justice system is contained in Jacob (1984), especially pp. 218–27. For example, on p. 223 of Jacob's book it is shown by a Milwaukee study that ghetto blacks are about three times as likely as middle class whites to agree with the statement, "I can't use the courts because legal proceedings are too complicated for me to understand them." Also, blacks were far less likely than whites to say that "local courts are doing a good job."

Chapter 10

1. The primary source of information for this section is Carter (1982), pp. 267–429. Materials quoted from this source are used with the kind permission of President Carter.

2. Carter (1982), p. 344. The quotation in the following paragraph is from p. 345.

3. Ibid. The quotations in this paragraph are from p. 349 and p. 350, respectively. Those in the following paragraph are from pp. 350, 352.

4. Ibid. The quotation here is from p. 355, while that in the following paragraph is from p. 359.

5. Ibid. The quotation in this paragraph is from p. 368. That in the following paragraph is from pp. 370–71.

6. Ibid., pp. 390–91.

7. Ibid. The quotations in this paragraph are from p. 391, 392, and 393, respectively.

8. Ibid., p. 396. The quotations in the following two paragraphs are from p. 397 and 401, respectively.

9. Ibid. Our final quotation is from p. 402.

10. The author here draws especially on a paper by Mohammed Abu-Nimer, "Can Western Conflict Resolution Approaches be Adopted in a Middle East Context?" presented at the 1994 meetings of the American Sociological Association.

11. For information on mediation in China, the author draws especially on Wall and Blum (1991), Wall et al. (1995), and on a paper by Xinyi Xu, "Quasi-justice: Conflict Resolution in Chinese Work Organizations," presented at the 1994 meetings of the American Sociological Association.

12. These findings are based especially on a paper by Jessica Pearson written for the 1993 National Symposium on Court Connected Dispute Resolution Research. The author found Marsha Bradford especially helpful in pointing out this paper and in summarizing for him some of Pearson's main points. For a further review of family mediation research, see Benjamin and Irving (1995).

13. Pearson and Thoennes (1988).

14. See Emery and Wyer (1987) and Emery, Matthews, and Wyer (1991). Our quotation is from the latter source, p. 410. Possible gender differences regarding mediation are also discussed in the literature review given by Benjamin and Irving (1995).

15. Medley and Schellenberg (1994a, 1994b, and 1996) provide the basic sources here.

16. The research here cited is that of Bercovitch and Langley (1993).

Chapter 11

1. Our primary source for these cases is Coulson (1986), especially pp. 67–69 and 90–93. Our presentations have been slightly fictionalized, but the basic events actually happened in a manner very close to that here recounted.

2. Our quotations for this case are from the summary report printed in *Arbitration in the Schools,* a periodical publication of the American Arbitration Association (March 1, 1983), Report no. 157-14.

3. Some of these details, including the words quoted, are from a summary report printed in *Arbitration in the Schools* (American Arbitration Association, July 1, 1983), Report no. 161-13.

4. According to Begin and Beal (1985, p. 393), "Over 95 percent of all American collective bargaining agreements provide for arbitration as the final means of settlement of grievances. However, many of these agreements specify that certain grievances are not arbitrable and, consequently, the strike remains as an alternative final policymaking step in the grievance procedure."

5. Our source for the Torrington case is Prasow and Peters (1970), pp. 38–41, 274–83, and 335–51.

6. Quoted by Prasow and Peters (1970), p. 39.

7. Our main sources of information regarding final-offer arbitration in major league baseball are Chelius and Dworkin (1980), Frederick and associates (1992), and Sully (1989).

8. The Don Mattingly case is discussed by Sully (1989), p. 165.

9. See especially Chelius and Dworkin (1980) and Frederick and associates (1992).

10. Our sources of information on this case include articles in *Aviation Week and Space Technology* (especially in the November 22, 1993, issue) and the *New York Times* (especially in the November 23, 1993, issue).

11. These quotations are included in the *New York Times* story published on November 23, 1993.

12. Quoted matter is from the source cited in note 2.

13. Quoted matter is from the source cited in note 3.

Chapter 12

1. Our description of the Spink county seat war is taken almost verbatim from Schellenberg (1974, pp. 69–71). An important original source for this conflict has been Bassford (1903). See also Schellenberg (1987, pp. 88–89).

2. Further information on specific county seat conflicts mentioned in this chapter may be found in Schellenberg (1987). The County and Town Index of that book (pp. 121–26) provides page citations.

BIBLIOGRAPHY

Adorno, Theodor W., Else Frenkel-Brunswik, Daniel J. Levinson, and R. Nevitt San-
ford. 1950. *The Authoritarian Personality.* New York: Harper and Row.

Aristotle. 1962. *The Politics.* Baltimore: Penguin (original date unknown).

Axelrod, Robert. 1984. *The Evolution of Cooperation.* New York: Basic Books.

Azrin, Nathan H., R. R. Hutchinson, and R. D. Sellery. 1964. "Pain Aggression Toward Inanimate Objects." *Journal of the Experimental Analysis of Behavior* 7:
223–27.

Bandura, Albert. 1973. *Aggression: A Social Learning Analysis.* Englewood Cliffs:
Prentice Hall.

———. 1977. *Social Learning Theory.* Englewood Cliffs: Prentice Hall.

Barnes, Harry Elmer, and Howard Becker. 1938. *Social Thought from Lore to Science.*
2 vols. Boston: Heath.

Bassford, O. S. 1903. "The Spink County War." *The Monthly South Dakotan* 6: 21–33.

Begin, James P., and Edwin F. Beal. 1985. *The Practice of Collective Bargaining.* 7th
ed. Homewood, Ill.: Richard D. Irwin.

Benjamin, Michael, and Howard H. Irving. 1995. "Research in Family Mediation: Review and Implications." *Mediation Quarterly* 13: 53–82.

Bercovitch, Jacob, and Jeffrey Langley. 1993. "The Nature of the Dispute and the Effectiveness of International Mediation." *Journal of Conflict Resolution* 37: 670–91.

Berkowitz, Leonard. 1962. *Aggression: A Social Psychological Analysis.* New York:
McGraw-Hill.

———. 1969. "The Frustration-Aggression Hypothesis Revisited." In *Roots of Aggression,* Leonard Berkowitz, ed., pp. 1–28. New York: Atherton.

———. 1993. *Aggression: Its Causes, Consequences, and Control.* Philadelphia: Tem-
ple University Press.

Bernard, Jessie. 1981. *The Female World.* New York: Free Press.

Bernoulli, Daniel. 1738/1954. "Specimen Theoriae Novae de Mensura Sortis." *Co-
mentari Acedemii Acientarum Imperialis Petropolitannae* 5 (1738): 175–92.

Translated as "Exposition of a New Theory on the Measurement of Risk." *Econometrica* 22 (1954): 23–26.

Bertalanffy, Ludwig von. 1955. "General System Theory." *Main Currents in Modern Thought* 11: 75–83.

———. 1968. *General System Theory.* New York: Braziller.

Blau, Peter M. 1964. *Exchange and Power in Social Life.* New York: Wiley.

Blumer, Herbert. 1969. *Symbolic Interactionism: Perspective and Method.* New York: Prentice Hall.

Bouchard, Thomas J., Jr. 1994. "Genes, Environment, and Personality." *Science* 264: 1700–1.

Boulding, Kenneth E. 1962. *Conflict and Defense.* New York: Harper.

———. 1973. *The Economy of Love and Fear.* Belmont, Calif.: Wadsworth.

Bower, Gordon H., and Ernest R. Hilgard. 1981. *Theories of Learning.* 5th ed. Englewood Cliffs: Prentice Hall.

Buss, Arnold H. 1961. *The Psychology of Aggression.* New York: Wiley.

Campbell, R. H., and A. S. Skinner. 1982. *Adam Smith.* New York: St. Martin's Press.

Carter, Jimmy. 1982. *Keeping Faith: Memoirs of a President.* Toronto: Bantam Books.

Chelius, James R., and James B. Dworkin. 1980. "An Economic Analysis of Final-Offer Arbitration." *Journal of Conflict Resolution* 24: 293–310.

Cook, Karen, ed. 1987. *Social Exchange Theory.* Newbury Park, Calif.: Sage Publications.

Coser, Lewis A. 1956. *The Functions of Social Conflict.* New York: Free Press.

Coulson, Robert. 1986. *Arbitration in the Schools.* New York: American Arbitration Association.

Cuzzort, Raymond P. 1969. *Humanity and Modern Sociological Thought.* New York: Holt, Rinehart & Winston.

Dahrendorf, Ralf. 1957/1959. *Class and Class Conflict in Industrial Society.* Stanford: Stanford University Press.

———. 1979. *Life Chances.* Chicago: University of Chicago Press.

Darwin, Charles. 1859/1927. *The Origin of Species.* New York: Macmillan.

———. 1871/1898. *The Descent of Man.* New York: Appleton.

Deutsch, Morton. 1949. "A Theory of Cooperation and Competition." *Human Relations* 2: 129–51.

———. 1973. *The Resolution of Conflict.* New Haven: Yale University Press.

Dollard, John, Leonard W. Doob, Neal Miller, O. Hobart Mowrer, and Robert R. Sears. 1939. *Frustration and Aggression.* New Haven: Yale University Press.

Douglas, Ann. 1962. *Industrial Peacemaking.* New York: Columbia University Press.

Druckman, Daniel. 1994. "Compromising Behavior in Negotiation: A Meta-Analysis." *Journal of Conflict Resolution* 38: 507–56.

Duke, James T. 1976. *Conflict and Power in Social Life.* Provo, Utah: Brigham Young University Press.

Eibl-Eibesfeldt, Irenaus. 1975/1979. *The Biology of Peace and War.* New York: Viking Press.

Einstein, Albert. 1933/1949. "A Manifesto." In *The World as I See It,* p. 81. New York: Philosophical Library.

Ellwood, Charles A. 1938. *A History of Social Philosophy.* New York: Prentice Hall.

Ember, Carol R., and Melvin Ember. 1994. "War, Socialization, and Interpersonal Violence: A Cross-Cultural Study." *Journal of Conflict Resolution* 38: 620–46.

Emery, Robert E, and Melissa M. Wyer. 1987. "Child Custody Mediation and Litigation: An Experimental Evaluation of the Experience of Parents." *Journal of Consulting and Clinical Psychology* 55: 179–86.

Emery, Robert E., Sheila G. Matthews, and Melissa M. Wyer. 1991. "Child Custody Mediation and Litigation: Further Evidence on the Differing Views of Mothers and Fathers." *Journal of Consulting and Clinical Psychology* 59: 410–18.

Fisher, Roger, and William Ury. 1981. *Getting to Yes: Negotiating Agreement Without Giving In.* Boston: Houghton Mifflin. [2nd ed. by Roger Fisher, William Ury and Bruce Patton, 1992. New York: Penguin Books.]

Frederick, David M., William H. Kaempfer, and Richard L. Wobbeking. 1992. "Salary Arbitration as a Market Substitute." In *Diamonds Are Forever: The Business of Baseball,* Paul M. Sommers, ed., pp. 29–49. Washington, D.C.: The Brookings Institution.

Freud, Sigmund. 1930. *Civilization and its Discontents.* New York: Anchor Books (no date; first published in 1930 by Hogarth Press, London).

———. 1964. "Why War?" In *The Complete Psychological Writings of Sigmund Freud,* vol. 22, 1932–36, James Strachey, ed., pp. 195–215. London: Hogarth Press.

Galtung, Johan. 1980. *The True Worlds*. New York: Free Press.

Garcia, Angela. 1991. "Dispute Resolution Without Disputing: How the Interactional Organization of Mediation Hearings Minimizes Argument." *American Sociological Review* 56: 818–35.

Gelles, Richard J. 1987. *The Violent Home*. 2nd ed. Newbury Park, Calif.: Sage Publications.

Gordon, Milton M. 1964. *Assimilation in American Life*. New York: Oxford University Press.

Gould, Stephen Jay. 1989. "The Wheel of Fortune and the Wedge of Progress." *Natural History* 98: 14–21.

Hamblin, Robert L. 1971. *The Humanization Process*. New York: Wiley.

Hamilton, Alexander, James Madison and John Jay. 1787/1949. *Selections from The Federalist*. New York: Appleton-Century-Crofts.

Hammermesh, Daniel S. 1973. "Who 'Wins' in Wage Bargaining?" *Industrial and Labor Relations Review* 26: 146–49.

Harrington, Christine B. 1985. *Shadow Justice: The Ideology and Institutionalization of Alternatives to Court*. Westport, Conn.: Greenwood Press.

Hastings, Max, and Simon Jenkins. 1983. *The Battle for the Falklands*. New York: Norton.

Haydu, Jeffrey. 1989. "Managing 'the Labor Problem' in the United States ca. 1897–1911." In *Intractable Conflicts and Their Transformations*, Louis Kriesberg, Terrell A. Northrup, and Stuart J. Thorson, eds., pp. 93–106. Syracuse, N.Y.: Syracuse University Press.

Heilbroner, Robert L. 1967. *The Worldly Philosophers*. 3rd ed. New York: Simon and Schuster.

Hobbes, Thomas. 1651/1909. *Leviathan*. Oxford: Oxford University Press.

Hoffmann, Fritz L., and Olga Mingo Hoffmann. 1984. *Sovereignty in Dispute: The Falklands/Malvinas, 1483–1982*. Boulder: Westview Press.

Homans, George C. 1958. "Social Behavior as Exchange." *American Journal of Sociology* 63: 597–606.

––––––. 1961. *Social Behavior: Its Elementary Forms*. New York: Harcourt Brace.

Honneth, Axel. 1987. "Critical Theory." In *Social Theory Today*, Anthony Giddens and Jonathan Turner, eds., pp. 347–82. Stanford: Stanford University Press.

Hunt, Chester L., and Lewis Walker. 1974. *Ethnic Dynamics*. Homewood, Ill.: Dorsey Press.

Isard, Walter, and Christine Smith. 1982. *Conflict Analysis and Practical Conflict Management Procedures.* Cambridge, Mass.: Ballinger.

Jacob, Herbert. 1984. *Justice in America: Courts, Lawyers, and the Judicial Process.* 4th ed. Boston: Little, Brown.

Jensen, Vernon H. 1974. *Strife on the Waterfront.* Ithaca: Cornell University Press.

King, Donald L. 1979. *Conditioning.* New York: Gardner Press.

Kriesberg, Louis, Terrell A. Northrup, and Stuart J. Thorson. 1989. *Intractable Conflicts and Their Transformation.* Syracuse, N.Y.: Syracuse University Press.

Kritzer, Herbert M. 1990. *The Justice Broker: Lawyers and Ordinary Litigation.* New York: Oxford University Press.

———. 1991. *Let's Make a Deal: Understanding the Negotiation Process in Ordinary Litigation.* Madison: University of Wisconsin Press.

Lewin, Kurt. 1948. *Resolving Social Conflicts.* New York: Harper.

———. 1951. *Field Theory in Social Science.* New York: Harper.

Locke, John. 1690/1956. *The Second Treatise of Government.* New York: Macmillan.

Lorenz, Konrad. 1963/1966. *On Aggression.* New York: Harcourt, Brace and World.

Lowie, Robert H. 1961. *An Introduction to Cultural Anthropology.* 2nd ed. New York: Rinehart.

Luce, R. Duncan, and Howard Raiffa. 1957. *Games and Decisions.* New York: Wiley.

Mann, Charles C. 1994. "Behavioral Genetics in Transition." *Science* 264: 1686–89.

Marshall, Eliot. 1994. "Highs and Lows on the Research Roller Coaster." *Science* 264: 1693–95.

Marx, Karl, and Friedrich Engels. 1848/1955. *The Communist Manifesto.* New York: Appleton-Century-Crofts.

McLellan, David. 1973. *Karl Marx: His Life and Thought.* New York: Harper & Row.

McNeil, Elton B., ed. 1963. *The Nature of Human Conflict.* Englewood Cliffs: Prentice Hall.

Medley, Morris L., and James A. Schellenberg. 1994a. "Attitudes of Indiana Judges Toward Mediation." *Mediation Quarterly* 11: 329–38.

———. 1994b. "Attitudes of Attorneys Toward Mediation." *Mediation Quarterly* 12: 185–98.

———. 1996. "Hoosier Attorneys Consider Mediation." *Res Gestae* (February 1996) 39: 40–42.

Milgram, Stanley. 1963. "Behavioral Study of Obedience." *Journal of Abnormal and Social Psychology* 67: 371–78.

―――. 1974. *Obedience to Authority.* New York: Harper & Row.

Miller, Neal. 1941. "The Frustration-Aggression Hypothesis." *Psychological Review* 48: 337–42.

Morganthau, Hans. 1948/1973. *Politics Among Nations.* New York: Knopf.

Moyer, Kenneth E. 1987a. "The Biological Basis of Dominance and Aggression." In *Dominance, Aggression and War,* Diane McGuiness, ed., pp. 1–34. New York: Paragon House.

―――. 1987b. *Violence and Aggression.* New York: Paragon House.

Nash, John F. 1950. "The Bargaining Problem." *Econometrica* 18: 155–62.

Nizer, Louis. 1961. *My Life in Court.* London: Heinemann.

Northrup, Terrell A. 1989. "The Dynamic of Identity in Personal and Social Conflict." In *Intractable Conflicts and Their Transformation,* Louis Kriesberg, Terrell A. Northrup, and Stuart A. Thorson, eds., pp. 55–82. New York: Syracuse University Press.

O'Barr, William M., and John M. Conley. 1988. "Lay Expectations of the Civil Justice System." *Law and Society Review* 22: 137–61.

Park, Robert E., and Ernest W. Burgess. 1921. *An Introduction to the Science of Sociology.* Chicago: University of Chicago Press.

Pearson, Jessica, and Nancy Thoennes. 1988. "Divorce Mediation Research Results." In *Divorce Mediation: Theory and Practice,* Jay Folberg and Ann Milne, eds., pp. 429–52. New York: Guilford Press.

Plato. 1968. *The Republic of Plato.* New York: Basic Books (original date unknown).

Plomin, Robert, Michael J. Owen, and Peter McGuffin. 1994. "The Genetic Basis of Complex Human Behaviors." *Science* 264: 1733–39.

Prasow, Paul, and Edward Peters. 1970. *Arbitration and Collective Bargaining: Conflict Resolution in Labor Relations.* New York: McGraw-Hill.

Pruitt, Dean G., and Jeffrey Z. Rubin. 1986. *Social Conflict: Escalation, Stalemate, and Settlement.* New York: McGraw-Hill.

Raiffa, Howard. 1982. *The Art and Science of Negotiation.* Cambridge: Harvard University Press.

Rapoport, Anatol. 1960. *Fights, Games, and Debates.* Ann Arbor: University of Michigan Press.

Richardson, Lewis F. 1960a. *Arms and Insecurity*. Pittsburgh: Boxwood Press.

———. 1960b. *Statistics of Deadly Quarrels*. Chicago: Quadrangle Books.

Rokeach, Milton. 1960. *The Open and Closed Mind*. New York: Basic Books.

Roos, H. Laurence. 1970. *Settled Out of Court: The Social Process of Claims Adjustments*. Chicago: Aldine.

Savage, Leonard J. 1954. *The Foundations of Mathematics*. New York: Wiley.

Savin-Williams, Ritch C. 1987. *Adolescence: An Ethological Perspective*. New York: Springer-Verlag.

Schellenberg, James A. 1974. "Conflict Resolution in County Seat Wars." *Journal of the West* 13 (October): 69–78.

———. 1978. *Masters of Social Psychology*. New York: Oxford University Press.

———. 1982. *The Science of Conflict*. New York: Oxford University Press.

———. 1987. *Conflict Between Communities: American County Seat Wars*. New York: Paragon House.

———. 1990. *Primitive Games*. Boulder, Colo.: Westview Press.

———. 1993. *Exploring Social Behavior*. Boston: Allyn & Bacon.

Schmitt, Emerson, P., ed. 1937. *Man and Society*. New York: Prentice Hall.

Schwartz, Barry. 1978. *Psychology of Learning and Behavior*. New York: Norton.

Scott, John Paul. 1975. *Aggression*. 2nd ed. Chicago: University of Chicago Press.

Serrin, William. 1973. *The Company and the Union*. New York: Knopf.

Simmel, Georg. 1908/1955. "Der Streit," In *Soziologie,* Georg Simmel, trans. in *Conflict and the Web of Group-Affiliations,* pp. 1–123. Glencoe, Ill.: Free Press.

Smith, Adam. 1759/1976. *The Theory of Moral Sentiments*. London: Oxford University Press.

———. 1776/1910. *An Inquiry into the Nature and Causes of the Wealth of Nations*. 2 vols. New York: D. P. Dutton.

Strauss, Anselm. 1978. *Negotiations*. San Francisco: Jossey-Bass.

Stryker, Sheldon. 1980. *Symbolic Interactionism: A Structural Version*. Menlo Park, Calif.: Benjamin/Cummings.

Suchting, W. A. 1983. *Marx: An Introduction*. New York: New York University Press.

Sully, Gerald W. 1989. *The Business of Major League Baseball.* Chicago: University of Chicago Press.

Sun Tzu. 1988. *The Art of War.* Boston: Shambhala (orignal date unknown).

Sunday Times Insight Team. 1982. *War in the Falklands: The Full Story.* New York: Harper & Row.

Svare, Bruce B. 1983. *Hormones and Aggressive Behavior.* New York: Plenum Press.

Thibaut, John, and Harold H. Kelley. 1959. *The Social Psychology of Groups.* New York: Wiley.

Thucydides. 1943. *The History of the Peloponnesian War.* London: Oxford University Press (original date unknown).

Tighe, Thomas J. 1982. *Modern Learning Theory.* New York: Oxford University Press.

Tilly, Charles. 1992. *Coercion, Capital, and European States, A.D. 990–1992.* Cambridge, Mass.: Blackwell.

Tucker, Robert C., ed. 1978. The Marx-Engels Reader. 2nd ed. New York: Norton.

Turner, Jonathon H., and Alexandra Maryanski. 1979. *Functionalism.* Menlo Park, Calif.: Benjamin Cummings.

Von Neumann, John, and Oskar Morgenstern. 1944. *Theory of Games and Economic Behavior.* Princeton: Princeton University Press.

Waal, Frans B. M. de. 1982. *Chimpanzee Politics: Power and Sex among Apes.* New York: Harper & Row.

———. 1989. *Peacemaking among Primates.* Cambridge, Mass.: Harvard University Press.

Walker, Laurens, Stephen LaTour, E. Allan Lind, and John Thibaut. 1974. "Reactions of Participants and Observers to Modes of Adjudication." *Journal of Applied Social Psychology* 4: 295–310.

Wall, James A., Jr., and Michael Blum. 1991. "Community Mediation in the People's Republic of China." *Journal of Conflict Resolution* 35: 3–20.

Wall, James A., Jr., Dong-Won Sohn, Natalie Cleeton, and Deng Jian Jin. 1995. "Community and Family Mediation in the People's Republic of China." *International Journal of Conflict Management* 6: 30–47.

Wallerstein, Immanuel. 1974. *The Modern World System.* 2 vols. New York: Academic Press.

———. 1987. "World-Systems Analysis." In *Social Theory Today,* Anthony Giddens and Jonathan Turner, eds., pp. 309–24. Stanford: Stanford University Press.

Walster [Hatfield], Elaine, G. William Walster, and Ellen Berscheid. 1978. *Equity: Theory and Research*. Boston: Allyn & Bacon.

Weber, Max. 1904–05/1958. *The Protestant Ethic and the Spirit of Capitalism*. New York: Scribner.

Wilson, Edward O. 1975. *Sociobiology: The New Synthesis*. Cambridge: Harvard University Press.

———. 1978. *On Human Nature*. Cambridge: Harvard University Press.

INDEX

CURRICULUM and ASSESSMENT for WORLD-CLASS SCHOOLS